Reporting That Matters

Public Affairs Coverage

John Irby
Washington State University

Kenton Bird
University of Idaho

Susan English
Gonzaga University

David Cuillier
University of Arizona

PEARSON

Boston   New York   San Francisco
Mexico City   Montreal   Toronto   London   Madrid   Munich   Paris
Hong Kong   Singapore   Tokyo   Cape Town   Sydney

Series Editor: Molly Taylor
Series Editorial Assistant: Suzanne Stradley
Marketing Manager: Suzan Czajkowski
Senior Production Editor: Karen Mason
Editorial Production Service and Electronic Composition: WestWords, Inc.
Composition Buyer: Linda Cox
Manufacturing Buyer: JoAnne Sweeney
Cover Administrator: Kristina Mose-Libon

For related titles and support materials, visit our online catalog at www.ablongman.com.

Between the time website information is gathered and then published, it is not unusual for some sites to have closed. Also, the transcription of URLs can result in typographical errors. The publisher would appreciate notification where these errors occur so that they may be corrected in subsequent editions.

Library of Congress Cataloging in Publication Data
Reporting that matters : public affairs coverage / John Irby . . . [et al.].
   p. cm.
  Includes index.
  ISBN 0-205-43462-2
   1. Journalism—Political aspects—United States. 2. Journalism—Social aspects—United
States. 3. Reporters and reporting—United States. 4. Public affairs—United States. I. Irby, John.

PN4888.P6R46 2007
071′.3090511—dc22

                                           2005057104

Printed in the United States of America

10 9 8 7 6 5 4 3 2 1   11 10 09 08 07 06

Photo Credits: pp. ix, 19, 29, 39, 51, 67, 85, 99, 115, 125, 139, 151, 195, 215, 229, 239, 251, 289, 299 by John Irby; pp. 1, 165, 179, 265, 279, 309 by Lisa Irby; p. 82 by John Harte

C O N T E N T S

PREFACE

BY KENTON BIRD AND JOHN IRBY

One stone is often pretty, but many pretty stones together are beautiful. Public affairs reporting is about putting together various elements—reporting, writing, research, fairness, accuracy, and so on—to serve the public well.

This book began as a series of conversations. When we saw each other at workshops sponsored by journalism organizations such as the American Press Institute, the Poynter Institute and the Pew Center for Civic Journalism, the question most often asked of the other was "What book are you using for Public Affairs Reporting next year?"

The answer always indicated dissatisfaction with the limited number of choices on the market and a desire for a fresh text that incorporated the thinking being shared by editors and journalism educators at those national conferences.

Reporting of public affairs has been described as coverage of government, politics, the courts and public issues. It traditionally has been the mainstay of local and regional newspapers across the United States, as well as some local TV and radio reports. It also includes advanced coverage of specialty beats whose complexity sometimes perplexes reporters and discourages readers.

The traditional approach to public affairs reporting relies heavily on covering the workings of government at all levels, especially meetings, reports and documents. But reporting of public affairs is much more.

It can include virtually everything that involves public life: from government to the arts, from religion to the environment, and from business to law enforcement. Ideally, public affairs reporting should be less about institutions and more about issues that concern people.

Following that approach, this book seeks to demystify news about government and public issues and show student journalists how to present it in ways that engage and empower readers, viewers and listeners.

In addition, we are committed to conveying to future journalists the importance of a multicultural approach to reporting. Many journalism texts focus on theory or skill development, or both. This text will also. But it will do so with a clear understanding of the importance of seeking a diversity of voices in reporting on public issues and controversies.

Reporting of public affairs has traditionally included a reliance on "official sources"—elected officials, government agency heads and public affairs officers. They are, indeed, important. But so are underrepresented communities and groups of people. There are not just two sides to a story—there are many points of view in the middle that have been neglected for too long.

Diversity is about more than skin color or ethnic background; it also means news coverage that reflects differences in ages, economic status, sexual orientation and ability/disability.

Journalists and scholars are increasingly questioning the role of journalism in the public sphere and reexamining the meanings of objectivity, detachment and neutrality. The civic journalism movement that emerged in the 1990s helped raise the visibility of innovative approaches to reporting on public issues—public listening, civic mapping and new frames for stories that seek consensus rather than promote conflict.

For instance, Jan Schaefer, former executive director of the Pew Center for Civic Journalism, and now director of the J-Lab at the University of Maryland, said: "Future news will be about story making rather than story telling."

This text will not be so bold, but it will reflect the latest thinking about civic engagement, public journalism and interactive media. Our approach is grounded in tradition, but focused on the future.

After we began our research and writing for this textbook, two additional voices were invited into the conversation, Susan English and David Cuillier, who brought significant professional newspaper experience and additional expertise to the project.

Finally, most of the reporting strategies and writing tips are geared toward print reporters. We recognize that strong reporting of public affairs is not exclusively a franchise of newspapers. However, we believe that writing and presenting news for radio, TV or the Web require a solid grounding in the fundamentals of reporting. Other classes and other texts address the particular challenges of writing and editing for electronic media.

Students sometimes struggle with the formality of textbooks, which can admittedly be somewhat terrifying. Terror, however, isn't always brought about by the material in the text, but sometimes by the way in which it is presented.

Presentation is one of the considerations of this text—not so much visual presentation, but in the words selected, tone and style.

Do work hard but also make sure that you work harder than others. Seek out people who can teach you and help you achieve your goals; look for opportunities to increase your skills.

Acknowledgments

Journalism has been a major component of the lives of the authors of this textbook. We acknowledge the professionals who provided tips and samples of their work for this text. We are grateful to the many journalism organizations and groups for their existence and the availability of the material that has been collected and presented. We also acknowledge our students and professional and academic colleagues and bosses; Allyn & Bacon for this opportunity, specifically Molly Taylor, Michael Kish, Karen Mason and Suzanne Stradley for their patience and their low-key encouragement as this project moved forward; Pat McCutcheon of WestWords, Inc., for his detail and thoroughness during the production process; and Cheryl Adam, an exceptional copyeditor.

John Irby also acknowledges his wife, Lisa, and children for their support and love, and Dr. Alex Tan, director of the Edward R. Murrow School of Communication at Washington State University, for his continuing support and encouragement.

Kenton Bird thanks Ted Stanton, formerly of the Moscow *Idahonian*; Colorado State University Professor Emeritus Garrett W. Ray; Ken Olsen, a reporter for the Vancouver (Washington) *Columbian*; Vicki Rishling, lecturer in the University of Idaho School of Journalism and Mass Media; and his wife, Gerri Sayler, for her patience and understanding why the dining room table was always covered with clippings and notes.

Susan English acknowledges Karen Dorn Steele, a veteran journalist at the *Spokesman-Review,* for inspiring her through hard work and perseverance and for writing important stories and unknowingly inspiring many journalists to pay attention to public affairs.

We would like to acknowledge the valuable contributions that the reviewers to this text made. The reviewers were Glen L. Bleske, California State University, Chico; Steven E. Chappell, Truman State University; Bradley J. Hamm, Elon University; Robert D. Highton, University of Nevada; Ann L. Landini, Murray State University; Edward G. Weston, University of Florida; and Sheila M. Whitley, North Carolina A&T State University.

Experts Who Supplied Professional Tips

- Chapter 1: Mark Briggs, content and strategy manager for interactive media, *News Tribune*, Tacoma, WA
- Chapter 2: Patrick Webb, managing editor, *The Daily Astorian*, Astoria, OR
- Chapter 3: Brye Butler, reporter, *Abilene Reporter News*, Abilene, TX
- Chapter 4: Bill Bell, editor-publisher, *Whittier Daily News,* Whittier, CA
- Chapter 5: Ken Olsen, freelance magazine writer, Spokane, WA
- Chapter 6: Steve McClure, managing editor, the *Daily News,* Moscow, ID
- Chapter 7: Christopher Smith, Associated Press correspondent, Boise, ID

When we began conversations about this text, we decided we would stray from the stiff, formal, academic format that is so often used. We favored a style of writing—and approach—we believe is more friendly, down-to-earth, fun, conversational and informal. This is in an effort to enhance learning.

Part of our attempt to portray a relaxed communication style is by placing bylines at the beginning of every chapter, and including short biographies and photos of the authors at the end of this preface. We encourage you to spend a few minutes reviewing that information in an attempt to get a better sense of our backgrounds.

As you begin reading *Reporting That Matters: Public Affairs Coverage,* don't be afraid of the term *public affairs reporting*—or the generally advanced nature of texts on public affairs reporting.

In its simplest form, reporting of public affairs is nothing more than informing the public of information that people need, information that comes primarily from public agencies or entities. It is about issues that concern people.

Obtaining information, however, isn't always easy. While the public's business certainly should be conducted in public, too many officials are less than forthcoming with information people need and want to know—and have a right to know.

This text is not remedial in nature, so begin by remembering some of the basic and key building blocks to good reporting and writing:

- **Use simple sentences,** usually with only one thought.
- **In most cases,** don't switch tenses. Find the best one to tell the story and stay with it.
- **Active voice is** always better than passive voice.
- **Avoid the safe** but formatted writing style of transition . . . quote . . . transition . . . quote . . . transition . . . quote. This is not good writing. It is the only transcription of linked thoughts.
- **Tell a story,** but don't force it. Let the story tell itself. Don't overwrite.
- **Use precision in** writing; the correct word for the correct usage. Avoid jargon and complicated words.
- **Use a dictionary,** thesaurus and stylebook.
- **Keep yourself out** of the story (avoid the use of *I, we,* and *us* except in first person stories, which should be rare and reserved for columns and other commentary pieces).

Reporting of public affairs isn't easy. But those who do it well make a difference in the world. Remember the words of Peter Bhatia, executive editor of the *Oregonian* and a former president of the American Society of Newspaper Editors (ASNE), spoken to the South Asian Journalists Association (SAJA) in 1999:

> I don't want to sound like an old man but I find that the current generation is not prepared to work hard. As baby boomers it was beaten into us that you can't expect things handed to you. You've got to have your own initiative and the willingness to go that extra mile.
>
> It's important to be focused on becoming the best journalist and create your own opportunities. Combine that with hard work and this is an industry where you can succeed.

- Chapter 8: Bill Morlin, investigative reporter, the *Spokesman-Review,* Spokane, WA
- Chapter 9: Bryan Gruley, Chicago Bureau chief, *Wall Street Journal,* Chicago, IL
- Chapter 10: Julie Sullivan, investigative reporter, the *Oregonian,* Portland, OR
- Chapter 11: Hannelore Sudermann, assistant editor and senior writer, *Washington State Magazine*, Pullman, WA, and Colleen McBrinn, assistant features editor, *Seattle Times,* Seattle, WA
- Chapter 12: Jim Borden, managing editor, the *Gazette,* Kalamazoo, MI
- Chapter 13: Vicki Rothrock, freelance correspondent, Hong Kong
- Chapter 14: Neil Modie, reporter, the *Seattle Post-Intelligencer,* Seattle, WA
- Chapter 15: Priscilla Salant, manager of rural policy and assessments, Department of Agriculture, Economics and Rural Sociology, University of Idaho, Moscow, ID, and Dan Popkey, columnist, the *Idaho Statesman,* Boise, ID
- Chapter 16: Maxine Bernstein, reporter, the *Oregonian,* Portland, OR
- Chapter 17: Sheila R. McCann, co-editor of Social Justice Team, the *Salt Lake Tribune,* Salt Lake City, UT
- Chapter 18: Hannelore Sudermann, assistant editor and senior writer, *Washington State Magazine*, Pullman, WA
- Chapter 19: Dave Boling, sports columnist, *News Tribune,* Tacoma, WA and Jim Kershner, columnist and theater critic, the *Spokesman-Review,* Spokane, WA
- Chapter 20: Anna King, reporter, *Tri-City Herald,* Kennewick, WA
- Chapter 21: Brent Champaco, reporter, *News Tribune,* Tacoma, WA
- Appendix A: Ralph Pomnichowski, freelance writer-photographer, Great Falls, MT
- Appendix B: James P. Medina, business editor, *Ventura County Star,* Ventura, CA

■ **Freedom of Information (FOI) requests:** Simply asking for an accounting of all FOI requests filed by other reporters covering an agency for a recent period will indicate what the competition is up to—and may give tips of story ideas that have gone unnoticed.

Common sense usually suggests where to begin a quest for public records. Some larger counties, municipalities and subdivisions of state government must designate a custodian of records who responds to all requests from the press and public. Most of the time, the office or person who compiles the document is the best place to begin. What's the best way to gather information from records? Some reporters swear by longhand notes on a legal pad or pocket notebook, but it's increasingly common to take notes on a laptop computer, particularly for police and court records when only a summary is to appear in print. For more complicated stories, projects and investigations, there's no substitute for photocopies of the entire documents.

Agencies are allowed to set reasonable prices for copying, so a reporter must be prepared to pay for copies at the time that he or she requests them. Knowing the approximate number of pages in advance—and having prior authorization from an editor to spend the newspaper's money—will prevent surprises when the bill comes.

Reporters need to weigh the value of having copies of the documents close at hand against the time needed to organize and retrieve the copies. Sometimes the inconvenience of going back to the agency to review a document outweighs the risk of losing the copy due to a haphazard filing system at one's office. If there is any concern that a document might be concealed or destroyed to cover someone's trail, it is prudent to make a copy the first time it's reviewed.

The more complicated the story, the greater the reporter's challenge in keeping track of notes from interviews, printouts from the World Wide Web and copies of documents. Experienced reporters develop filing systems using color-coded file folders, cardboard bankers' boxes or plastic storage bins. Some reporters keep files for investigative projects at home to avoid intermingling with notes for daily stories.

Strategies for requesting records under state and federal Freedom of Information laws are discussed in the chapter on access (see chapter 7).

Finding Stories in Records

Ronald Campbell, a reporter for the *Orange County (California) Register,* says that journalists, by nature, aren't suited for the laborious process of searching for information through records.

"We expect instant results and tend to get distracted when we don't find something exciting quickly," Campbell wrote in "The Zen of Documents," a tip sheet prepared for an Investigative Reporters and Editors conference. Campbell says reporters need patience, an ability to see patterns and openness to new ideas. "In following a paper trail, be mindful that a sidetrack may be more productive than the main road," he wrote.

Here are two examples of reporters who discovered important—and interesting—stories through documents.

Alexis Bacharach, a reporter for the 8,000-circulation *Moscow-Pullman Daily News,* knew something was awry with plans for a University of Idaho building project in Boise, three hundred miles away from the main campus in Moscow. She had heard rumors of cost overruns and undisclosed financial transactions. But nothing appeared on agendas of the Idaho Board of Education, and officials were close-mouthed when asked about the project. Then the university's financial vice president abruptly resigned.

Bacharach called a university official who she knew had reservations about the project. "Does this have anything to do with Boise?" she asked. The answer helped her frame an open-records request for documents about University Place, as the three-building campus was to be called.

"The source steered me in the right direction to put the documents in context," she explained. "Without his help, I would have drowned in documents."

The official told her the university had lent money to its affiliated foundation to cover expenses associated with planning and design. That gave Bacharach enough information to narrowly frame her request. She wrote to the university attorney (the designated records custodian) and asked for "Any statements of transfers at or exceeding $1 million to the University of Idaho Foundation from all University of Idaho endowments, scholarship funds, retirement funds and any other university account not associated with the foundation in the past 12 months. . . . Any statements showing said transfers from said accounts signed by Vice President of Finance and Administration and UI Foundation Treasurer Jerry Wallace within the last 12 months. . . . Any documents including notes, memos and e-mail correspondence . . . that make reference to the transfer of university funds to the UI Foundation for the purpose of giving financial support to the Idaho Water Center and/or Idaho Place."

Bacharach's request for information triggered an eleven-hour meeting of the Board of Education, setting in motion a series of events that caused the university's speculative funding scheme to come under public scrutiny. After most of the records Bacharach asked for were released two weeks later, she and her editors spent the weekend reviewing them. The story—which began on page 1 and continued on most of an inside page—began as follows:

A 6-acre parcel of land sits vacant on the corner of Myrtle Street and Broadway Avenue in Boise. The property is the intended home for the University of Idaho Foundation's University Place.

On an academic level, university officials have dreams of a combined Boise operation for UI and Idaho State University. There even have been rumblings that University Place could provide the location for the state's first medical school.

About three years and $28 million later, the Boise site has gone from UI's pet project to the center of a state investigation into questionable expenditures of university and foundation funds. How University Place went from promise to problem plays out in a series of documents and memos obtained from the UI by the *Moscow-Pullman Daily News.*

The project started simply in 1999 when the property sought for University Place became available for purchase. The university established an agency account in the fall of 2000 to start the project, according to a confidential memo sent to Jerry Wallace, then–vice president of finance and administration and foundation treasurer. The same document reported there was never approval to set up the account. An unsigned document obtained from the UI describes the agency account as an

(continued)

(continued)

unlimited line of credit extended from the UI to the foundation.

Without immediate state funding available, the UI loaned the foundation $1.9 million to secure the property in Boise. The transfer of funds was made without approval from the State Board of Education and with no guarantee of state money.

The university's president later resigned after the extent of the debt and deception became known, and state and federal investigations followed.

Other newspapers, including the *Idaho Statesman* of Boise, pursued the story with their own records requests. *Statesman* reporter Dan Popkey filed a detailed request that produced "a room full of documents"—including architectural drawings, memos, reports and a computer containing more than 6,000 e-mail messages. Popkey's report, published three months later, detailed a web of intrigue and corner-cutting that reached to the governor's office. Nonetheless, it was Bacharach's initial request (focused by an internal source) that caused the university's financial house of cards to collapse when it did.

Court records can be just as useful in uncovering bad decisions that cost taxpayers money. Scott North, a reporter for the *Herald* in Everett, Washington, wondered why Snohomish County paid a $412,000 settlement to a burglar whose foot had been partially chewed away by a police dog during his arrest.

"The attorney who negotiated the settlement for the burglar told me that the paper trail was rich and explained why the county had paid out as much as it did as quickly as it did," North said.

North and two colleagues began an investigation that turned up a series of behavioral problems with the dog—and pointed out that Washington state had few rules for training police dogs or determining when a dog was unfit for duty.

North said the county resisted the paper's efforts to investigate the problem dog's history. County officials released some records, redacted details from other documents and asserted "attorney work product" exemptions on still others.

"Instead of getting angry, we got busy," North recalled.

Because Washington law requires government agencies to explain why they withhold certain records, the *Herald* reporters learned about a lawsuit focused on the dog's work at another police department in the state. That led to a contact with the plaintiff's attorney, who authorized the release of key documents showing that the dog had been sold to the Snohomish County Sheriff's Department after being found unacceptable for police work in Tacoma.

The Internet as a Reporting Tool

Computer terminals arrived in many U.S. newsrooms in the late 1970s and early 1980s as part of "front-end" systems intended to streamline copy editing, headline writing and the production of news pages. But they were primarily internal networks designed to share stories among reporters, editors and designers. Their only link to the outside world was to the Associated Press (AP) and/or other news services, from which they received a stream of news, sports, feature stories and photographs, first by telephone lines and later by satellite.

PROFESSIONAL TIPS

Bill Morlin

Bill Morlin earned a journalism degree at Eastern Washington University. He began his journalism career in 1967 with the Associated Press, working in Spokane, Seattle and Olympia, Washington. In 1972 he was hired as a reporter for the *Spokane Daily Chronicle,* where he worked until the *Chronicle's* merger with the *Spokesman-Review* in 1983. As an investigative reporter for the *Spokesman-Review,* he specializes in criminal justice issues, with emphasis on extremist groups, terrorism and organized crime.

Question: As more and more government documents become available electronically, what types of records are still best inspected at the source, on paper, and why?

Inspecting public records electronically takes the human contact component out of the reporting process. Clerks behind the counter (when you meet them eyeball to eyeball) can frequently provide anecdotal information that no computer search or telephone interview will ever turn up. There will never be a replacement or substitute for shoe-leather reporting, and don't forget that.

Of course, it's great while under deadline to go online and quickly retrieve public records. But frequently, as in the case of many criminal court cases, only brief information is available. Some online court records don't provide names and phone numbers of attorneys involved. Bankruptcy filings don't show all the creditors.

And, despite growing numbers of public records, many still are not online. For example, in a story a few years ago, I wanted to see state Department of Transportation forms filled out by various nonprofit groups using freeway rest stops to offer "free coffee" as a fundraising activity. A woman and her son running a charity scam were using the state-operated rest stops to haul in hundreds of dollars a day from unsuspecting motorists

who took the "free coffee" and threw coins and dollars bills into a donations jar. The state forms that I obtained by visiting a state office tied the scam artists to use of the rest stops.

More recently, to find the gravesite of the late leader of the Aryan Nations, I had to visit a Coeur d'Alene cemetery and ask to see its publicly available site map, showing various graves. Such information often can't be found online.

In short, despite the advantages of modern computer technology, it can often breed laziness for reporters. They should learn to push away from their desk and mouse, grab a notebook and hit the street.

Question: What are three essential documents to understanding how a state or local government agency works, or doesn't work as well as it should?

Court calendars; agendas for city council and school district meetings, and their annual financial budgets; and reports from state auditors and the General Accounting Office (GAO).

Court calendars are daily roadmaps, showing how various criminal and civil cases snake their way through our crowded courts and legal system.

Agendas for city councils and school boards provide the "fresh meat" issues that are scheduled

(continued)

PROFESSIONAL TIPS   Continued

to come before these governing bodies. Agenda packets given to council members and board members frequently also include relevant background information on topics—often a windfall for reporters. An agency's annual budget also shows where the money will be spent.

State auditors' reports of all state and local governmental agencies can be a minefield of information for reporters. GAO reports, looking at federal agencies, also can be essential documents to understanding how a government agency does or doesn't work.

Question: Which independent groups or agencies keep records that might be useful in evaluating the performance of a city, county or school district?

Clearly, the state auditor in most states is "one-stop-shopping" for reporters who want to see how various governmental agencies are operating. Frequently, state audits turn up irregularities and even criminal acts.

The unfortunate part of this watchdog function is that many times, the agency or government officials accused of wrongdoing get to see and respond to the state audit report before the public and the press get a copy.

A tip: stay plugged into the state audit process, and find out when the next audit report of a particular agency will hit the public file.

Question: Given the abundance of both good and bad information on the Internet, what tests do you apply to assess the credibility of records retrieved from Web sites?

Some documents, by their mere nature, are self-authenticating. But it's also easy with scanners and computer technology to manipulate and or make altered documents. That may have been the case in 2004 when *CBS News* producers got documents they thought were Texas Air National Guard records of George W. Bush.

One way to avoid being tricked is to attempt to get the same document from more than one source. Compare the copies to make sure there has been no adulteration.

Question: What suggestions do you have for avoiding errors when using documents in a story?

If possible, find the author of the document—the prosecutor in a criminal case, the defense attorney in a civil suit, the legislator who drafted the bill—and have that person explain its contents or what it means. Often, reporters think they know it all and are afraid of "appearing dumb" with news contacts.

Sometimes, even if you think you know the meaning or significance of a document, playing dumb with the document's source can peel loose great quotes or insights you might not have thought about.

The World Wide Web—a user-friendly, visual-based system to find information on the Internet—is such a large part of commerce and culture today that it's hard to believe it is a recent phenomenon.

Frank Bass, director of computer-assisted reporting for the AP, points to two developments in the 1990s that made the Web such a boon to newsgathering: the development of Mosaic, the first point-and-click interface in 1993; and America OnLine's decision to offer unlimited Internet access for a flat rate of $19.95 a month.

"Prior to AOL's offer, many newsrooms had been reluctant to make full use of the Internet's potential because of the possibility of outrageous fees," Bass wrote.

Numerous Web sites are devoted to strategies for assessing the accuracy of information on the Internet. In general, the advice is similar to that for dealing with paper documents: determine who has produced the Web site, what their qualifications and motives are and how recently the information has been updated. Be skeptical of Web pages that advocate a particular point of view, are secretive about who produces the content or merely recycle material from other sources.

Bob Greene, an investigative reporter for *Newsday,* had a series of tests to measure a source's credibility. Although intended to assess the validity of information from human sources, they apply equally to Web pages. Here is his list:

- **Has this source** proved accurate in the past?
- **Can the source** provide the names of other witnesses or documents that confirm the information?
- **Was the source** in a position to know the facts that he or she is relaying?
- **Is the source's** motive in supplying the material rational?
- **Does the information** fit the facts?

Journalists usually use the Internet as a starting point for background information, not as the final word. Once they find information online, they should call the primary source to verify it and gather other information not provided online. Online information helps point journalists in the right direction, such as finding contact information. Journalists should know what's on the Web and have useful sites bookmarked and ready for when they are needed. If a story is due in twenty minutes, it is too late to search for information online and be sure of its veracity or timeliness. In fact, it is often faster to pick up the phone and call someone than to find information on the Internet. Getting out of the office to talk to people face-to-face is still one of the best ways of gathering information.

Computer-Assisted Reporting

Bernstein would have given up his cigarettes and Woodward his corduroy suits to have the power of a computer at their disposal. A scene in *All the President's Men* shows the two *Washington Post* reporters digging for hours through boxes and boxes of thousands of library cards, trying to find out whether a particular official checked out certain books. In today's world, a search for a name in a computer database of 2 million records would take a few seconds.

Computer-assisted reporting—also referred to as *computer-assisted journalism* or *database journalism*—is the use of computers to acquire and analyze information. Although online information gathering has been an important element to computer-assisted reporting, the power of the computer resides in its ability to analyze large amounts of data, typically in spreadsheet programs such as Excel or Lotus, database managers such as Microsoft Access, mapping software such as ArcView and sometimes statistical software such as the Statistical Package for the Social Sciences (SPSS).

Computer-assisted reporting is also a relatively new tool for journalists. Although a select few reporters used mainframes to analyze data as early as in the 1960s, computer-assisted reporting did not become widely used until the early 1990s with the advent of cheaper personal computers and Internet connections. The National Institute for Computer-Assisted Reporting (NICAR) also helped raise awareness of the technique through workshops, training camps and conferences. Yet the ability to work with data is still a relatively rare skill found among journalists. News organizations value reporters who know how to do it well.

Acquiring and analyzing data helps journalists write stories with conviction, to go beyond anecdotal evidence and "he said, she said" muddiness. Computer-assisted reporting is power reporting. Indeed, Bill Dedman used his experience in database journalism to create his "power reporting" Web site (www.powerreporting.com), which provides tips for computer-assisted reporting. Dedman won the Pulitzer Prize for a series of stories in the *Atlanta Journal and Constitution* that revealed racist policies in home-loan lending.

By analyzing data, including linking different databases, journalists have found stories previously uncovered. For example, some journalists have matched school-bus driver databases against criminal conviction data to find school bus drivers with drunk driving records, prompting schools to start implementing background checks.

Data analysis can help reporters better examine their communities. Brad Branan, a reporter for the *Tucson (Arizona), Citizen,* wanted to find out where crime was occurring in the city. He downloaded free crime data from the FBI's Web site and used Microsoft Excel to find out that Tucson was ranked fifty-fifth in the nation for violent crime out of 280 metropolitan areas. But he wanted to know more about where the crime was occurring in town.

Branan's next step was to get from the city of Tucson specific crime data that included every reported crime and its location by block and street. He imported the data into ArcView mapping software to show where crimes were occurring. Branan found neighborhoods that were having problems, and after applying U.S. Census data to the map, he found that the crime was driving people out of their homes and causing unstable communities. His story, "Crime Magnets," began this way:

Daniel F. Armenta checked into a Miracle Mile motel in January 2002 and started to party. He picked up a prostitute and bought crack cocaine.

The 34-year-old Tucsonan ended up dead in his room at the Riviera Motor Lodge, 515 W. Miracle Mile.

He was shot, stabbed and whacked with an ax. Two people Armenta had sought for drugs were convicted of murdering him.

Armenta died in the most violent section of the city, a *Tucson Citizen* analysis of violent crime reports shows. The newspaper mapped about 8,500 violent crime reports handled by the Tucson Police Department through the first three months of 2004.

The reports were grouped by the department patrol. The . . . highest rate of violent crime—murder, manslaughter, rape, robbery and aggravated assault—generally is between Interstate 10 and a line that runs roughly along First, Euclid and Park avenues.

The three northern sectors had a higher combined rate than the three downtown sectors—198 violent crimes per square mile, compared to 187 for the downtown sectors. . . .

A volatile mix of strip clubs, prostitution, drug dealing and criminal predators makes the area Tucson's most violent, police say.

Branan deftly mixed details from police reports, interviews with police officers and neighborhood leaders and personal observations of the high-crime areas. But it was the matching of crime reports to Census tracts that demonstrated the extent of the crime problem.

City officials could no longer rationalize the disparity between downtown and the northern neighborhoods. They could not argue with the data. In response to the story, the federal government formed a task force to tackle crime in Tucson, and the city approved $4 million to hire seventy-one more police officers.

Computer-assisted reporting is a skill that young journalists can learn quickly, but it's more than just knowing how to use software—it's a way of thinking. Reporters first must identify data that can enhance their stories, then figure out how to get them, analyze them, and present them in an engaging way:

- **Identifying data:** Most government information is stored electronically, which makes computer-assisted reporting even easier today, even at the local town hall or high school. Any information written on a government form is likely to be entered into a database, so look at the forms to get an idea of what might be in the data. Most databases are composed of thousands or millions of individual records, and each record contains information separated into different categories. For example, a city's parking ticket database might contain thousands of individual tickets, or records, and each record might include a variety of categories, such as the person's name, vehicle license plate number, the date, location and violation. Each of those categories is called a *field.* When looking at the parking ticket database on the computer screen in an Excel or Access grid, each horizontal row would be an individual ticket and each vertical column would be a category or field. In that format it becomes easy to sort the tickets alphabetically, group the most common ticketed locations, find individuals or add up the total fines. A spreadsheet program is excellent for examining and calculating large reams of numbers, such as from a city budget. Sometimes a database you need for a story does not exist, so you'll have to create it by typing in the information yourself, often from boxes and boxes of paper files. Sometimes this is the best type of database because you know the data are accurate (you entered them yourself) and they can be tailored to a specific, important story.

- **Getting data:** Sometimes data, such as national FBI crime statistics, are available for free downloading from the Web, but more often you will have to ask a government agency for the electronic file. Legally, computerized data are generally treated the same as any paper government record, so if you are allowed to get a copy of a parking ticket, then you should be allowed to get a copy of the parking ticket database. Working through the technical issues, however, can be tricky. First, find out what is in the data. Ask for a copy of the *record layout,* which lists the different fields of information included for the records. Talk to the person who created or maintains the data to find out what it means and its limitations. When starting out, it is best to begin with simple data that can be easily verified and checked. Just because data are in a computer does not make them correct. Data can be "dirty," and are only as accurate as the people who typed them in. Almost all data can be exported from a government computer, usually in common software such as Excel. If that is not possible, ask for the data in a generic form that can be imported into an Excel file, such as a tab-delimited text file. Files can be transferred as e-mail attachments or burned onto CDs. Be prepared to haggle over data because you might be the first person who has asked for them. Also, be prepared to juggle several data requests at the same time because responses can drag on for months.

■ **Analyzing data:** Once you have the database, check it out and make sure you understand it. Peruse it to see what is in it and whether a lot of information is missing or appears inaccurate. Clean it up, and figure out what you can do with it. Software programs allow you to do a variety of analyses. Some of the common ways of thinking about data include:

- **Extremes:** Find the biggest, smallest, highest, lowest, richest or poorest, such as the highest paid employee on campus. Rankings, including a "top 10" list, can be interesting to readers and lead to good stories.

- **Trends:** Look at the numbers from year to year, such as enrollment during the past ten years or the change in campus burglary rates over time.

- **Individuality:** Look for well-known individuals who might be of public interest in such databases as tax evaders.

- **Linking:** Get two different databases and link them together to find new information, such as drunk-driving records with transit drivers. Each database will have to share at least one field of similar information to link, such as an identification number or name.

■ **Writing:** Some of the best computer-assisted reporting stories won't appear to readers to be based on numbers. Too many numbers crammed into a paragraph can send readers fleeing or shivering from memories of math class. In many computer-assisted reporting stories, the months of data work are compressed into a single paragraph or a single fact—but an important fact that supports the story. For relevant numbers and facts, try developing simple, easy-to-read graphs or charts. Focus the story on people. To assure accuracy, it helps to run the data analysis past an expert, such as a university statistics professor, another reporter skilled in computer-assisted reporting or possibly the director of the agency that collected the data. It is better to discover flaws in the data or analysis before publication, not after. Ultimately, the best way to learn computer-assisted reporting is to do it. Reporters at small news organizations need to carve time out of their busy days to teach themselves how to use the software and work through technical problems. Once you have done a story or two that incorporated data acquisition and analysis, your boss might be willing to send you to advanced training, such as a NICAR two-week boot camp.

Five Basic Rules

The following tips were presented by Jim Steele, *Time* magazine; Joe Stephens, the *Washington Post;* and Mike McGraw, *Kansas City Star,* at the Investigative Reporters and Editors conference, June 6, 2003:

- **Never view documents** in a vacuum. Combining two or more documents, or documents and interviews, is often the key to investigative stories. Such "triangulation" unlocks the full potential of unsung documents and sources.

- **Always view documents** over time; compare this year's annual report to ones published five and ten years ago.

- **Please help short-circuit** the troubling trend of journalists failing to use the federal Freedom of Information Act and state open records laws. Yes, it takes time; yes, there are delays, especially in the aftermath of September 11. But sometimes they work and work well. Either way, we have a constitutional obligation to keep them well greased.

- **If someone refers** to or reads from a document during an interview, ask for a copy. Carry a floppy disk with you so there's never an excuse for someone not to download what you want.

- **Make copies of** your documents before you start marking them up. That way, when the graphic folks ask for copies for art work, you won't feel so dumb.

CHAPTER EXERCISES

1. Go to the U.S. Census Bureau's Web site (www.census.gov) and find population figures for your city, county and state. Compare figures from the regular Census (conducted every ten years) to the most recent estimate. Then find predictions for the next two to five years. What observations can you draw about population growth patterns?

2. Visit the city clerk's office, and ask for a copy of the agenda for the next city council meeting. Ask whether the same information is available on the city's Web site. Visit the site and compare the two agendas. Then attend the council meeting. How closely is the agenda followed? What supplemental documents are mentioned by council members and city staff during the meeting? Where would you obtain them?

3. Contact the international programs office of your college or university, and ask for a breakdown of international students for 2000 and the most recent semester they are available. (Some colleges make this information available on a Web site.) Which countries or parts of the world send the most students to your university? How has this pattern changed since September 11, 2001? Which majors are most popular for foreign students?

4. With the permission of your instructor, do a public records profile of her or him. Find out as much as you can about her or his residence, finances and public activities through the following methods:

   a. Web search, using Google, AltaVista or another search engine.
   b. Your college's news bureau or media relations office. If your institution is public, you might also be able to find her or his salary in a budget document.

      c. University and public libraries.

      d. State auto license and driver's license records.

      e. Property ownership and tax records (usually through county assessor's and treasurer's offices).

      f. Voting history (through county clerk or elections office).

      g. At least one other governmental agency.

CHAPTER 9

Leads

BY JOHN IRBY

One important aspect of a lead is to catch a reader's attention, much like this Mardi Gras mask. Leads have been described as the most difficult part of writing. Although the process might sometimes be painful, there is often satisfaction in a job well done.

It was a dark and stormy night!

Snoopy, the crafty and loveable beagle, is often credited with that lead. Unfortunately, some might consider him a dog of a plagiarist as he didn't write those words. Victorian novelist Edward George Earl Bulwer-Lytton, who died at the age of 70 in 1873, is the author.

Bulwer-Lytton, however, is better known for his lead "The pen is mightier than the sword," which he wrote in 1834 in *The Last Days of Pompeii*.

Leads are critically important to all stories, yet far too many reporters and editors fail to understand their significance.

Inverted Pyramid

Newspapers, like most other businesses, have a tendency to format processes. That is sometimes a good thing, but not always.

Journalism students are generally taught in lower-division courses to follow the inverted pyramid format of writing. It is what it says it is—an inverted pyramid; place the most important information at the top, followed by information in order of importance to the bottom (or top) of the pyramid.

Writing in an inverted pyramid format is a tradition in journalism, which began at a time when there was value to following the rule because it aided not only editors but also compositors who cut stories from the bottom, as legs of printed type were cut and pasted onto a page. It was part of an antiquated production process that was often performed on deadline.

There was little time to think through what actually should be trimmed to make the story fit the predetermined spot, so it was cut from the bottom, hoping that is where the reporter placed the least important information.

Another reason dates back to the early foreign correspondents during wars. Often they would phone in their stories, possibly being disconnected or cut off in midstory, unable to reconnect. So, the most important information was crammed into the beginning of the story.

Newspaper readers are also believed to often want stories that are "to the point." Researchers tell us that readers seldom spend more than twenty minutes to read or scan their entire newspaper.

But many journalists, however, believe readers will make time for good, solid, interesting, compelling narrative writing. They claim there are more effective writing formats today—especially in public affairs stories, which often demand a more thorough analysis of the news.

Such stories require much more thought in the lead process.

When a reporter uses the inverted pyramid format, he or she is placing the climax of the coverage topic or subject at the front of the story—in the lead—saving readers the time of having to wait for or find the information.

But when a reporter fails to build suspense, it is difficult to encourage or train readers to read the rest of the story, because they know they can get the basics and move on.

Probably more than 75 percent of news stories written today are written in inverted pyramid style. It is a format that needs to be mastered. By using this format, you will learn the art of making news judgments and prioritizing information.

In this format it is also critical to write the story as simply and clearly as possible, while still providing background and context. The best place to start is the lead, which sets the tone for the story.

Mission Impossible

The lead is often the most difficult part of writing, at least for most beginning journalists. There are some basic reasons:

- **It isn't easy** to sum up five hundred or more words into twenty-five or fewer words. The same can be said for writing headlines.

PROFESSIONAL TIPS

Bryan Gruley

Bryan Gruley is the Chicago bureau chief of the *Wall Street Journal*. He directs a group of eight reporters who write about agriculture, food companies, restaurants, airlines, banks, manufacturing, newspaper publishers and anything interesting in the great Midwest. Previously, Gruley was a senior editor in the *Journal*'s Washington bureau, where he helped reporters in Washington and elsewhere write difficult stories for page 1, and wrote some himself, on a wide variety of financial and nonfinancial subjects. He wrote one of the page-1 stories on September 11, 2001, that won the *Journal* a 2002 Pulitzer Prize for breaking news.

Question: What thought processes do you use in coming up with leads?

I do better when I'm not thinking at all, when the lead just presents itself as something obvious that I'd be stupid not to use. First hunches are often right when it comes to leads, I think. I recall a story I did once about these massive metal sculptures alongside a county road in North Dakota. I wrote almost exactly what I thought when I first crested that road and saw the sculpture in the valley below: "The grasshopper crouches in silence at the highway's edge, a monstrous rust silhouette on steel-gray sky. At 30 feet tall and 50 feet long, it looks like it might, at any moment, spring from its muddy perch and devour a passing pickup truck."

It's usually easier with news stories, where all you want to do is tell what happened and, actually, it's the second 'graph, where you tell the readers why they ought to read about the Kalamazoo County Board of Commissioners raising parking fees by 25 percent, that's trickier. But when I wrote the lead for the *Journal*'s front-page story on what happened on 9/11, I couldn't just say: "An estimated 4,000 people died when two planes commandeered by terrorists slammed into . . . " It demanded something more, some impossible perspective, some attempt to reach out to the reader and say, "I know, it was unbelievable, but it really

happened." Again I conjured how I felt when I saw the towers burning on the television sets at the front of the newsroom: "They were like scenes from a catastrophe movie. Or a Tom Clancy novel. Or a CNN broadcast from a distant foreign nation. But they were real yesterday. And they were very much in the U.S."

Truth in advertising: I wrote everything up to "yesterday." Larry Rout, a superb *Journal* editor, attached the last line, which was perfect.

In the end: be simple. Direct. Concise. Sometimes it helps to listen to how you tell someone else about what you're working on.

"Hey, Gruley, what are you working on?" . . . "Man, you wouldn't believe this, I'm driving down this road in South Dakota and I come over this hill and down in the valley I see this huge grasshopper the size of a city bus. I'm thinking the thing's gonna jump out and devour my rental car."

Question: What is the all-time favorite lead you have written (or read), and why?

Too many all-time favorite leads to count. Or remember. But one that always sticks in my head, because I'm a hockey player, is one written by a UPI [United Press International] sportswriter in Detroit sometime in the 1970s. The Detroit Red Wings played the Montreal Canadiens to a 1–1 tie on the night of a vicious ice storm. The lead was: "You know you're going to see a good hockey

(continued)

PROFESSIONAL TIPS   Continued

game when you have to put your skates on just to get to the rink."

It was clever, it incorporated a wider swath of news (the weather), and it hooked the reader. Even though it didn't tell you precisely what happened—the 1–1 tie—it made you want to read. That's really all a lead needs to do—make you want to read the next 'graph. And the next 'graph should make you want to read the next 'graph. And so on.

I can share what I believe to be the worst lead I've ever read, or at least in memory. Maybe I denigrate it unfairly because it appeared on the front page of the *New York Times,* where I guess we should expect better. The truth is, though, that the big "writerly" papers frequently publish leads that would make a self-respecting journalism teacher retch if he or she wasn't aware that it didn't run in one of our "best" newspapers. Don't get me started . . . : "INDIANOLA, Iowa, Feb. 2—White is the color of cold in Iowa this winter, with perennially white skies folding into silent white pastures and fields of corn stubble. Behind white clapboard farmhouses, only the white tanks, shaped like snub-nosed submarines, offer protection from a winter that began as the coldest recorded around here and has almost two months to go."

Do you have any idea what this story is about? Go ahead, read it again. You still don't know, do you? I've read this aloud to dozens of journalists. Not one has guessed what the story was about based on the first fifty-six words. Thank God for the copy editor, who wrote this headline: "Price of Propane Making It Harder to Keep Warm."

Question: What are the things to avoid in writing leads?

Leads aren't supposed to dazzle readers with brilliant writing. They aren't supposed to crystallize every damn thing in the universe of the story in a sentence or two (although that's fine, if the subject is simple enough). One of the biggest and most common mistakes reporters make on feature stories is to lead with a lengthy anecdote. Usually it takes so long that the reader has moved on to the crossword puzzle or her backyard garden before

she finds out what happened in the scintillating cloakrooms of the House Subcommittee on Maritime Idiosyncracies. The writer says, "But that was my best stuff." Well, often your best stuff doesn't make any sense to the reader because he needs to read the story before he can comprehend the meaning of your best stuff. It's like giving someone the punch line before the joke. If you have to explain the punch line, it falls pretty flat. And why the hell use your very best stuff in the first two 'graphs? Why should I keep watching the movie if I've already seen the best stuff?

For instance, I wrote a goofy front-page story that had all sorts of juicy scenes I could've used. I chose to start it this way: "MANISTEE, Mich.—Five weeks ago, David Gutowski, a self-employed painter in this little town, killed a six-point buck with his bare hands and a brown leather belt."

Reader says, "He what?"

Betcha he reads on.

That's really all a lead is required to do: make the reader read the next 'graph.

So, OK, rather than the lead, per se, let's talk about the top of the story—the first three or four 'graphs, say. The top should do two things. One, get the readers' attention—provoke 'em, make 'em laugh, make 'em wonder, shock 'em. Two, give them a hint what the hell the story is about and why they ought to spend time with it. Don't make them wait until the twelfth 'graph to find out what the story is about. Unless your anecdote includes aliens, Elvis, the Mafia, Terry Bradshaw, Teri Hatcher and Osama bin Laden, give us all a break and just tell us why you've taken the trouble. Which reminds me of a buddy who used to write for the *Los Angeles Times.* Great reporter, great writer, although a little self-indulgent at times. He showed me the top of a story he was writing that had something to do with graveyards, an inherently interesting subject. It was very well written, in a colorful-language-and-well-constructed-sentence sort of way. But I just really wanted to know what the hell the story was about, and after the eighth or ninth 'graph, I hadn't a clue, so I asked him, "Do you plan at some point to tell the readers what this story is about?"

- **In writing the** lead, the writer is attempting to hook the reader.
- **Beginning journalists develop** mental blocks about writing leads because journalism teachers tell them it is the most difficult part of writing.

Although leads might be the most difficult part of writing for many, it doesn't have to be mission impossible. Don't think of the lead as difficult. Think of it only as something that will "advertise" the rest of your story—what is coming—a brief, simple but creative synopsis of the most important information in the story. As Bryan Gruley said, what is the story about?

The best writers don't sit down immediately after an interview and pound out their lead and story. They first try to organize their thoughts and think about the relevance, usefulness and interest for readers. They will ask themselves two questions:

- **So what?**
- **Who cares?**

For instance, if you are sent to cover a relatively minor house fire, asking, "So what?" and "Who cares?" might reveal that the only person who cares is the owner of the house. But if the information you gathered includes the fact that it was an arson fire started the exact same way as ten others that month in the general area, then the number of those caring has just dramatically increased.

"So what?" and "Who cares?" aren't all that matters in helping to set up or structure a story lead. Make sure you have a good understanding of the other basics you have been taught in previous courses: who, what, where, when, why and sometimes how?

Next, try to rank or prioritize the information you have obtained, as this will start to help crystallize the focus or approach of a lead. It is temping to disregard this step, especially for veteran reporters who might be working on deadline. Veteran reporters sometimes magically think they can rank the information as they write. But far too often, they find they are doing a lot of rewriting, either on their own or by the mandate of an editor, because they skipped the five or ten minutes it takes to prioritize the importance of their information.

Tips for Leads

After a thoughtful foundation has been laid, it is now time to write your lead, considering the following guidelines:

- **Keep your leads short.** Generally speaking, the first sentence should be under twenty-five words. Leads, however, can and often are more than one sentence or one paragraph, but, generally they are a sentence or two.

- **A reoccurring theme** for journalists is accuracy. Never include a name in a lead without checking the spelling. And consider the importance of using the name, as it might easily be delayed if the act is more important than the name of the person involved in the act. When a name is delayed it is called a *delayed-identification lead,* and when it is included it is called an *immediate-identification lead.*

- **Keep your opinion out of leads** (and news stories). Opinion usually doesn't make a good lead, even if it is attributed to a proper source.

- **Although the five W's and H** should almost always be included in every story, as the information is appropriate and available, don't feel compelled to include all of the information in the lead. Determine the most important *W* for the lead, and save the rest for the body of the story. Avoid wordy leads like the following: "Susan Washington, a student in the Edward R. Murrow School of Communication at Washington State University (WHO), has been selected for a fellowship for journalism students at Indiana University (WHAT), to be held at Indiana University in Bloomington, Ind., (WHERE), June 17–23 (WHEN), based on her winning essay (WHY), and made possible by a grant from the Poynter Institute. (HOW)."

- **Remember that too** many numbers will bog down a lead or story.

- **Active voice is** generally better than passive voice.

- **Be careful with** time elements. Make sure they are not confusing to the reader, and only use when they are necessary.

- **Attribution in leads** isn't always necessary, especially if the information is common knowledge, factual and not potentially libelous.

There are times when alternative leads—non–inverted pyramid style—should be considered. But one that should be avoided almost all the time is the "quote lead."

Paula LaRocque, former assistant managing editor and writing coach at the *Dallas Morning News,* said this about writing and quote leads: "Selecting the quotes isn't so hard; it's presenting them that causes the trouble, and the worst place to present them is at the beginning. Quote leads deserve their terrible reputation. Yet they still appear regularly in both print and broadcast journalism. We can make three generalizations about quote leads. They're easy, lazy and lousy. They have no context. The readers don't know who is speaking, why, or why it matters. Without context, even the best quotations are wasted."

There are, however, some very effective alternative and stylistic leads that work well, including those with "flair or novelty." This is a good approach when novelty is actually present. Here's an example: "Three men were lectured and released by police officers Monday after their involvement in a prank at Denny's Restaurant."

That is a basic lead that works. But the only real hook in the lead, something that might get the reader to keep reading, is the word *prank.*

A more enticing lead, however, might be something like this: "This is the naked truth. Three men were caught Monday with their pants down after a prank at Denny's Restaurant."

The story, a true one, took place when three men thought it would be funny to streak a Denny's Restaurant in Spokane, Washington. They drove up to the restaurant in their birthday suits, jumped out and streaked the Saturday morning customers.

One diner, however, played a prank of his own. He noticed the men had left their car running. He walked outside and drove off, leaving the jaybirds stranded.

You leads are another alternative that should be used with caution. The use of the word *you* implies a personal relationship with the reader, and many readers don't feel that closeness: "If you study hard you will get good grades. But if you party hardy, you will reap the grade you sow."

In most cases it is best to drop the *you* and play it straight: "Appropriate study generally results in good grades. But too many parties will generally have a negative effect on grades."

Using clichés and mixing metaphors should also be avoided in leads (and stories): "You will reap the grades you sow."

Although accuracy is paramount in leads (and stories), so is clarity. What is wrong with the following lead? "Moscow City Clerk Chris Bainbridge said three candidates have filed for the Nov. 2 City Council election. Candidates include Aaron Ament, Jack Hill and Councilman Steve Busch."

It shouldn't be an immediate-identification lead. Moscow City Clerk Chris Bainbridge certainly isn't the most important person in the story. Also, alphabetize the candidates to minimize complaints.

A delayed-identification lead is the right call in the following, but there are other problems: "A 27-year-old Ball State student found dead in his room in a residence hall died of an accidental prescription drug overdose."

Most readers would not recognize the name. But how does the reporter know the death was "accidental" as the rest of the story did not support that statement? Important facts need attribution. "Accidental prescription drug" isn't clear. Was it an accidental overdose of prescription drugs? Maybe the student knew he was taking an overdose; thus, it was suicide.

Taking a Chance

Children attending story hour at the library know storytellers start at the beginning and build to the climax or ending of the story. They don't speak in monotones, but rather add inflection for reader interest. Inverted pyramid is only one way—oftentimes not the best way—to tell a story.

Storytelling is best when it uses chronological narration, scene re-creation, anecdotes, foreshadowing and dialog. And it can also be used in just about any story, except possibly breaking news.

As appropriate, take a chance with lead writing. Use your creativity. In crafting leads and re-creating scenes, attempt to have the reader see, smell, feel, taste and hear what you are writing.

Foreshadowing is an extremely effective lead technique. It helps build the suspense of the story by telling the reader what might be coming. These leads can be very simplistic and enticing. "John Jones knows he is lucky to be alive. Yet he can't smile about it."

As a reader, you immediate want to know why Jones is lucky to be alive and why he can't smile about it: "The bullet that traveled through Jones head, entering his neck and exiting his jaw, would be deadly for most. But the most damage it did to this 24-year-old student was damage nerves that keep him from smiling."

Anecdotes can also make interesting leads. They are the stories within stories. They inform and entertain: "Mary Sullivan was the last person to complete the half-mile open-water swim. Others were pulled out, but at least Mary finished, even though more than 300 competitors beat her out of the water. Sullivan, however, made up considerable time in the 25-mile bike and six-mile run portions of the Lake Castaic Triathlon, to finish in front of more than 100 other athletes. It was quite an accomplishment for the 24-year-old student who lost her sight just six months ago."

That is a story lead within a much bigger story.

Reporters—students and professionals—have a tendency to shy away from considering and writing creative leads. The hard-news lead is the one seen most often, frankly because it is easier to write.

They are used to summarize the news and are most often used on breaking news. Unfortunately, they are also often used on news that isn't breaking. Consider the following two leads in the *Daily Evergreen,* the student newspaper at Washington State University:

- **"Pullman is ready** for construction growth, said developer Duane Brelsford Jr."
- **"The WSU network,** as networks across the country, has been battling assorted computer viruses and worms for the past month."

Both summarized the stories that followed. But although neither of the stories was breaking news, they both had breaking news leads.

The *Evergreen,* like possibly several other newspapers in small towns, faces a daily dilemma. It doesn't have much breaking news to cover—or it avoids covering breaking news for other reasons—yet it wants to appear newsy, so it often forces hard-news leads, which read more like "ho-hum sleepers."

There is more risk in taking chances with leads and being more creative, but more rewards in increased readership. For instance:

- **"Bigger isn't always** better and people are often protective of their sleepy, small and friendly environs and cities. But growth is on the way for Pullman and Duane Brelsford Jr. says bigger is better when it comes to business development."

- **"While they aren't** slimy, slinky brownish-red worms, they are nonetheless yucky, disgusting and troubling. They are computer worms and viruses that are clogging and infecting the Washington State University network."

Breaking news leads, however, must be appropriate. For instance, if there was a power outage at Pullman Regional Hospital and three patients died, this lead would not be advisable: "Bad things sometimes happen to good people. Sometimes it isn't really anyone's fault. So no one can really be blamed for the death of three patients Thursday as a result of a power outage at Pullman Regional Hospital."

A better hard-news lead would be: "Three patients died Thursday during a two-hour power outage that shut down vital life-support systems at Pullman Regional Hospital which also had its back-up generators fail."

Leads, although clear, concise and clever, must not overstate, mislead or be judgmental. Whatever is written must be supported or backed up in the body of the story. Leads must be based on fact, and they should not be cluttered or contain unimportant material. For instance, what's wrong with this lead? "At Friday night's meeting of the Pullman City Council, attended by 25 people, a decision was made that had great impact. The council voted, 6–0, to impose a onetime assessment on all property owners, due in 30 days."

Although this lead is laughable, it is all too common. It is cluttered with mundane and unimportant information. Those who waded through the drivel would have found in the sixth paragraph of the story that the onetime assessment was $5,000. Shouldn't that be the lead?

Try also to stay away from dark, gloomy, melancholy or "say-nothing" leads: "The war veterans stood silently as they honored their dead in a somber ceremony Monday."

There might be a time for such a somber lead, but make sure these are used sparingly.

Reporters will also from time to time write illogical leads. "Seeking consensus on faculty raises, university administrators are floating a plan to raise faculty, student, staff and visitor parking fees."

How would raising parking fees foster consensus on faculty salary raises? The lead is unclear. It could be possible, however, if the funds from the parking fees were dedicated to faculty salary increases.

Quality Work

The following leads came from news reporting and writing students:

■ **About a local mortician:** "They looked happy. The infant had a bow in her brown little curls and a pink ruffled dress which draped over her mother's arms. Her mother had her hair wrapped in a modest bun which gave her a look of elegance. 'I'm pretty good with the curling iron,' Bob Warnock said, 'but it does take me a little while with the rollers.' Warnock is not your typical hair stylist and he does not work in a beauty salon or photography studio either. He is director of Kimball Funeral Home and a licensed mortician and embalmer."

■ **About a student nearly killed in a car accident:** "Screecch . . . bam. All is silent. The smell of rubber on hot cement engulfs the air. Steam rises from a trail of destruction to a 1991 Isuzu Stylus, embedded in the guardrail of Highway 195 just outside of Colfax. It was a road trip that soon would completely change the life of one Washington State University student. Just ask Tony Zammit, who was pinned to the steering wheel, internally bleeding. Lying there helplessly, Zammit realized his life would never be the same."

■ **About a student with a brain tumor:** "The ragged edge stretches from the top of her head to the tip of her right ear. For many, the scar would be a reminder of pain and anger, but the scar means something much different to Jen Crompton."

■ **About a young woman's birth decision:** "It was the longest three minutes of her life. Two lines would mean she was pregnant; one would mean that she wasn't. Two lines would mean disappointing her friends and family, shame, uncertainty, reliving a mistake she thought she had learned from. One line would mean a second chance. She knew if she was pregnant, she would have the baby. She didn't believe in abortion. She knew she wasn't perfect, but she also knew what she believed in, and with that faith she always tried to face her mistakes with integrity."

C H A P T E R   E X E R C I S E S

1. Write a breaking news lead from the following facts (watch for included style mistakes, misspellings and typos):

   WHO: Sally Johnston, 37, 2990 W. Stadium Wy, Dallas Texas

   WHAT: $500 reward for return of Dog

   WHERE: Lost or stolen near Safeway

   WHEN: Saturday evening, around 12 P.M. midnight

   WHY/HOW: The dog was left in the car while shopping. The doors were unlocked and the windows were down about 4–5 inches.

   OTHER NOTES: Dog five yrs. Old.; Guide dog for daughter, mary, 12; Cost 3800 dollars for dog and traing; Money raised by members of The Church of Christ; Church members also paying reward money; Sally thinks the dog was stolen; "Toby wouldn't leave. He was to well trained. He loved mary to much. He had to be stolen or tricked. He's not just a guide dog. He's mary's friend." Sosinski slept in car Saterday night in park lot hoping do would show up; she serched area several hours.

2. Assume that the dog discussed above has now been missing for a week. Write a non-breaking news lead from the above facts.

3. Interview your classroom neighbor about what he or she did last night. Write a lead about it.

4. Select five stories in your newspaper. Critique the leads.

5. Select five different newspaper leads. Rewrite them, using as much creativity as is appropriate.

10 Storytelling Techniques

BY SUSAN ENGLISH

Storytelling is like building a house. Although it must be built on a firm foundation, there is beauty in a work that is well done and a story well told.

Reporting public affairs requires diligent, thorough and intuitive reporting. The results of the reporting, though, are not the story. Good reporting should reveal the story. The story requires more than facts. Storytelling requires a plot, characters, a beginning and an ending (although they don't necessarily have to occur in that order) and a voice or a perspective.

The lure in public affairs reporting that must be resisted is to begin writing just as soon as great information, stunning facts and some revealing quotes are gathered. What happens is that the facts overwhelm the story. This does not just happen. Rather, reporters let it happen because they fail to plan to write a narrative.

In newsrooms, writers and reporters call much of their work *stories,* but it really does not mean they are narratives. Much public affairs reporting results in what might more accurately be characterized as reports, to distinguish them from narratives.

Reporting is a vital part of this process. But although a reporter needs a game plan to report a complex story, he or she also should spend just as much time and effort preparing to write the story.

Sometimes mere reports happen because in this type of journalism, just getting the critical information is difficult. Reporters file Freedom of Information requests and get back documents with most of the information redacted. Reporters file appeals and more FOI requests. They cross-reference databases and spend hours mining information from Web sites. When they finally get the information they need from multiple independent sources and are ready to write the story, reporters sometimes become so enamored with the facts, data and quotes that they forget the story. They struggled so hard and for so long to get the information that they focus on facts rather than narrative.

Narrative wraps context around the facts and quotes. The story informs readers in important ways that raw information does not. Narrative reveals meaning and explores the why and how. Narratives can lead to problem-solving stories, as they prompt readers and journalists to ask where the community can go from here. And increasingly, those solutions are framed in narratives as people imagine what the solution might look like.

People think in narratives. They understand that communities of people, whether a neighborhood or a virtual community, are connected in a complex web of common interests or issues.

Good narratives include historical context, and journalists need to remember that the stories they work on did not begin when they became interested in them.

Journalists move frequently as they advance from smaller newspapers to larger markets. It is vital to remember that issues, conflicts, problems and sometimes solutions usually began before the reporter moved to town or to a new beat. Many issues have deep roots and complex causes. Reporters must ferret out these roots and understand the stories before attempting to write them. Without historical context, stories become a one-dimensional recounting of existing and usually known facts wrapped with information the journalist obtained through investigative reporting techniques. These stories leave the readers wondering, "What does this all mean?"

In too many newsrooms, narrative-style writing is considered the franchise of the features department. Reporters who want to try their hand at narratives gravitate to the features department or are told to pitch their stories to the lifestyles editor. This has changed in some newsrooms over the past decade, as readership surveys repeatedly show readers want stories about people, relationships and connections. They say they want more details from newspapers than they get from TV news reports and they want to know what the news means in their lives.

How does a good reporter also become a good writer? By storytelling: by spending as much time at the beginning of the process and at every step along the way, thinking about and planning the narrative.

Reporting and writing are different skills, and journalists become better at both through practice. In some newsrooms, journalists spend time with both a good reporting editor and a good writing editor when working on a complex story. Some newsrooms are lucky enough to have a writing coach. But unless young journalists start their careers in one of the large metro newsrooms, they will have to seek out the editors in their newsrooms that like to spend time working on reporters' writing. You will recognize these editors because during the editing process they pepper their conversation with talk of cadence, voice, tone and structure.

When reporters find a good writer's editor, they seek ways to spend more time with him or her. One way of fostering a good writing environment in a newsroom is with a writers' group. These ad hoc groups might meet over a weekly brown-bag lunch to talk about writing techniques, review examples of well-written stories from other newspapers and critique some of their own work.

Sometimes the writing coach or one of the editors leads the sessions. More often, group members volunteer in turn to lead a discussion. Most managing editors welcome this type of staff development and will allow time for the weekly discussion leader to do some research, or will at least offer to buy some books about writing for the newsroom library. If your newsroom does not have such a group, start one. After you leave the college or university environment, much of the responsibility for getting better at the skills you have and becoming adept at new skills is up to you.

Scene-Setting Leads

Inverted pyramid leads that serve breaking news stories so well are not always the best choice for public affairs stories. Although such stories might break news, often the more important aspect of these stories is the context, the narrative that explains what this news means to the reader.

In the past decade, the use of scene-setting leads, even on breaking news stories, has become almost a cliché as reporters attempt to create narratives on deadline from reporting efforts that neglected to gather narrative material.

Reporters return from writing workshops where they were told to set readers down in time and place, and then tell them the story. Use details, writing coaches tell reporters. People think visually so describe the scene so they can visualize where the story is happening, editors tell young reporters. So reporters respond by topping most of their stories with a paragraph or two describing what one key source was doing, and where, when he or she revealed the information to the reporter. These paragraphs are usually written in present tense so that it seems to be happening even as the reader is diving into the story on the front page of the Sunday paper.

A typical scene-setting lead might describe the CEO of a company sitting behind an oak desk seemingly the size of an aircraft carrier deck, on which sits only an engraved pen and pencil set and a framed photo of his family. Behind him, through the corner office windows, the reporter can see the Rocky Mountains looming in the distance, or the Pacific Ocean or a forest of skyscrapers.

The TV mounted in the corner opposite his desk is tuned to CNBC with the sound muted, but the stock market quotes continually scroll across the screen for the duration of the interview. The offerings on the bookshelf flanking the aircraft carrier desk are spare but do include executive self-help books with titles about playing to win, habits for effective people and having grace under fire. The CEO is wearing a tie, loosened, and a white shirt. He leans back a little in his desk chair when he answers the reporter's questions. The chair is always big and leather.

The reporter often recalls the scene and tries to re-create telling details only when he or she sits down to write the lead and presumes it will be revealing and important. And the scene juxtaposes nicely with the rest of the story that will explain how this company got into trouble for dumping toxic waste in a river, downsized its workforce and was caught hiring undocumented workers or robbed its pension fund to boost its profit picture, leaving hundreds of retirees without their retirement income after thirty years with the company.

Experienced writers know they need to plan how they will make the transition, called the *turn,* from the lead of the story into the rest of the story.

The problem with using such scene-setting leads is they are not usually revealing or important. For example, the fictional lead about the CEO reveals nothing about the story. In fact, despite the details, it contains no new or unexpected information. We expect CEOs to have corner offices with views, large furniture and a bookcase. We expect them to wear business attire and to have mannerisms that indicate their status.

The reporter would serve readers better by taking them to the scene of the toxic dump, the no-tell motel where some of the undocumented workers were housed or the mobile home park where some of the retirees live and worry if they can continue living there.

In addition to choosing the wrong scene in which to set the story, reporters sometimes choose another wrong turn. With the narrative-style lead out of the way, they follow with a recitation of facts uncovered during the reporting process, sometimes delivered in descending order of difficulty in obtaining them.

They think that *context* is explaining the process the reporter used to get this information and the hurdles he or she cleared in getting it. Storytelling is forgotten in the rush to deliver important or stunning facts.

There is nothing inherently wrong with scene-setting leads. Indeed, it is vital to place the reader in time and place, which are important components of context. But to plop such a lead on top of a complex story involving a public issue and saying that it answers the context question is akin to adding windshield washer fluid to a car that won't start and declaring the car fixed.

Writers who understand storytelling know that the narrative is the front story and the facts, information and documentation are all part of the back story. Building a narrative is something like building a house. The facts are the infrastructure, the foundation, frame, floor joists and rafters. The narrative is the sheetrock, roofing and shingles, the stuff that wraps the infrastructure and makes it a house. The writer provides readers with windows so they can see the infrastructure and see for themselves that it is strong, sound and plumb, and holds up under the weight of the story.

Literary Journalism

Great journalists think in stories. They see themes in their ideas, what some journalists call *universal truths.* Many of these truths are captured in clichés—what goes around comes around, justice prevails, hard work and perseverance get you ahead, America is the land of opportunity. Journalists who are good narrative writers work at seeing the big picture, or the theme, and then work to write that story at a local level. It is a skill that can be learned.

Readers want context and narratives, and this has prompted a boom in literary journalism. This genre of writing in news reports is an American style developed in the late nineteenth and twentieth centuries by such writers as James Agee and Joseph Mitchell. The genre, called for a time *new journalism,* was popularized in the 1960s and 1970s by such writers as Tom Wolfe, Truman Capote, Joan Didion and Hunter Thompson.

Now, many colleges and universities offer a course in literary journalism in their curriculum. It is the style de rigueur for magazines and online publications such as Salon.com. An increasing number of newspaper writers have embraced the techniques. A quick look at the most recent journalism contest winners will show just how popular it is.

Literary journalism utilizes writing techniques borrowed from fiction and the cinema. All journalists, whether they write obituaries, cover sports, cover the judicial system or do investigative reporting, should be adept at using the writing tools of literary journalism, for these are the tools of telling stories.

Narrative Ideas

Well-written stories begin at the idea phase. Weekly and sometimes daily story conferences between a reporter and his or her editor are where stories begin. Reporters are expected to show up with a couple of stories they want to work on that week, often a daily story and another for the Sunday paper.

These stories might spin out of a news event. For example, a reporter might want to look at long-range sentencing patterns after a judge has handed down a particularly brief prison sentence to a career criminal. Or a reporter might look at land-use data and growth management plans after the county commissioners grant a variance for a new high-density subdivision in an agricultural area not far from town.

The key to these ideas in terms of seeing the narrative is that something has to happen; there must be action. That is one of the differences between a narrative and a mere description. Certainly there have been some great literary journalists who used description almost exclusively to tell a story, Mitchell and James McPhee among them. But at the core of public affairs reporting is the news delivered in a timely fashion.

Let's use the hypothetical zoning variance as an example, because this would be a typical story a young journalist would write repeatedly when covering local government. With a zoning variance, the reporter has the bones of a good idea.

What would it take to turn this into a good story? First, the reporter needs to gather some historical context to make sure this is a change. Perhaps this is business as usual in this community. If that is the case, a few phone calls to the state agencies that enforce growth management plans would be in order, to see if such variances are allowable under state regulations.

If this does, indeed, represent a change, the reporter then needs a plan for finding out what this means to the community and its residents.

Before even pitching the story to his or her editor, a writer should be able to answer the following questions:

- **What is the story?**
- **Why am I doing it now?**
- **What does it mean?**

Narrative writers would at this point already be thinking of the theme of this story. The key to writing great stories is to gather, at every step of the reporting process, the type of information needed to tell that story.

What would the theme of the hypothetical zoning variance story be? In thinking of narratives, it is helpful to take one step back to see the larger picture. What might be the midrange view? It is also helpful sometimes to think like a moviemaker. Directors use close-up views to reveal important details of the story, midrange views to move the story line along, and long-range views as scene-setting devices to set the movie viewer in time and place. Because the midrange view is where the narrative happens, it might be productive if the reporter starts thinking of this story theme as land use rather than a zoning variance. Although this particular variance might not be significant, if it is part of a pattern, it can be used to tell the story of how land use is changing in the community over time.

Before any in-depth reporting is done, a focus statement should be written, one that answers the basic questions of "What is the story?" "Why am I writing it now?" and "What does it mean?" The last question is not necessarily answered at this point, but reporters should be aware that it needs to be asked throughout the reporting process.

The theme or story line might change during the reporting process, and in many cases it should change as the reporter gathers more information. But good storytelling involves insight at every point in the process. Writers build some time for reflection into their process. After each key interview, the reporter should spend a little time thinking about how this new information fits into the working theme of the story. If it doesn't, the story might have changed. The theme should continually be tested as information is added to the structure of the story.

We jumped ahead in the process a little, but most reporters will be engaging in several stages of this process constantly. Few reporters who have just one idea at a time survive in the news business. Multitasking is a required skill, and most reporters have at least a couple of stories going simultaneously. Veteran reporters usually have a long idea list to which they are continually adding ideas and thoughts.

Telling the Story

Several other chapters explore the reporting process in detail, so let's assume the reporter has all of the information he or she needs to start writing.

The focus statement should in some form become part of the nut 'graph of the story, for it tells the reader what the story really is about. The top three or four paragraphs must reveal to the reader the theme of the story and at least summarize what it means.

Before writers dive into the main body of the story, they should have a good working outline. The outline includes a list of the main characters, or players, in the story and what role they play. It includes the plot points of the narrative and where each portion of the story takes place. It includes a list of who is affected by this story and how.

At this point, some writers find it helpful to write the ending of the story as well. Being able to see where they are heading keeps some writers from taking off on interesting but unnecessary tangents.

PROFESSIONAL TIPS

Julie Sullivan

Julie Sullivan is an award-winning investigative reporter for the *Oregonian* in Portland, Oregon. She was a member of the team that was awarded the Pulitzer Prize in 2001 for a series of stories on systematic problems with the U.S. Immigration and Naturalization Service.

Question: Can and should all stories that fall under the area of public affairs reporting be written as narratives?

Of course not. For me, form follows function, and the news, the point of the story and the sources should always determine the story form. The material determines what kind of a story I produce—whether it is the short form, the inverted pyramid, the investigative piece or narrative.

Finally, narrative can actually obscure news by focusing on stage direction or elevating the significance of something the reporter observes above all other events. This is how so many news reporters in Oregon missed the story of the Immigration and Naturalization Service for so long. The paper consistently produced narratives about individual immigrants in epic struggles instead of saying, "Wait a minute; this is the story of one agency that is failing in its mission and harming people."

Question: In what ways does narrative writing change your reporting process?

All stories require reporters to be prepared with background information, thoughtful questions and a tentative story framework before they ever begin reporting, otherwise reporters waste their own time and worse, their sources' time.

That said, all reporters could benefit from considering what they would need in a narrative. For instance, after a long negotiation session that averts a teachers' strike, a good reporter will slow the source down and ask for a step-by-step description of what happened in that negotiation room, who was there, and what the turning point was.

Narrative requires a reporter to gather as many details as possible and observe as much as possible. These are also elements that can be used in any story form.

Question: There are so many stories that deserve to be told. How do you choose the stories you want to pursue? What aspect of the story idea convinces you that this is a story you will spend time reporting and writing?

News always trumps. Ask, "What do readers need to know tomorrow?" Basically, newsworthiness should determine what you pursue, followed by how interesting or unusual the subject is.

Question: Journalists at the *Oregonian* work in teams. How does that environment affect the way you report and write a story?

One benefit is that you collaborate far more with other reporters on your team. That collaboration is the best way to train young reporters, reinvigorate midcareer people and produce more thoughtful pieces because you constantly bounce story ideas off one another and share sources. It also produces a lot of double bylines, which can produce strong stories in a hurry.

The loyalty to the team works like it does on any team, causing people to compete and work harder to impress your teammate.

The drawbacks occur when news falls into the dead space between teams, where the responsibility

(continued)

PROFESSIONAL TIPS   Continued

for that news is not as clear and tips and sources can easily get lost. It takes a lot of communication and managers who see the big picture.

Question: What do you know now as a journalist that you wish you had learned in college or early in your career? What advice would you give to journalists just entering the field?
I wish I'd had more formal training in interviewing. There is a science to preparing and conducting interviews that I wish I had learned earlier.

I would tell young journalists to worry less about their leads and more about producing a body of work that has an impact on their community. Journalists must have impact—they must change laws, illuminate wrongs, educate or entertain readers, or they won't be relevant.

One tactic for writing the body of the narrative that many writers find effective is to clear their desk or at least close their notebooks and simply focus their attention on writing the story. They ask themselves, "What is the story I am telling?"

Writers fall into two general categories in terms of writing style: those whose stories improve with repeated telling, and those for whom the first time they tell it is the best. You will have to discern for yourself which way you produce the best work. It is pretty easy to see in a newsroom the writers who practice one of these styles. The tellers want to verbally walk through their stories with their editors, and often reporters sitting near them, before sitting down and writing. Sometimes this is seen as a stalling technique, because writing is harder work than telling. But for these writers, the time spent honing their story is productive (although they need to be aware that others around them might have a different style and this might not be productive time for them).

Those who need to get the story down on the computer screen before telling it verbally sometimes come into the office early or stay late, or frame the story at home, as working solitary serves them best.

Just as you need to discern your writing style, you will also need to learn when your most productive time of day falls. Although journalists certainly must learn to work on demand and on deadline, they have some control over the time of day they work on longer or more complex stories. Many freelance writers and novelists say they either work best in the early morning hours or late at night. To accommodate this, they set the alarm and are at their writing desk by 6 or 7 A.M., or arrange their lifestyle so they can write for several hours after 9 or 10 P.M.

Journalists seldom have this type of freedom to arrange their workday, but if they are most productive in the morning, they should carve out some early morning hours to write and leave afternoons for opening mail, doing follow-up interviews and arranging story conferences with their editor. Night owls are usually in good writing form by afternoon.

Once writers have the narrative on the screen, then they can open their notebooks and start working important and key quotes into the proper places in the story. Some writers, as they draft the narrative, will leave themselves notes in the text as to what facts, numbers or quotes should be inserted at various points.

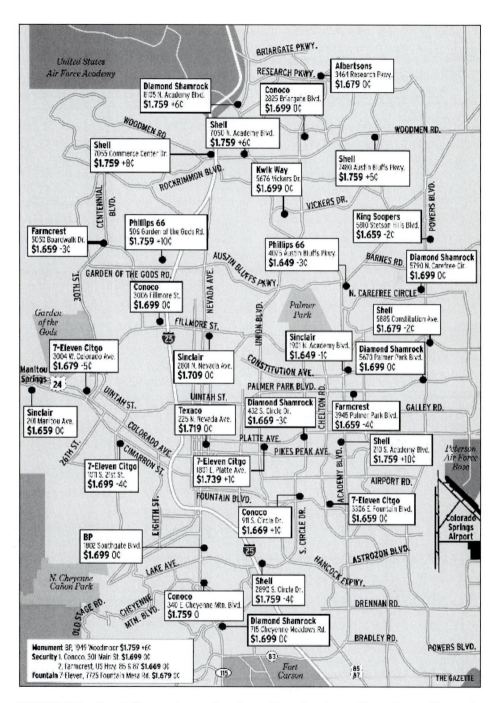

FIGURE 10.2 Storytelling can be greatly enhanced by using photos, illustrations and/or graphics like the one above that told the story of gas prices in Colorado Springs, Colo.

The Gazette

Remember, information is used to support the story. Without documentation such as quotes, numbers and facts, the story has little credibility.

Some reporters like to transcribe their interviews, gather the data onto the computer scene and fill in the story around all of the reported information. The danger of this, as noted earlier, is that the story thread gets lost among the facts; it becomes the back story.

Beginning journalists sometimes transcribe their interviews in the order in which they were done, insert key facts, cut out some quotes and call it a story. This is typing rather than writing. They sometimes think that by organizing their interviews in order of importance, they can skip the outline phase of the writing process. The story always suffers by doing it this way.

During the outline phase, the writer determines the best structure for this story. Should it be circular in which the ending is the lead, then the writer returns to the beginning of the story and leads the reader back around to the end? Or should the story take an hourglass shape in which it starts large by exploring a trend, then narrows to an anecdote or two and grows larger again while explaining what this trend means to the reader?

Perhaps two stories are best written in parallel fashion with a timeline being a key component. Perhaps the writer will time travel, taking the reader back and forth in time and place as the story happened in this fashion.

The writer should be in firm control of this aspect of writing. The structure determines the cadence of the story—how fast does the writer move the reader through the story? One effective way of doing this is with sentence length. Readers speed through short sentences. The periods stop readers. Sentences seem abrupt. But they are easy to read. Longer, flowing sentences, rich with adjectives and complex with dependent clauses, serve to slow the reader and add gracefulness to the story.

Good writing has varied sentence lengths. Writers also use punctuation to control cadence and pacing. They also favor words with fewer syllables over longer, less familiar words. They work to make it easy for the reader to navigate their stories.

During the reporting process, the writer should have determined the voice of the story or the perspective from which it will be told. This is an important decision in that it is one level at which diversity can be added to the news report.

Let's return to the land-use/zoning variance example and look at the various perspectives possible in such a story. Because they are easily accessible and often articulate, the land developer and government officials often are the logical and first choices of journalists

GOOD WRITING TIPS

- Think in themes.
- Write more stories about how things work. How are decisions made by the city council or state legislature?
- Write stories that give readers context and perspective.
- Write about life as it happens every day. String it together for the reader. Try to figure out what the ordinary person would do day-in and day-out if he or she had the time. Then be there and write about it.

working on such a story. Certainly they need to be part of the story, as theirs is an important perspective.

But perhaps the developer plans to include middle- and low-income housing in the new development, which will allow low-income renters in town an opportunity to become homeowners. Perhaps this story is best told from the perspective of nearby farm families trying desperately to maintain a traditional rural lifestyle.

Reporters should consider all of the major perspectives from which a story could be told and choose a voice that is not often heard. When we talk about *diverse voices,* or including diversity in our news reports, we think of ethnic diversity. Certainly that is an important aspect of diversity. But journalists need to broaden their efforts to include the many other perspectives that have a stake in our communities and the events and issues that constitute the news.

Although a broader discussion of diversity is included in the chapter on ethics and the law (see chapter 6), it is incumbent on the reporter to purposefully choose the perspective or voice he or she will use to tell a story.

Getting It Right

Accuracy goes beyond getting facts correct and quoting sources exactly. Writers must produce stories that are fair and balanced. Too often, this is characterized as "telling both sides of the story." If writers have fully explored the perspectives from which each story can be told, they know that balance and fairness often includes more than two perspectives.

Balance means representing the perspectives with the relative weight of their stake in the issue. In the land-use story, yes, the developer has a substantial financial stake in the issue, but the financial stake should not always determine the perspective. In this issue, the community also has a big stake in that a change in land use will dramatically change the character of the community as it grows from a small town in a rural area to a more urban community with suburbs.

Weighing the perspectives and writing a balanced story are intuitive processes, and writers should ask themselves what would be fair to all voices.

It is natural when the writer reaches the end of his or her story to consider it done. But really, this is only a good draft of the story. At this point some editors want to start looking at the story, knowing revisions and polishing are in order.

As the story is being crafted, the editor is working with the photo and graphics departments to pull together a well-rounded and thorough package. The page designers and online editors are also aware of the package and are beginning to think about placement in the paper or Web site and about an effective presentation.

When this good draft is completed, the next vital step is double checking the facts, quotes, attribution and organization of the story. Reporters should verify each number and each quote with his or her notes. If need be, call the source to confirm the information. Make sure that names and source titles are correct. Reread each quote to ensure they accurately reflect the source's viewpoint and the conversation.

On a printed-out version of the story, note beside each paragraph or section the voice that it represents. Then look over your notes to make sure there is a good balance in perspectives, and that they are represented in the order that is fair to their relative weight.

Run the spell-checker. Then go for a short walk or take a coffee break, but avoid socializing. This is not the time to take your mind off your story, but you want to use a short break to let your mind roll the story around. Sometimes you will think of a key quote or fact you forgot to use, or doubt arises about a quote and you will decide to call back the source for verification.

You need to breathe, take a break from the intensity of writing and renew you energy level. Don't start cruising the Internet and reading other material. You need to maintain focus on your story. This also gives your editor a chance to do a first reading of your story. Then it's back to your desk to start working with your editor's suggestions and questions, and to take care of any thoughts you had during the break.

It is not unusual to call key sources back two and three times during this editing process, to verify information or answer questions your editor had. Sources rarely resent or question these callbacks because they, too, want the information and their quotes to be correct. Indeed, they often are grateful the reporter is taking such care to get it right.

Good writers take a printed copy of their story and step into the hallway or interview room to read their story aloud. They are checking for punctuation missteps and hearing the cadence and tone and voice of their story, making notes where the cadence needs polishing or where the voice can be improved. Only by reading aloud can writers hear how readers will navigate their stories and improve the pacing.

Then, after your editor's last few queries are addressed, print yourself a final version and file the story. Many writers take hard copies of their stories home with them. On major stories, a copy editor or page designer will often call the reporter with minor questions. Or sometimes the information in the photo caption, which was gathered by the photographer, is inconsistent with information in the story. Sometimes writers will reread their story after a break at home and want to tweak a sentence or paragraph. Most copy editors are willing to do this, but will resist any major editing without getting your editor involved in the revision.

Be proud of your work, and be aware that all writers think they could have done better. Writers suffer from a form of buyer's remorse when they read their story after it is published; they wish they had written a paragraph or the lead or the ending in a different, more effective way that only now has occurred to them. This is normal. During the writing process, focus and do the best reporting and writing you can do given the time frame and resources you have to work with.

Writers should think like athletes: they practice and improve, and when the game is at hand, they go through whatever ritual will get them in the zone, then they perform at their peak until deadline and go home satisfied they have done their best.

Powering Up Your Writing

Read good writing, and read constantly. One of the characteristics of good writers is they are voracious readers. They graze Web sites, browse the shelves of bookstores and libraries, read posters on telephone poles while waiting for the traffic light to change and subscribe to a plethora of magazines.

Many writers keep a file of well-written magazine and newspaper articles at their desk and read for ten minutes before they begin writing so, as a ritual, they can start to hear the music of good writing.

Only through reading good writing can you start to recognize the writing devices and techniques that ramp up the quality of prose that is merely adequate and serviceable. Writers spend their careers working on their writing, making it more concise, graceful and clear. They strive for what writing coaches call *writing that sings*. When you begin to hear the music of others' writing, you will be able to hear the high notes in your own work.

CHAPTER EXERCISES

1. Using a narrative approach, write a personal essay/story about the most difficult thing that has happened in your life.

2. Review an issue of your campus newspaper. Select one story you believe could have been improved by using narrative storytelling, and explain why.

3. Select a current event. Obtain coverage of it from a newspaper and magazine. Analyze the two, and write a report contrasting the coverage and styles. Include a paragraph of the style you prefer, and explain why.

4. Volunteer to tell a story (i.e., read a book) at an elementary school or library storytime hour. Practice your pace and tone in advance. Write an essay on the experience.

5. Take a newspaper story and read it out loud. Make note of areas where tone or pace needs attention.

6. Find a typical story in your campus newspaper. Identify the voice or perspective of each paragraph.

7. Review a country music video. Write a one-page essay on the story that was being told. Include its application to news writing.

CHAPTER
11

In-Depth Stories, and Series and Team Reporting

BY SUSAN ENGLISH

It often takes teamwork to tell in-depth stories and write a series of significant stories concerning issues that affect the general public. In the food processing industry, for instance, health and safety are ongoing concerns.

Shrinking newsroom staffs and growing expectations of producing stories for both printed and online versions of newspapers have added another skill to the repertoire required of good journalists: they must be able to work well with others.

Newsrooms used to be filled with hard-drinking, cigar-smoking reporters (mostly men) who swore often and loud and threatened editors with physical harm if they even thought about changing one word of their stories. Reputations were made on big scoops, and balance and accuracy were not necessarily the hallmarks of their prose. Late last century, these rough-living reporters were replaced by well-educated journalists packing big egos who picked off the plum assignments and expected to be treated like stars. Editors became valued for their ability to tolerate pouting and to soothe the ruffled feathers of these journalists sometimes referred to as simply "the talent."

Journalists' salaries rose, drinking and smoking were banned from the newsrooms and reputations were made with contracts to write books or screenplays or with guest appearances on TV.

But with the dot-com bust, the tolerance of prima donnas in the newsroom shrank along with editorial department budgets. Generalists—reporters who can snap a photo or two, and photographers who can at least contribute notes to a story—are still highly valued at small newspapers. And increasingly, all journalists are valued for their ability to contribute to a team effort.

Team Newsroom

This can play out in a couple of ways. One is a change in the way newsrooms are structured. A few newsrooms, most notably the *Oregonian*'s in Portland, Oregon, were restructured as a number of small teams. Rather than individual reporters having a beat, each team focused on a specific area or issue. The teams include visual journalists—a photographer, graphics person and/or page designer—as well as reporters, writers and an editor. The beats are broader than in traditional newsrooms, so the typical city hall, county government and cops reporters, and possibly the courts reporter, would cover local government as a team. Other teams might specialize in social issues, the economy, health or the environment.

One of the strengths of team reporting is that stories are reported within context and are more often seen as indicators of a larger community trend rather than a series of isolated and discrete events. The newsroom structure also provides a way for journalists to consistently cover an issue or group that might fall between traditional beats or that doesn't warrant the attention of a full-time beat writer.

For example, the construction of a few miles of bicycle lanes along city streets might result in a single story by a general assignment reporter in many newsrooms. But in a team environment, the issue of bicycles as one means of alternative transportation would stay on the radar of the transportation team and probably have consistent presence in many stories.

But the strength of pulling the umbrella of a team's interest over many smaller and seemingly unrelated events or issues can also be a weakness. Critics of the team structure say a lot of news of local interest goes unreported because teams tend to work on projects with larger scopes. Critics say the bar for how large an event must be to attract news coverage is too high, that news stories of robberies and wrecks, speeches and planning meetings, and profiles of community leaders just never get written. For this reason, some newsrooms organized by teams also have a team of general assignment reporters and photographers just so the franchise of most newspapers, local news, still gets in the paper.

Efficiency is not the lone motive driving editors to reorganize their newsrooms into teams. Often it is the journalists themselves who crave the time and encouragement to work on projects that wrap context around the events in the community and help readers take the long view on their worlds.

Given that most newsrooms are not organized by teams, but rather along traditional beat structures that have been tweaked this way or that, journalists find other ways to work on projects that require the efforts of a team. Most often, these teams are assembled for a short-term project, such as covering an unfolding news event from several perspectives or shining the spotlight on an issue of community concern.

In 1999, as the turn of the century approached, the *Spokesman-Review* was among the many newspapers that published millennium projects of one sort or another. Spokane grew as a typical frontier boomtown in the American West in the late 1800s and still grapples with issues such as water use, cattle grazing rights and the historical use of the land by Native American tribes. The millennium team spent the year writing about the myths of the frontier West—from settlers to saloon girls and cattle rustlers to cowboys—and what those myths looked like a century later.

A couple of writers, one photographer and an editor were the team core. But through the year, a half-dozen reporters, a columnist and a couple of photographers also rotated onto the team roster. Everyone involved still had his or her beats to cover, or daily assignments. They carved out time in creative ways and spent significant amounts of their own time reporting and crafting their stories.

While some newsrooms have the luxury of having a project team in addition to the traditional beat structure, more often reporters and photographers gravitate toward others who might make a good ad hoc team for one of the journalist's pet projects.

"Sometimes you have an idea and have to wait years for the right opportunity or right teammate to come along," says Chris Anderson, a veteran photojournalist at the *Spokesman-Review.*

Most often, a team is simply a core of a reporter or two and a photographer who want to work on a project or story badly enough that they are willing to work on it on their own time. "Time and energy are two of the biggest challenges of working on a project," Anderson says.

The Same Story/Two Perspectives

Anderson teamed with veteran reporter Hannelore Sudermann to produce a four-part, in-depth look at what the wheat harvest meant in the small communities in the Palouse in southeast Washington state. Anderson worked in the *Review*'s headquarters in Spokane. Sudermann, who covered higher education, lived and worked in the *Review*'s Palouse office, about a two-hour drive from Spokane.

"We both had to produce for the daily paper and were trying to get out into the harvest at odd times like nights and weekends," Anderson says. "You wind up doing a full day's work and then heading out into the fields. Or I would drive to Colton [in the heart of the Palouse] at the end of the day so we could be out in the fields at sunrise."

Anderson likes working closely with a writer on a project. "I liked hearing from a reporter about what they sensed—the smells of the barn, the light at sunset etching the field, the dust and grime on a face."

The collaboration of photographer and writer enriches a project. "Sometimes when you are not looking, you see a lot more. Sometimes when you are not writing notes, you hear a lot more," Anderson says.

Like most projects, this one included maps and graphics. A page designer got involved to pull it together, and as it was being published, it was turned over to an online editor to be organized on the newspaper's Web site.

The challenge with a project is to stay focused on the original idea and to have fun with it, Anderson says.

Whether it is producing a series on a wheat harvest or covering a tragedy, the process of working together remains essentially the same.

Everyone on the team must agree on what the story is and why they are doing the story. Unless the story is spinning off of breaking news, the writer and photographer often talk over an idea and the possible narratives before pitching the project to an editor.

In the cases of breaking news, the whole newsroom is expected to know how to work as a team. Anderson recalls working with a number of reporters and editors when an Air Force tanker crashed at Fairchild Air Force Base in Spokane, killing everyone on board. When dozens of journalists from national media arrived in Spokane to cover the long standoff between Randy Weaver and the FBI and ATF at nearby Ruby Ridge in north Idaho, the *Review* journalists became highly competitive as a team.

"A big story hits and the newsroom works like a team and everyone wants a piece of the action," Anderson says. When Ruby Ridge happened, reporter Jess Walter was not included on the initial team, so he sat at his desk the first day and tried to figure out what the paper was missing. He got on the phone, called the Midwest, got the Weaver family and wrote a story, Anderson recalls. Walter went on to write a book and a screenplay about the Ruby Ridge incident, during which Weaver's wife and son were shot and killed.

"No good journalist wants to miss out on a great story," Anderson says.

Reporters should remember that although they might have been working on a story or a beat for a long time and hence are experts on the subject, photographers more resemble general assignment reporters. They work across the traditional boundaries of beats or newspaper sections and could bring a more contextual perspective to the story.

The key to being a successful team member is being able to contribute to each other's work as well as to the published project. That means getting along with others on your team and working to create an environment in which ideas for story leads can come from the photographer, and the writers might toss out photo ideas for consideration. A great journalistic package is better than any of its individual parts—photos and text tell the same story, but the narrative is enriched by both, as well as by maps, graphics and thoughtful design.

Increasingly, the ease and gracefulness of moving a story package online are being considered during the idea stage of the process. It certainly should be part of the reporting process. Newspaper Web pages are being used increasingly to offer readers the opportunity to read entire documents and transcripts that reporters might have excerpted from their stories. This means the online editors must also be considered part of the team.

PROFESSIONAL TIPS

Hannelore Sudermann

Hannelore Sudermann covered higher education for the *Spokesman-Review* in Spokane, Wash., and is now assistant editor and senior writer for *Washington State Magazine*. She and photographer Chris Anderson teamed up to produce a four-part Sunday series on wheat harvest in Eastern Washington.

Question: From your experience, can you estimate the percentage of stories that originate with writers? Do stories that result from ideas pitched by writers have a different perspective or flavor from stories that come from photographers?

Most newspaper stories, maybe 80 percent, originate with writers. Most of the remaining 20 percent come from editors. That's unfortunate. Photographers can be excellent resources for story ideas and sources. Because they are often working a variety of assignments during the day, they are out meeting people and looking around in their communities far more than the reporter, who spends so much time at his or her desk writing and doing interviews over the phone.

Reporters often have general ideas, for example, of the state of health care in a community and how it fits into the national perspective. Once the idea is set, the reporter goes out and looks for subjects who might illustrate the story. A photographer may actually notice that there's a segment of the community that's not getting health care and he might come in and suggest it as a story, already knowing that there's a group out there to write about. In a way, photographers are truer community journalists than reporters.

As a writer, I've tried to interact with photographers every day. Whether it's wandering through the photo lab and looking at work they're doing for other stories, or tracking them down and telling them I liked a certain photo in that day's paper. I always ask if they have a project they want to shoot or if they know of a story we should be covering.

Question: When a reporter and photographer are assigned to a story, what do you like to see happen before you both start doing your work on the story? How much of the story line or narrative do you want to talk about with the photographer before he or she sets up the photo shoots?

Once I know the story and I know who will be working on it with me, I seek that person out. We talk about what I think the story will be, who might be important characters in the story, and what might make for good journalistic photographs. Often the photographer has his or her own perspective on how the story could shake out and maybe even ideas of good sources and subjects.

As I'm working on a story, I'll check in with the photographer and describe what I have at that point. I'll sometimes e-mail a draft of the story to the photographer. I try to go along on the photo shoots, of course I take care not to step into the shots or distract the subjects in a way that affects the photographer.

On the other hand, a reporter can be an important participant in a photo shoot. He or she can distract the subjects so they are more at ease while the camera is pointed at them. The reporter can also point out important components of the story that might be illustrated with a photograph. On the flip side, the photographer also can ease the reporter's job by asking a question while the reporter is focused on taking notes or speaking up

(continued)

PROFESSIONAL TIPS   Continued

if he or she notices something the reporter has missed.

Photographers and reporters should take care not to get in each other's way. I knew one reporter who, while the photographer was trying to shoot a family having dinner, pulled a chair right up to the table and inserted himself in the scene. I also once worked with a photographer who was so absorbed in his passion for hunting he interrupted my paced interview with a bee scientist to talk about deer in the area.

If this happens, it's a good idea to talk about it diplomatically after the shoot and interview. And reporters, don't be offended if a photographer reaches over and pulls you out of the frame. Just apologize for it later.

Question: Do you ever ask the photographer to see some of the photos while you are working on early drafts of stories?

Absolutely. One of my favorite things to do is wander into the photo department and see what came across on the camera. Sometimes I'll notice details I hadn't seen while on assignment. Sometimes the photographer and I find the shot that ties perfectly with the story. If I'm working on an important project, I like to have images of the places and people we covered tacked up around me while I'm writing.

Now that photographers are using digital cameras, they'll sometimes stop mid-shoot to look at what they've captured. I sometimes just sidle up to them and peek over their shoulders for a glimpse at how the story is coming across in images.

Question: What were the challenges of working with a photographer on a project such as the wheat harvest project you two produced?

The biggest challenge was time. We were dealing with daylight summer hours, farmers itching to harvest, and a not-so-flexible newspaper schedule. Our reporting took us all around Eastern Washington over several weeks. It took extra effort to get to places early enough to catch that golden morning light or to hang out in a dusty field long enough to catch the moon at sunset. And this wasn't a project that we had extra hours budgeted for, so we found ourselves working after hours and during Chris Anderson's vacation.

Question: What allowed you two to work so well as a team on that project?

We were lucky to have worked on other projects together, we knew each other's styles, and we both liked the stories we were covering. Chris was the real driver of the series. He had ideas about what he wanted to shoot. I started there and found the stories to build around his initial photos. That work then led to more sources and stories, allowing us to develop a nice multi-story project.

Question: How often in your years in the news business has the process worked this way? Is it dependent on the two personalities involved in producing the story, or is there something in a newsroom environment that fosters great team reporting?

In the more than 10 years as a journalist, it has always worked this way for me. I've been lucky to find photographers who have the interest, talent and energy to find and tell real stories.

The newsroom typically isn't going to set up these collaborative projects. Most of the time it's up to the reporter and the photographer to step forward, pitch an idea and argue for time to do it right. Timing is also a factor. We knew with our harvest series that it would be a slow period in the summer news cycle and that the editors would welcome strong features with beautiful photographs. It paid off with a lot of front pages and well-played photos.

And personalities are important. Being a journalist is a rare experience. Getting people to let you into their lives and tell you their stories is unparalleled. Sometimes the only person you can share that with is the reporter or photographer who was there with you.

Convergence: A Short History

Some time in the economically wild 1990s, the virtual world spawned virtual companies in garages and unbelievable virtual wealth. Media owners and publishers began to envision a virtual media world in which the traditional impenetrable walls between print journalism and broadcast journalism would crumble, or at least become opaque.

They called it *media convergence.* Some envisioned a converged newsroom that would produce news reports for both media. Reporters would write one story for the next morning's newspaper, and another version for the 5 P.M. newscast. Some executives even thought the reporter would just step into a TV studio adjacent to the newsroom and tape the segment for the 5 P.M. newscast.

The convergence of the visuals staffs would be even easier, they said. The photographers could carry both a camera to take photos for the newspaper, and a camcorder to shoot footage for the broadcast version. When technology caught up, they said, the same piece of equipment would yield both photos and video of acceptable quality for each medium.

Naysayers abounded, especially inside newsrooms, but also among some in the highest ranks of the industry.

Robert J. Haiman, president emeritus of the Poynter Institute in Florida, said this of convergence in a speech he delivered in 2001: "I believe that the converged media world is one from which good journalism, and good journalists, are going to be in great need of defense.

"I say that because my notion of the mission of good journalism is still the same today as it was when I first learned as a young cub reporter from Nelson Poynter, more than 40 years ago: 'To inform the public about the public's business, creating a society that is equipped with the knowledge it needs to make the right civic decisions more often than it makes the wrong civic decisions, and thus helping to perpetuate self-government and democracy.'

"That is the prime obligation of the news media. And the more I hear about convergence—about which so many journalists and journalism professors seem so enthralled these days—the less I am persuaded that it has much, if anything, to do with that obligation."

Critics of convergence also addressed tangible hurdles. Newspaper reporters were not equipped, and in many cases were unwilling, to report stories on the air, they said. Shooting video was very different from capturing a single image for the front page of a newspaper, photographers said.

Skepticism did not reside just in newspaper editorial departments. Those in the broadcast industry expressed little interest in recrafting their reports for the print media.

Dan Garrity, assistant professor and the director of the broadcasting program at Gonzaga University, worked in the network affiliates in Seattle (KING-NBC) and Spokane (KREM-CBS and KHQ-NBC) prior to joining the GU faculty in 2002. He says that convergence between the KHQ newsroom and the newsroom at the daily newspaper, the *Spokesman-Review,* was not happening even though one family owns both media outlets.

"No facility with which I've been associated suggested having broadcasters write for print. KREM and KING had no such partnership (with a print product), and the KHQ–*Spokesman-Review* relationship would not allow such a thing. The relationship was amicable, but I got the impression the paper was quite happy with the reporters they had doing the work."

Substantial arguments against convergence came from those who talked about the different roles of print and broadcast media. Newspapers have yielded timeliness to broadcast media, which can go live as soon as they get a crew on the scene. Providing depth and context has become the franchise of the print media.

The discussion spanned years and all the while, media mergers made convergence between newspapers and television look like a fait accompli. But that was last century.

Still, convergence is alive and a consideration at some newspaper and television newsrooms across the country.

Virtual Newspapers

Convergence, as it has played out, is something quite different from what visionaries talked about a decade ago. In fact, *Newsweek*'s Steven Levy says that convergence is no longer a buzzword anymore, not because it went bust, but because the media have converged.

In his coverage of the annual Consumer Electronics Show in Las Vegas in January 2005, Levy explained convergence in this way: convergence "embodied the elusive idea that different media, including every variety of sound, image and data, could be served up and consumed like a giant main-course salad, with fantastic benefits in the process. Now you rarely hear it, because the concept is so here and now that it would be like commenting on air."

What happened on the way to a joint print–broadcast newsroom was the Internet. The new virtual medium could accommodate both the contextual issues coverage that is the hallmark of print journalism, and the video that is the hallmark of broadcast journalism. In short, journalism from print and broadcast media converged on the Web.

"When I was at KHQ, our understanding was we would be responsible for rewriting the story for the Web, and adding appropriate content for that venue," broadcast veteran Garrity says. "For example, if you were on a court case, you do the 5 P.M. hit with a live package, then come back to the station and rewrite the story for inclusion on the station's Web site. If there were some lengthy documents that were not included in either report, you could hyperlink them, then offer other sites the consumer could visit for more info."

Not all journalists embrace convergence, even if it is on the Web rather than on TV, and arguably many veteran reporters remain skeptical. Some see convergence as an attempt by newspaper owners to require more work from news staffs that are shrinking, and if the Web sites ever become revenue streams, the revenue might not flow back into Spartan newsrooms.

Nevertheless, virtual convergence offers print journalists the opportunity to excel in what has become their franchise: in-depth reporting that can be sourced and expanded in ways not possible in the printed product. And print journalists can recapture timeliness as a competitive edge, because news reports can be posted on the Web site as soon as they are written and can be updated at will.

Simply flowing them onto a newspaper Web site will not enhance all stories. But the unlimited space of the Web and the possibilities of hyperlinks offer vast opportunities for good public affairs reporters to strut their stuff.

The *Seattle Times* used its Web site to let readers see pages of official documents their reporters had obtained to write a series of stories about high school coaches having inappropriate, and sometimes illegal, sexual contact with students and players. The ability to invite readers to review the documents in full for themselves enhances the credibility of the newspaper stories immeasurably. This is especially useful in volatile stories such as this one, and it takes some of the pressure off of reporters to include long sections of text dense with legal language culled from the documents.

Many newspapers are beginning to use their Web sites to post not only documents obtained through Freedom of Information (FOI) requests but also longer versions of interviews and more photos than were possible to use in the printed packages.

The relationship between the printed product and the online version of newspapers is still evolving, but journalism students, whether on the print or broadcast track, need to enter the job market with some understanding of the possibilities this convergence offers, and some skills.

The new vision in some media companies has the work of print journalists joining the streaming video of their broadcast peers on the company's media Web site—the merging of the strengths of both traditional media. Hence, print journalists will not have to step in front of a camera and broadcast reporters will not have to produce thirty-inch stories for page A1 of tomorrow's newspaper. But journalism students should step up their awareness as well as skills of how best to pair the work from different media.

Gonzaga's Garrity tells his broadcast students that to succeed in a converged media world, they need two things: good writing skills and an understanding of the needs of the consumers of each medium.

"The biggie is writing skills," Garrity says. "I believe there is (or should be) a big difference in how print and broadcast media write, and we should be equally skilled in both. It's just not adequate to re-purpose your script from TV and slide it into the print or Web site. Yet that's what I find happening too often in newsrooms today. The added writing skills used to be a nicety. They'll soon be a necessity.

"And students must be able to identify and satisfy the needs of the consumers of each medium. By understanding what people are looking for when they open a paper, log onto a site or tune into a broadcast, they will be better able to accomplish this goal. I liken it to a writer challenged to compose a haiku, a short story and a novel on the same topic. While each ought to contain the same basic idea and meet the same commitment statement, each also deserves its own unique treatment. As news operations continue to condense, we must realize that we in academia can't send out one-trick ponies any longer."

PROFESSIONAL TIPS

Colleen McBrinn

Colleen McBrinn is assistant features editor for the *Seattle Times*. She graduated from the University of Oregon with a journalism degree and has worked as a journalist for the Yakima (Washington) *Herald-Republic,* and at the *Times* as education reporter, assistant editorial page editor, and editor of NEXT, a section of commentary by young people that appeared online as well as in the *Times'* editorial section.

Question: You have worked with stories that appear in the print version of the *Seattle Times* and the Web version. Are there routine changes made in the format of the copy to make it more apropos to the online environment?
Not typically. Usually what runs in the paper runs intact online. However, for special projects (investigative stories, political polls, online chats, etc.), we will do more online such as include audio, more photos and text, and/or interactive features. You can see our recent projects online at http://seattletimes.nwsource.com/tableofcontents/special_projects.html.

Question: Is the demographic of the online readers of the *Seattle Times* different from the print demographic? If so, does this influence the variety or types of issues your writers address as they consider the different demographics?
Some of our research indicates that more younger readers view us online than in the paper. At this point, we haven't done anything exclusively online to specifically address this younger demographic. In other words, what runs in the paper runs online

and vice versa for the most part. However, we do have a *Seattle Times* company site called nwsource.com that we link from the homepage that has all kinds of local entertainment info, etc., and some of that info does not run in the paper.

Question: What types of news stories lend themselves well to the online environment?
Again, special projects where we can expand and add different features work very well for the site, and we get a lot of interest and hits.

Question: In a converged media world, are there skills beyond good writing and reporting you would advise journalism students to acquire to equip them for today's newsrooms?
Creativity! Young journalists should always be looking for different ways to tell a story using audio, video, etc. At bigger papers, you'll typically have online news producers with the expertise to do a lot of this, but in most cases they need the ideas to come from you and for you to be prepared to do a lot of the front-end work to achieve a great package online. At smaller papers, this may be harder to achieve for lack of staff resources.

(continued)

PROFESSIONAL TIPS   Continued

Question: As a young journalist not too many years out of college, are there classes you wished you had taken outside the journalism department that would have better prepared you for a newspaper career?

Yes, math and economics! Honestly, I use both often and wish every day that I had not blown them off . . . and maybe more classes on how to more effectively dig for hard-to-find info on deadline—various ways to mine the Web in a hurry.

Question: Some people say online versions will make printed newspapers obsolete. You work in both environments. Are the two environments redundant? What are your thoughts about the future of the printed products?

I think printed newspapers will be around for a long time, *but only if* we adapt to readers' changing needs and appeal to younger audiences. Many newspapers are too slow to change and are threatened by some things like blogs when really, we need to be jumping on new things and making them work for us.

CHAPTER EXERCISES

1. Select a project from a newspaper, and compare the stories, photos, documentation and graphics in the printed version with those elements posted on the Web site. Identify the strengths of the printed version and the strengths of the online package.

2. Invite the team editor or city editor of your local newspaper to class to discuss how ideas for good projects are pitched at his or her paper and the process for producing projects.

3. Using a project from a newspaper, find Web sites that could be linked from the project online that would be appropriate and credible and would enhance the project.

4. As a class, generate six ideas for projects that revolve around the campus community, and develop a plan for producing the best of the six ideas using a team approach.

CHAPTER

12 Working with Editors, Designers and Photographers

BY KENTON BIRD

A pine tree's branches intermingle amid a blue sky to form a pretty picture. When reporters, editors, designers and photographers work together, a story is much more clear, interesting and enticing.

Except at the smallest weekly newspapers, a reporter is not a soloist—he or she is part of an ensemble of journalists. A beginning reporter's success in the newsroom depends on working cooperatively with other reporters, as well as editors, photographers and designers. The degree of teamwork influences everything from the original assignment to how and where the story is displayed.

Explanatory headlines, information boxes, photographs and charts are essential to making public affairs stories interesting and useful to readers. Without them, a story will be ignored by many readers and noticed only by insiders or those with a direct stake in the outcome. At newspapers and magazines that value attractive and readable design, visual

151

considerations are built into the reporting, not tacked on after the story is written. Planning is critical to effective packaging of stories, photographs and graphics.

This chapter offers tips for promoting dialogue between reporters and their coworkers, identifying ways to illustrate stories and meeting editors' expectations.

Coaching

Most of the vocabulary about *coaching*—a rethinking of the relationship between reporters and editors—comes from the Poynter Institute in St. Petersburg, Florida. Poynter faculty members Roy Peter Clark and Don Fry articulated the need for better newsroom dialogue in their book *Coaching Writers: Editors and Reporters Working Together.* They describe the differences between fixing stories (the standard approach to editing) and coaching reporters. The first approach meets an immediate need—correcting problems before publication—but invites a recurrence of the same reporting or writing flaws the next time the reporter tackles a similar story. The second strategy has a permanent benefit: helping reporters do their jobs better. A few minutes spent on focusing a story or suggesting additional sources in the prewriting stage take less time than rewriting on deadline, they argue.

Coaching is almost as old as ink on paper. Experienced reporters reminisce about helpful editors who took them aside after deadline and reviewed a story paragraph by paragraph, showing how to move the news to the top of the story, emphasize essential facts and provide telling details. Yet other writers recall editors whose stock in trade was making wholesale changes in the story without ever explaining to the reporter the reasons why. The result in many newsrooms was mutual distrust between reporters and editors. Clark and Fry summarized the impasse: "Traditionally, both groups would rather bitch and moan than consult and collaborate."

Their book, as well as Poynter videos and tip sheets, recommend a variety of strategies for rethinking the relationship between the reporters who gather and organize facts, and the editors who assign, shape and critique their work.

The dialogue often begins with a budget memo or a digest line: an opportunity to pitch a story to the editor and outline a strategy for reporting it. News organizations of all sizes do this on a daily basis, but the larger the organization, the further in advance a reporter must plan. Sunday page A1 features are often scheduled weeks ahead of time, subject to breaking news. Memos typically list the premise of the story, sources the reporter intends to consult, the probable length and when it might be ready. Ideally, the reporter should suggest possible art—a photograph, information graphic or illustration—at the time the story is conceived. A sample budget memo is located at the top of the next page.

Because the editor will use the reporter's memo as the basis for pitching the story in an editors' meeting or news huddle, the reporter shouldn't promise more than can be delivered. The memo should accurately reflect the significance of the story—and the prospects of finishing it before deadline. There's nothing more frustrating for an editor expecting a story strong enough to lead the local section front to receive a brief that would be best buried next to the crossword puzzle or horoscope.

> TO: Ann Editor
>
> FROM: Roger Reporter
>
> I'd like to look into changing enrollment patterns in the Coeur d'Alene public schools. I'm curious why the schools at the north end of town are bursting at the seams, while those in the south, closer to downtown, seem to have empty classrooms. I'll review enrollment figures for the past ten years, talk to the elementary school principals and contact the parent–teacher organizations.
>
> We probably need a map to show the location of the schools and possibly a chart to show overall district enrollment. And I'd like one of the photographers to accompany me to each school.
>
> This will take at least thirty inches to cover thoroughly, though it might work as a two-part series. I will need at least a week to report the story, so the soonest it could be ready is the first Sunday of next month.

In many newsrooms, these memos are sent and acknowledged by e-mail. But even a routine story benefits from a face-to-face meeting between the reporter and the assigning editor. The first objective is to agree on the focus and length of the story before any reporting begins. Another exchange, hours or days later, should come after most of the reporting has been finished but before the reporter begins to write. The key question at both stages is "What is the story about?" If the reporter can't sum up the key facts quickly, the editor needs to ask other questions. One approach is to determine how much knowledge readers have about the topic already and what they need to know next.

The best coaching is quick, informal and constructive. A reporter just back from a meeting, crime scene or spot-news event should recount what he saw and heard. The editor should ask what was most interesting, unusual or contrary to expectations. "What surprised you?" or "What do you know now that you didn't know before?" might be better questions than "What's your lead?"

Meanwhile, the reporter shouldn't hesitate to ask for advice about how to organize facts, resolve contradictions and provide context. The resulting story will be easier to follow than one in which the reporter charges back to the office from an assignment, flips open her notebook and starts writing off the top of her head. The next step is to submit a lead or, better yet, a first draft to the editor early enough for quick review well before deadline. This helps a reporter know whether he or she is on track while there's still time to call back a source for clarification. The closer to deadline a story is finished, the less time remains for productive coaching. Reporters who earn a reputation for pushing deadline lose valuable opportunities to improve their writing.

Another form of coaching takes place once the story is in print—a postpublication critique of what worked and what didn't. At this stage, editors should be candid and reporters willing to listen.

Brian Beesley, design editor at the Lewiston (Idaho) *Tribune,* says that if reporters really want to improve their writing, "They need to check their egos at the door." He recommends finding time to consult with an editor off-deadline. Find someone whose judgment you trust and approach that person, he says.

"Editors like to edit, they like to be asked to evaluate other people's writing and they're generally happy to be of service," Beesley says. "All reporters need to do is ask."

Fry and Clark devote a chapter of their book to "How to Get Coached." Among their tips: praise good editing; warn editors about surprises (such as an unconventional approach to a story); cultivate relationships with copy editors, newsroom clerks and librarians; and recognize the pressures on editors. A dozen years after *Coaching Writers* was published, Clark and Fry's suggestions for creating more productive newsrooms through better communication are still valid and have been widely emulated.

Story Planning

Two models for stronger visual presentation expand the reporter–editor dialog to include photographers and page designers. One strategy, Writing-Editing-Design (WED), originated at the Poynter Institute; the other, the Maestro Concept, came from University of Kentucky journalism professor Buck Ryan.

Don Fry and his Poynter colleague Mario Garcia first outlined WED, which implies a marriage between words and images, in the late 1980s. "Good editing means good planning, and that means design considerations have to come into play early in the process," they write. Reporters are at the heart of the process. They must start thinking visually from the moment the story is assigned. At small newspapers, reporters often take a camera with them to news events. This often gives them an advantage over someone who relies on a staff photographer to illustrate the story. Fry encourages reporters to "scoop up every piece of visual material they see . . . photos, diagrams, maps, charts"—anything that could become the basis of an illustration or information graphic.

George Rorick of Knight-Ridder Tribune Graphics agrees: "Every time you take a trip, bring back a map for the graphics staff to put on file." See Figure 12.1.

Fry says writers benefit in several ways from WED. By viewing stories as packages of words and visuals, they are likely to be more perceptive observers at the scene of the news event. "Reporters who think graphically see better, and therefore write better," he says. In addition, by gathering materials for illustrations themselves, reporters gain a larger voice in how a story will be displayed. Designers, meanwhile, welcome the opportunity to be involved earlier in the process, instead of being asked to improvise a visually interesting package after the reporting, writing and text editing are finished.

The Maestro Concept became popular at U.S. newspapers after Ryan, then at Northwestern University, presented it to the American Society of Newspaper Editors in the early 1990s. He devised the system in response to several problems: new software needed for editors to produce pages, newsroom inefficiencies that frustrated staff members, source-driven stories that neglected readers' needs and newsroom bureaucracies that got in the way of good work. "Interesting ideas get dulled down as they move through the maze of desks, departments and shifts that constitute the traditional newsroom," Ryan wrote.

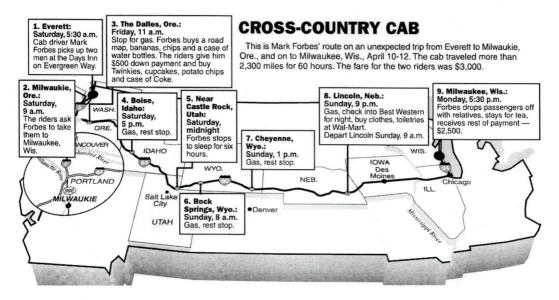

FIGURE 12.1 This graphic from Everett, Washington, shows the route and a basic timeline of a $3,000 cross-country cab ride.

Judy Stanley, *The Herald*. Copyright 2004, The Daily Herald Co.

In place of the maze, Ryan proposed a flattened newsroom structure aimed at bringing "reporters, photographers, designers and editors together as a team at the beginning of a story." Using the metaphor of an orchestra conductor, Ryan's model calls these planning meetings *maestro sessions*. At a small newspaper, the managing editor is the maestro; at larger organizations, a metro, sports or feature editor leads the discussion. Ryan says a maestro session usually runs fifteen minutes, less for breaking news and more for complicated stories. "The session is designed to ensure that the story is fully reported and that it will be reported in the most compelling way for readers," he explains.

At each session, participants use a story-planning form, which replaces separate photo assignment and graphic request forms. It lists readers' likely questions, provides space for headline suggestions, asks participants to picture it on the page and defines challenges for reporting and illustrating the story.

Tim Harrower, author of the *Newspaper Designers' Handbook,* created a similar worksheet that contains a list of sidebar options and space to sketch a rough layout. Harrower's list of reader questions begins with "Why should I care?" Editors can design their own forms to reflect their newspaper's particular needs. Similar to coaching, story planning works best when it's incorporated into the early stages of deciding how to cover an event, issue or controversy. Harrower observes: "Most newsrooms are like factory assembly lines: the reporter reports. The photographer photographs. The editor edits. And then—at the last minute—the designer designs. The assembly line process works fine if you're making sausages, but it won't consistently produce award-winning pages. Lavish layouts rarely succeed when they're slapped together on deadline."

Monica Moses, deputy managing editor for visuals at the *Star Tribune* of Minneapolis, says the best planning meetings involve no more than six people—"More than that and you are unlikely to get the creative brainstorming you need to find really interesting solutions."

Ideally, the participants will follow a story from concept to publication. But if that isn't possible, the system should make provision for "handoffs" to other staff members, as well as an expectation that the successors should stick to the original plan (except if the story changes dramatically or if someone comes up with a significantly better way to display it).

Moses also observes that none of these models works for everyone—"[T]hey must be adapted to your newsroom's rhythms, values [and] eccentricities." And avoid having a meeting simply for the sake of a meeting—sometimes, a story writes itself and the best editors simply stay out of the way.

Photography

As newspapers seek to lure young readers away from television and the Internet, they give more attention to good design. Strong local photographs are essential to establishing a paper's visual identity and its connection with a community. Pictures of a community's triumphs and tragedies, landmarks and landscapes, heroes and victims all contribute to readers' connection with the newspaper. A paper that takes photojournalism seriously always engages readers with more intensity than one that views photography as something to fill the space between stories. Photographs add authenticity and credibility to stories, while attracting casual readers who might bypass a story told only with text. It's no wonder that savvy reporters like to work with photographers who have reputations for telling stories visually.

At Idaho's *Lewiston Tribune,* design editor Beesley says inexperienced reporters don't always see the value of visuals, erroneously believing that words alone will carry the story. "You have to sell them on the premise that having a photograph or graphic or illustration to accompany their story increases the chances people will read it," he said.

Reporters who think only in terms of text are at a disadvantage to those who recognize the value of visuals. That's where a probing question from an editor—even something as simple as "What's the photo?"—is helpful. For stories about people, the photo assignment is obvious: a head shot or environmental portrait of the subject of the story. For more complicated issues or trend stories, the photo assignment is more subtle. Photographers like to be part of these discussions, though their schedules often keep them out of the office at times when key decisions are made. Another dividend is that the photographer often brings a fresh perspective to the way a reporter "sees" the story, particularly in the prewriting phase.

The best photographers are multipurpose journalists, almost as nimble with a notebook as they are with a camera. Photographers who collect names, phone numbers and

PROFESSIONAL TIPS

Jim Borden

Jim Borden is the managing editor of the Kalamazoo, Michigan, *Gazette.* He previously was an editor at the *Gazette* in Colorado Springs, Colorado, for fifteen years, the last six as assistant managing editor, supervising the editing, art and design departments. He has been an editor for newspapers from Spokane, Washington, to Eugene, Oregon, including what is now the *Moscow/Pullman Daily News* in Moscow, Idaho. He is a graduate of the University of Idaho.

Question: From an editor's standpoint, what's the biggest challenge in working with reporters?
Every reporter has strengths and weaknesses. Some are very good at digging out information, conducting interviews, combing public records and searching databases, and some need assistance with those things. Some are very organized and methodical, while others have stacks of paper two feet deep on their desks and can't find today's notes, let alone notes made last week or last month. Some are able to assemble their stories in clear, logical fashion, and others need help figuring out where to start, what to include, what to leave out and how to end a story.

The biggest challenge is figuring out a reporter's specific personality, needs and style and tailoring a coaching and teaching approach to that reporter. For some, it's helpful to heavily "front load" the process, so that even before much reporting has been done the editor and reporter have thought carefully about what kind of story we're after and where and how to get it. Some benefit from talking the story through with their editors after the reporting is done but before writing begins. But they all thrive on praise and recognition, whether they want to admit it or not.

Question: What strategies have you found effective in getting reporters to think visually about how their stories might be illustrated and displayed?
It's imperative to get reporters thinking about visuals at the beginning of the story process. A series of sharply focused questions can help uncover visual possibilities. Photos often are fairly obvious; stories about people need photos of people. But graphics and charts are often less obvious.

For a story on the economic effects of the deployment of Colorado soldiers to Iraq, editors at the *Gazette* talked about juxtaposing two graphics: the first would show the numbers of troops departing and then finally returning over an eighteen-month period. From the basic data we had, we developed a bell curve, showing partial deployment, full deployment and then the return of soldiers over the period. The second graphic tracked sales tax collections by local governments. It produced a curve that started high, dipped when the soldiers were fully deployed, then rose again after they returned. Together, the charts helped us show how much local governments—and businesses—depend upon soldiers and suffer when they're gone.

The strategy for developing the ideas was simple: we asked several people to meet to brainstorm ideas for covering the next deployment.
Continued

PROFESSIONAL TIPS   Continued

We jotted ideas on a board, and drew out and ran with the ones that had visual and other potentials.

Question: Sometimes it seems like reporters and photographers speak different languages. How do you get them to talk to each other?

Most of the time, reporters and photographers are smart enough to communicate before each has begun to report the story. Where the ball most often gets dropped, however, is when they neglect to communicate during or just after each has done his or her reporting. A reporter and photograph might be assigned to cover the county fair. But if the reporter interviews a 7-year-old bull showman and the photographer shoots an 80-year-old carnival ride operator, the package isn't going to work.

Question: What kind of coaching do you give to reporters before they begin work on a story?

A lot of up-front coaching is more in the form of questions than directions, for two reasons: the first is that it's important for an editor to know what the reporter knows. How else can the editor make good recommendations? The second is that reporters work best with editors they feel are engaged in their work. Usually, reporters have a pretty good idea beforehand what potential stories could come out of a single event. By asking the reporter about those possibilities, an editor can help provide focus and make clear what is and isn't wanted in the final product.

Question: If a reporter wants to improve her or his writing, what's the best way to approach an editor?

Unfortunately, not all editors are great writing coaches. They're good former reporters, or can get things done efficiently or were too shy to be reporters in the first place and went straight to the desk. The way reporters develop writing talents most often is:

- Study carefully and gain mastery over the language. You're lost if you can't assemble clear and logical sentences and paragraphs, or if you can't spell or [if you] bumble with grammar or style.
- Read great journalism in the best newspapers and magazines, and take the time to dissect the best stories to understand how they were constructed.
- Remember that deep and thorough reporting is the foundation for everything, and that writing without reporting is like serving a coffee lover a cup of hot water.
- Talk with your editor, yes, but talk with lots of other editors and reporters, too, and have group discussions and analyses and pass around examples of great work. Be proactive about the learning process. When the student is ready, the master will appear, it is said.

Question: What other advice would you give to reporters about the care and feeding of editors?

Don't make them have to dream up story ideas for you. Keep a tickler file of stories to do when the beat is slow. But also listen to and work interactively with editors. Their experience makes them valuable, and they can keep you from covering the same ground or making errors. Be meticulous about the facts, spellings of names and places, times, dates and so on. Nothing will get you in trouble with an editor faster than sloppy work.

Finally, be sure to thank them occasionally for their effort. They generally do not get a byline, but many editors work many hours on some stories, and when a story comes out well, everybody pats the reporter on the back. They may not know that the story had to be redone from start to finish and that the original contained many errors or glaring omissions. Editing is called a thankless job, but it doesn't have to be.

key facts at an accident or crime scene earn their paychecks; others see their job description so narrowly that they can't be bothered to gather basic information for a caption. Reporters who seek productive partnerships must recognize that photographers are the artists of the newsroom—and sometimes have artistic temperaments. A well-timed compliment can soothe a photographer's fragile ego and will pay dividends on the next assignment.

Here are five ways for reporters to bring photographers into the process earlier:

- **Have a clear** concept of the story—breaking news, feature or investigative piece— and be sure the photographer knows when it's scheduled to run.

- **Invite the photographer** to go with you on interviews. In addition to getting photos of the subject at home or in the workplace, the photographer often notices details that a reporter misses because he's so busy taking notes.

- **If the photographer** can't go along, the reporter must collect essential information: phone number, work schedule and best time to call. If the subject has had previous experience (positive or negative) with the newspaper, be sure to pass along that background, too.

- **If the photographer's** schedule allows, debrief her as soon as she returns from the assignment about what she saw and the images she intends to use. Don't wait until the finished photograph is ready to go on the page before pointing out the picture doesn't match the story's focus.

- **Alert the photographer** as soon as possible if the story has changed since the initial interview or if additional major characters have emerged. If someone is important enough to be quoted in your story, he probably should be part of the visual package, too.

Informational Graphics

Reporters at small and medium-sized newspapers are under the mistaken impression that information graphics are only for the metros—newspapers with artists and designers who do nothing but create news illustrations. In fact, editors with limited artistic skills can easily create attractive graphics that enhance the readability of stories. Designers talk about *entry points*—visual elements that entice a reader into a page. The reporter can help this process by gathering information for graphics in the reporting process, suggesting several options for graphics and starting early.

Harrower, in his popular *Newspaper Designers Handbook,* makes a strong case for sidebars (short stories that accompany a longer piece) and information graphics (boxes or figures that convey supplemental facts or figures). He explains why they're important: "Because they're tight, bright and entertaining, they add reader appeal to any story, whether news or features. In fact they often attract higher readership than the main story they accompany."

Harrower lists eighteen categories of sidebars and graphics, from the obvious (pie charts) to the offbeat (quizzes and how-to guides). Here are the six examples that require minimal graphic skills to assemble, along with other types of information aids:

- **Bio box:** This is essential for news stories or features about people in public life. By moving basic biographical information (education, work history, current position) to a graphic, the writer can concentrate on conveying a sense of the subject's motivations and goals. Poynter's Don Fry calls this "tackling the block"—relocating the résumé. As a result, the profile doesn't bog down on the details of schooling or career, and the reader gets another entry point to the story. Harrower suggests this technique also can be used for key facts about companies, communities or organizations.

- **Locator map:** The more widespread a newspaper's circulation, the more important it is to show where events originate. These range from neighborhood maps to show the location of a crime to regional maps that show towns affected by a government agency's decision. Even if the information is contained in the story, readers appreciate seeing at a glance the geographical context for the news.

- **Timeline:** A chronological listing of past events is essential to providing historical context to a running story. As with a profile, putting this information in a box keeps the story from bogging down on what came before—and allows the reporter to concentrate on what's new. Timelines are also effective organizing tools for reporters, especially with investigative or interpretive stories. By keeping a chronology on file for reference, a reporter can easily update it to reflect the latest twist in a story.

- **"What's next?" box:** This projects the story into the future by reporting the next step in the process: a public hearing, reconsideration by an agency or a judicial review. It also can refer the reader to a source of additional information or a relevant Web site. If it suggests a way for citizens to contact elected officials or influence a decision, some designers call it an "empowerment box."

- **Fast facts:** A quick way to summarize a story, listing key facts or figures. This works especially well for budget stories: last year's spending, this year's spending, percentage change, source of additional review, new programs. This step forces reporters to be more precise in their reporting by assuring that the numbers in the fact box and story match up with those in the original document.

- **Glossary:** If writing about a scientific or technical topic or a bureaucracy that thrives on specialized jargon, give the reader a list of frequently used terms and their definitions. Sometimes, deciphering the *alphabet soup* (commonly used abbreviations) is all that a reader needs to make sense of a complicated subject.

- **Other types of information aids:** Illustrations, bar charts, pie charts and tables are helpful, especially for financial information, but typically require knowledge of a design or graphics program. With enough advance notice, a skilled page designer can create simple but appealing graphics. Bring them into the planning early.

Survival Skills

Getting along with newsroom colleagues is not just common sense but also a matter of self-interest. A reporter who wants to move to a better beat or a bigger newspaper needs a strong portfolio and good references. Sometimes, factors beyond a reporter's control—a new city editor, a new computer system, the whims of the publisher—conspire against doing one's best work. The best remedies to those situations are paying attention to editors' preferences, staying neutral in squabbles and keeping cool under pressure.

A reporter who knows his or her beat and covers it thoroughly is usually left alone. Conversely, the quickest way to invite second-guessing by editors and poaching by other reporters is to miss a major story or to develop a reputation for sloppy reporting. Accuracy matters. When a reporter makes a mistake—and that error makes it into print—the reporter should be the first to tell the assigning editor. Then, he or she should get on the telephone to the sources or subjects of the story to apologize and tell them the paper will publish a correction. Finally, follow up with an editor to be sure the correction actually runs.

Reporters need to find a balance between "feeding the beast" (with daily stories) and the projects and investigative pieces that anchor a section front and win prizes for newspapers. Editors want both, and at small and medium-sized papers they often have unrealistic demands about how much a reporter can produce. Determining these expectations at the beginning of a new job (or a new beat) is essential to setting up a reasonable work schedule. It should be understood that many community newspapers expect at least one bylined story a day, plus briefs and other small assignments or requirements.

Reporters should seek a balance between quick turnarounds and long-term projects, and between hard news and features. Writers should negotiate for time to clear a backlog of stories and ask for backup from other reporters to provide a window to finish a project. Editors, for their part, should avoid overloading reporters in the middle of a big project with daily stories.

Respect the work of photographers, copy editors and page designers. They face different kinds of challenges and often work more weekends, holidays and odd shifts than reporters. A reporter should never underestimate the value of an editor—no matter how seasoned the reporter or green the editor. Many times, a copy editor has saved a reporter from embarrassment by questioning a fact that seems out of place or catching a minor error. Even a veteran reporter can benefit from an editor's critical eye.

Form alliances with photographers, and enlist their assistance in getting the space and time to do the big packages. When you see a stunning photograph, a clever headline or a package that sings, praise the staff members responsible—and make sure their bosses hear about it, too. The designers and photographers will remember the compliment when it's time to design or illustrate your next page A1 feature.

Avoid becoming embroiled in newsroom politics. Long-term survival means diplomacy. "Don't publicly embarrass your editor," says Ken Olsen, a reporter for the *Columbian* in Vancouver, Washington. "If you have a problem, talk to the editor privately." Think twice about doing battle with the editors over a story, Olsen advises. Reporters will write thousands of fifteen- to twenty-inch stories in the course of a career. Few are worth going to the mat over a word choice, quotes or punctuation. Save your political capital for stories worth fighting for.

Sidebar: The Value of Planning

By Monica L. Moses, Deputy ME/Visuals, Minneapolis Star Tribune

Why is planning so hard in the average newsroom? Well, for starters, we are caught up in the daily miracle that is newspaper production. Unlike people in other industries, newsroom staffs are at work almost "round the clock." We can't take a week off to take a deep look at what we do and to retool it. So we cling to our old assembly-line habits; they get the paper out, more or less accurately, more or less without libel lawsuits.

Of course, those habits give us too many story packages that communicate poorly to the scanning reader (that is, every reader not confined to bed). Our less-than-great newsroom communication becomes the reader's less-than-great reading experience.

The key to the well-known story-planning methods—such as Buck Ryan's Maestro system and the Poynter Institute's Writing-Editing-Design process—is an efficient, cross-discipline conversation as early as possible in the production process. It's a simple, fifteen-minute talk that includes reporter, line editor, copy editor, designer, photo representative and graphics person. What do the planners need to decide? Four main things:

- **The focus of the story.** If the story can't be summed up in twenty words or less, it's not ready to be planned. The more focused the story, the better the headlines and visuals are likely to be. Specific is always more interesting than general. If the story is about artichokes, what about them? What's new, what's different? If the reporter can't say for sure what the point of the story is, suggest the meeting be postponed.
- **Why readers will care.** If you run a seventy-inch story that is not relevant to readers, you're throwing copy (headlines, visuals, your hard work, etc.) down a hole. Probe story ideas for the bits that will hook readers—will concern them, delight them, captivate them, annoy them, whatever.
- **What's the best visual approach?** The best story form? Is it a photo package? A graphic? Should the story appear in three parts with three inches of intro text?
- **What is the working headline?** Headlines need to go with visuals, first and foremost. The first connection the reader makes with a story is visual-headline. It's crucial the two work together coherently.

Look behind the most dazzling, most powerful visual journalism, and you almost always find passionate people who talked early and deeply about a story. If you keep at it, you build rapport, a common language in the newsroom, and—above all—better stories for readers.

(Excerpted from "The 5 Ws and 1 H of Planning," www.poynter.org, QuickLink: A14306)

Finally, be willing to accept routine work or undesirable stories without grumbling. The late Sylvia Harrell, a longtime business reporter at the *Lewiston Tribune,* often observed: "Every job has its dirty dishes." In other words, step up to the plate when the city editor needs a weather story, a preview of a community festival or a roundup of the Christmas shopping season. A reporter's readiness to tackle mundane assignments when no one else is available will pay dividends in the long run.

CHAPTER EXERCISES

1. In a class session, or as homework, break into groups of three. One person will play the role of a reporter, another will think as a photograph and the third will assume the role of a graphic artist. Take an assigned story idea from your professor and brainstorm the various components. Put together a report of your findings, including the various elements and how you worked as a team.

2. Select a page-1 story in your campus newspaper that was published without photos, graphics or illustrations. Provide ideas for additional elements that could have helped tell the story.

3. Write a two-page essay on the importance of working with editors, designers and photographers.

4. Attend a story-planning session (budget meeting) of your campus or community newspaper, and write a summary of how effective the meeting was in terms of involving all internal stakeholders (reporters, editors, designers, photographers, etc.).

BY JOHN IRBY

Data and numbers have a tendency to scare some reporters, but understanding their power and importance is essential. Gasoline prices are a business and public affairs story, especially when humor is employed to soften the shock of the high cost of a gallon.

"I want to be a journalist because I'm no good with numbers."

   Students in news reporting and writing courses across the country must have a telephone tree where they chant that mantra from coast to coast. Or at least it seems that way.

There is only one problem. Journalists, even though students are not always yet aware of it, work with data and numbers every day. Almost every story will include some data, and virtually every aspect of life has a connection to numbers.

In the days after September 11, 2001, newspapers across the United States heralded the tragic terrorist attacks with the following headlines:

- **Acts of mass murder:** *Newsday* (September 12)
- **Acts of war:** *Los Angeles Times* (September 13)
- **Confronting the terror:** *Boston Globe* (September 14)
- **Bush vows war on terror:** *Philadelphia Inquirer* (September 14)

All of those stories were awash in data and numbers, as illustrated below:

- "Investigators have now identified the **18** people who hijacked the **four** planes."
- "**4,763** were reported missing in the Trade Center attacks."
- "New York Mayor Rudolph Giuliani said the remains of **184** people had been recovered."
- "In New York, officials ask for **6,000** body bags."

Numbers and data have much power. If used correctly, with the proper context, they can show impact and relevance.

For instance, the *Daily Evergreen* student newspaper at Washington State University reported that administrators said there would be a tuition increase from $4,435 to $4,745 (7 percent, or $310). On the surface it seemed a small increase.

But an increase of $1,349 is much more serious in the cost of education, and that is how much tuition had been raised in five years. That's almost a 40 percent increase, and if that data had been provided in the story it would have added context and background.

Additional context could also have been included by noting that the University of Washington and Washington State University had the highest in-state tuition and fees among public institutions in fifteen western states, with the exception of the Colorado School of Mines.

Reporters can't be afraid of data and numbers, or back away from them. They are the foundation of quality reporting.

Thinking about Business

Many young reporters, when they think about business stories, don't get overly excited. But if you open your mind and expand the scope of what you consider to be a business story, the possibilities are endless.

Business stories are much more than just writing about interest rates. They can be about what those interest rates mean to the buyer of a new car or house—how much additional money will be paid beyond the sales prices because of financing.

Reporters sometimes think business stories are writing exclusively about such topics as what happens on Wall Street. A downturn in the market should be reported, for many reasons, including the impact on retirees playing the stock market. But this is not only a business story; it is also a quality of life story.

Business stories are, in their most simple format, writing about money and how it relates to people. But they are also about personal finance—and most people are interested in personal money matters.

Stories about business must be written in commonsense language, explaining how people make money, how they spend money and how they save and invest money.

Like most any other subject, preparation is a key ingredient for business writing. If you are going to write about the pros and cons of fifteen- versus thirty-year home mortgages, you need to understand something about mortgage and real estate rates.

If you are going to write about art as an investment, then you probably should have a basic understanding of painting, sculpture and other artistic media.

And before you start writing about mutual funds, stocks, the Dow Jones Indexes, the New York Stock Exchange or NASDAQ, you should learn something about how the money markets operate, including the risks and rewards.

The best business stories, however, although inclusive of data and numbers as appropriate, aren't usually awash in mathematical or statistical analysis.

Some of the best business stories will report issues that have personal impact or relevance, using only basic math and statistical perspective. Data are best used in illustrative ways, not as a focus.

For instance, it is a business story to write about the high cost of gasoline and the impact it has on travel. OPEC, cartels, cost per barrel and production levels can be used to illustrate the story, but the real story is how much more consumers are paying for gas than they did a year ago, and how much more it will cost on a driving vacation to visit Grandma this summer in Michigan.

But in such a story, don't forget to factor in inflation. You might find that the 50 cents per gallon you paid years ago was more expensive than the $2.50 paid today, considering all the data of inflation, cost of living, median household income and so on.

Business stories can be as bright and as interesting as any story in any section of the newspaper. It all depends on how they are approached—and written.

Covering a business beat, however, does have some peculiarities. Reporters need to have the knowledge and know the language necessary to ask the right questions, recognize newsworthy answers and write the story in a way the reader without specialized knowledge will understand. Reporters must be able to speak the technical language, but not default into including inappropriate jargon in their stories.

The biggest challenge for business reporters is to figure out how to get information from people who usually don't have to tell you anything. The information controlled by CEOs, managers and business employees usually isn't public, unlike much public information that can be obtained from government officials.

Many businesses are reluctant to make information public because of a basic distrust of the media, even when it might be in their best interest to release the information. The best business reporters will concentrate on gaining the trust of those in business by reporting fairly and accurately about the business.

Far too many businesses seek a chamber of commerce, "booster" approach, and they are often willing to "pay" for it.

Detroit automakers, for years, made "test" cars available to auto writers—for as long as they wanted to "test" them. Some offer discounts on car purchases.

The same relationship has existed between other businesses and reporters. For example, professional sport is a business and teams seek positive coverage. One professional football team used to take steps to ensure that by providing every beat writer with a color television set as a Christmas present.

Disneyland, another business, doesn't offer members of the media free tickets or junkets out of the kindness of its corporate heart. The opportunities are offered to curry favor in reporting.

For more information and consideration of ethics in business coverage, see the chapter on ethics (chapter 6).

Some of the best stories are generated by enterprise, a reporter following a hunch or tip. For example, a routine announcement of an executive appointment should make a reporter stop and wonder what happened to the person who is being replaced. Was he or she fired? Promoted? Did he or she quit because of some unhappiness? The answer to those questions can be the beginning of exceptional business stories.

The source of much business news is usually an announcement by a company of a new product or reaction to a governmental action. Covering annual meetings or reviewing annual reports can also produce good business stories.

Data Collection

Unfortunately, we all seem to end up at the doctor's office from time to time with some malady. After the examination, the doctor makes a diagnosis and assigns a prescription.

At the drug store we pick up the small medicine bottle and pop two green pills. In looking at the label, we see *Rx1227564.*

Rx1227564 is the prescription number. It is also data. Although *data* is a plural word, many consider it a singular word and a synonym for *information.*

Data is factual information, but generally has no real meaning on its own. Used in stories, contextually, it takes on meaning and becomes information that can be organized for analysis, used to supply reason, used to make decisions or used to make writing clear.

Data, records and reports, however, lose much of their power when not accompanied by human sources such as company officials, financial analysts, academic experts, association officers, the chamber of commerce, former employees and/or labor leaders.

Although many find accounting and numbers uninspiring, it is critical for reporters to understand the basics of business, such as an annual report. There are five basic concepts or terms in such an analysis:

- **Balance sheet:** This is nothing more than a snapshot of a company that shows assets (what the company owns), liabilities (what the company owes) and shareholder equity (dollar value of what shareholders own).

- **Income statement:** The income statement will show how much money the company made for the year. It will also generally provide yearly comparisons.

- **Return on sales:** This is the relation of net income to sales, a tool used to understand the financial health of an organization. For instance, it might cost a company $1 million in salaries and expenses for its sales force, but the company might bring in $3 million in revenue—for a $2 million net income to sales.

- **Return on equity:** This is a ratio that shows how effectively a company's invested capital is working.

- **Dividends:** This is a share of profits to be received by stockholders.

Business reporters must also acquaint themselves with six key economic categories the government uses routinely, to better explain and predict current and future economics and trends:

- **The Index of Leading Economic Indicators:** This monthly index is a summary of twelve areas of economic activity. The twelve areas are manufacturers' new orders, private housing building permits, daily stock prices, manufactured goods inventories, factory worker layoff rate, industrial worker workweek average, the nation's money supply, net new business startups, shipping rates for finished goods, consumer goods new orders, factory equipment orders and commodity prices.

- **The Dow Jones Industrial Average:** This is a listing of the stocks of thirty major companies and their total average sales price per share for that day.

- **The Wholesale Price Index:** This is a monthly statistical mix to achieve an average of wholesale prices of farm and industrial goods.

- **The Consumer Price Index:** This is a measurement of fixed goods and services in five major categories—housing, food, health and leisure spending, transportation and clothing.

- **The unemployment rate:** This is computed by dividing the total number of people in the civilian workforce by the number of those out of work. A monthly sample of 50,000 households is used.

- **The gross national product (GNP):** This is the total output of goods and services in four categories—personal consumption, new housing and industrial development, direct government purchase and net exports.

Although data is readily available, it is not always provided and must be gathered by the reporter, who sometimes has a tendency to go to the same people—officials—or sources to gather information.

As an example, a reporter living in a community—or even a student growing up in a community—has gathered a great deal of data or information about that specific community and the people in it just by being there.

So, in some cases, it might only take an additional ten to fifteen minutes for a reporter to gather necessary background, as he or she might already have the names of key sources, context and perspective.

But sometimes reporters must start at the beginning, or rely on reference materials that can include a newspaper's electronic archives, libraries, phone books, reverse directories, local directories, maps, almanacs, encyclopedias, media stylebooks, dictionaries and virtual resources and links.

And don't forget secretaries and clerks. They are the gatekeepers of much data, and if cultivated properly these sources will often supply you with data.

Some of the best public source documents, or data, can include property records, corporation records, court records, campaign and conflict-of-interest reports, loan records, minutes and transcripts. And some of the best nonpublic records, if you can find someone to provide them, include investigative files, past arrests and conviction reports, bank records, income tax records and credit checks.

The Internet, obviously, has changed the way many reporters do background work. In the past if a reporter needed background information on a business, he or she would have to call the company and ask for annual reports or trek to the library and look up information. It is much different today. In many cases, if you type www.companyname.com as an address on the Internet, you will have immediate access to basic—and often expanded—company data.

The same tactic will generally work when you are trying to find background information for nonprofit organizations. For instance, if you type www.nameofnonprofit.org, you can get basic information.

Also, data from city governments can often be found by going to www.ci.cityname.stateabbreviation.us.

The Internet, however, isn't a magical information warehouse, and there is nothing that equals knocking on doors and working phones and sources for information.

Caution is the watchword with the Internet. It can be slow, frustrating and sometimes misleading, even though much data can be located by using search engines, various techniques, subject indexes or discussion groups.

For instance, a little-known California-based cult called Heaven's Gate once staged a mass suicide. Because of the Internet, reporters had little problem finding out information about the group. All they had to do was type the words *Heaven's Gate* into one of the four or five leading search engines and the information was available—taking only a few seconds of download time, dictated by the speed of the computer processor.

Some of the information, however, wasn't fit for publication. On one Heaven's Gate link, there was a message from an E.T. living on earth in a human body. The E.T. wrote, in part:

> In the early 1970's, two individuals (my task partner and myself) from the Evolutionary Level Above Human (the Kingdom of Heaven) incarnated into (moved into and took over) two human bodies that were in their forties. I moved into a male body, and my partner, who is an Older Member in the Level Above Human, took a female body. (We called these bodies "vehicles," for they simply served as physical vehicular tools for us to wear while on a task among humans. They had been tagged and set aside for our use since their birth.) We brought to Earth with us a crew of students whom we had worked with (nurtured) on Earth in previous missions. They were in varying stages of metamorphic transition from membership in the human kingdom to membership in the physical Evolutionary Level Above Human (what your history refers to as the Kingdom of God or Kingdom of Heaven). It seems that we arrived in Earth's atmosphere between Earth's 1940's and early 1990's. We suspect that many of us arrived in staged spacecraft (UFO) crashes and many of our discarded bodies (genderless, not belonging to the human species) were retrieved by human authorities (government and military).

Really?

PROFESSIONAL TIPS

Vicki Rothrock

Vicki Rothrock is a freelance correspondent based in Hong Kong. She covers topics ranging from Hong Kong film to the textile and fashion industries for U.S. trade publications. Rothrock began her freelancing career after a stint as a copy editor on the *Wall Street Journal*'s overseas copydesk in Hong Kong and an even shorter stint writing business scripts for a CNN news program. Born in Tacoma, Washington, she graduated from Washington State University with a B.A. in speech communication in 2000.

Question: How important are numbers and data in stories?

When writing a story, I'm constantly trying to remind myself what was drilled into me during my Intro to Journalism class at Washington State University: show your readers, don't tell them. It's one thing to say an industry is doing exceptionally well; it's another to say that a specific industry's revenue jumped 40 percent compared with last year's figures. The latter gives a more precise picture.

Question: What are some of the cautions in using numbers and data?

Numbers can be tricky. If you use too many of them, your story will resemble a complicated math formula that no one will want to read. Consider asking for a detailed graph to accompany your story if the text gets too bogged down with digits. If you use too few numbers, then your story might lack detail. It's important to find the right balance.

One way to make things less cumbersome is to use round numbers. Instead of saying something costs $45,899, you might want to write that it was nearly $46,000—it's easier on the eyes, and how important is the remaining $101? When it comes to calculations, do the math for your reader: use a percentage increase or drop instead of writing last year's figure compared with this year's figure.

Question: How hard is it to keep numbers and data in the proper context?

Some things are easier explained with words, while some information lends itself to numbers. When I'm reporting a story, I want to collect as much data as possible, whether it's from interviews or documents. Once I'm at the writing process, I have a tendency to let my enthusiasm spill over and I regurgitate number after number. I always have to ask myself whether yet another number adds to the story.

Question: Is there anything else you'd like to add concerning the use of numbers and data in reporting and writing?

Mistakes go hand in hand with numbers. Ask yourself: Does the number make sense in that particular context? Does it make sense that a big multinational company's stock ended in single digits? Double check! When giving your story a final read, try highlighting all the numbers in your story, and check one last time against your notes and redo your calculations. You can never be too careful.

The *Wall Street Journal*

The *Wall Street Journal* is clearly the leading business newspaper or publication. Charles H. Dow and Edward D. Jones left their jobs at a news agency in 1882 and established Dow, Jones & Company. In 1889 they had fifty employees and produced the first edition of the *Wall Street Journal,* a four-page publication. Today, the *Wall Street Journal* produces four newspaper editions with 160 pages and has a circulation of 2.3 million, the largest daily in the county.

Some of the other leading business publications are *Forbes* magazine, *Business Week* and *Fortune* magazine. *Time, Newsweek* and *U.S. News & World Report* have also expanded their business coverage dramatically over the years, as have major newspapers.

As a business reporter, read the work of other business reporters from such publications. Not only will it make you more knowledgeable, but it will also make you a better reporter and writer.

The *Wall Street Journal* seems to define business reporting liberally, and includes some of the best writing in the world. That is a good tip for you—define business reporting liberally.

Following is the lead of an exceptional example of reporting and storytelling in a "business publication," written by Bryan Gruley, Chicago bureau chief of the *Wall Street Journal.* The story pulls at humanity's heartstrings but is full of numbers and data, but these are not crammed down the reader's throat:

The two young men stood trembling before Army Lt. John Withers, dressed in the rags they'd worn at the recently liberated Dachau concentration camp. Sores pocked their bony arms and legs. Decades later, the lieutenant would remember how their sunken eyes sought mercy.

But in 1945, near the end of World War II, they posed a problem. Lt. Withers was a black leader in an all-black supply convoy. In violation of Army orders, his men were hiding the refugees. Lt. Withers planned to have the strangers removed—until he saw them.

They stayed with his unit for more than a year, two Jewish survivors of the Holocaust hiding among blacks from segregated America. The soldiers nicknamed them "Peewee" and "Salomon." They grew close to Lt. Withers. By the time he bid them farewell, they'd grown healthy again.

Mr. Withers never forgot them. Over the years, he told and retold their tale to his two sons. When one son set out to find them, he discovered that Salomon had died in 1993. But Peewee, he learned, was alive.

Unlike Mr. Withers, Peewee had buried his past. His children and grandchildren knew almost nothing about his time in Auschwitz, Buchenwald and Dachau. When his grandson asked about the number tattooed on his left forearm—A19104—all he could say was, "Bad people put that down."

He couldn't bring himself to talk about it.

Then John Withers reappeared—and changed Peewee's life yet again.

Consumer News

Jane takes her red favorite blouse to the dry cleaner, hoping to get it back in time for a Friday night party. Joe, the guy behind the counter, fills out a claim check and tells her he can have it ready on Friday morning. It will cost her $5.

John walks through the door as Jane is leaving. He has a light blue dress shirt. He tells Joe he needs it back for a Friday afternoon interview. Joe says, "No problem," fills out the claim check and hands it to John. It will cost him $3.

Why does it cost Jane $2 more than John, whose shirt, by the way, is an extra large, compared to Jane's size 10?

Dry cleaners might say it has something to do with the "frilly" nature of a woman's blouse, or the type of material (polyester versus cotton) or the color. But are those legitimate reasons?

This is a consumer story.

Consumer news is a bit different than business news, but it is actually somewhat redundant because virtually all news is directed toward consumers. But the basic definition of consumer news, in the business arena, is events or ideas that affect readers in their role as buyers of goods and services.

Consumer news coverage exploded in the 1960s with the rise of vocal consumer groups, the chief leader in the movement being Ralph Nader, a former U.S. presidential candidate. Consumerism previously, and to many today, still means looking for the best bargains and clipping coupons, but Nader directed his attention to taking a hard look at corporate and government power, and pointing out what he believed to be wrongdoing and the enormous power wielded by business and government.

Consumer news can generally be found in three areas:

1. **Government agencies:** Cases of consumer fraud, in which people pay for something they don't receive or the product quality is suspect, are handled by government agencies at state and federal levels. There are many regulatory commissions in all states policing the practices and services offered by utilities, transportation companies, banks, savings and loan associations and other groups. For instance, the Washington Utilities and Transportation Commission (WUTC) "ensures reasonable rates, consumer protection and public safety associated with the provision of utilities and utility services such as electricity, natural gas, telephone, water, household goods and solid waste collection services. In addition to regulation of utilities, the UTC also provides regulatory oversight of certain transportation services."

2. **Quasi-public consumer groups:** These organizations are not associated with government and generally have been formed by individuals to represent consumer interests. There are many, such as Common Cause and

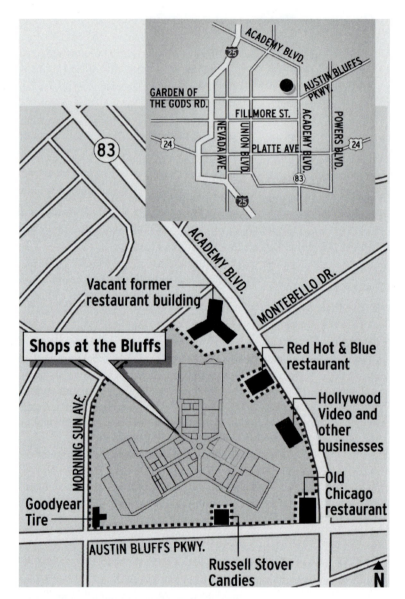

FIGURE 13.1   Newspapers will organize coverage by teams or beats. The business beat isn't just about data and numbers about stocks and bonds, or the gross national product or interest rates. The *Orange County Register* in Santa Ana, California, was the first to establish a "mall beat" because it understood that although the beat was business focused, it also has social significance as a gathering place. The graphic above from Colorado Springs, Colo., illustrates how a locater map/graphic can help business coverage.

The Gazette

the Sierra Club. Common Cause, as an example, "is a nonpartisan nonprofit advocacy organization founded in 1970 by John Gardner as a vehicle for citizens to make their voices heard in the political process and hold their elected leaders accountable to the public interest . . . remains committed to honest, open and accountable government, as well as encouraging citizen participation in democracy." One of its issues in 2005 was to: "Make certain that our government is held accountable for the costs, in lives and money, for the invasion of Iraq."

3. **Private business:** Consumer news is generated in virtually every large corporation, and many small businesses, often through recalls and/or charges of knowledgeable or unconscious wrongdoing. The U.S. Product Safety Commission, for instance, lists thousands of recalls from private businesses for defective products (go to www.cpsc .gov/cpscpub/prerel/prerel.html). For instance, the following two recalls were listed in early 2005:

   ■ **"In cooperation with** the U.S. Consumer Product Safety Commission (CPSC), Royal Appliance, of Glenwillow, Ohio, is voluntarily recalling about 20,000 Dirt Devil® Sweeper Vac™ vacuum cleaners. The vacuum's rotor can lock and overheat during use causing a smoke and fire hazard."

   ■ **"In cooperation with** the U.S. Consumer Product Safety Commission (CPSC), The Step 2 Co., of Petersboro, Ohio, is voluntarily recalling about 9,300 toddler swings. The straps on these swings could break, causing a child riding in the swing to fall to the ground and suffer injuries."

Consumer stories can be some of the most fun to write, as well as provide invaluable information.

Finances/Budgets

In covering financial news of companies, there are lots of places to start, or consider, but what matters most in financial analysis is the actions executives take and the company's financial performance.

It is always a good idea, when possible, to begin gathering information by analyzing or seeking an accounting of how much money has been spent (and on what), how much money has been obtained through the various revenue venues and how it all relates to the budget. That, very simply, is financial analysis.

It is the process by which numbers clearly show, or paint a picture, of how well a company is doing, has done or plans to do. Without this kind of analysis, reporters have very little story or reporting foundation.

In the most basic format, companies will have an income statement showing the financial performance over a specified period of time, usually broken into the following categories on the following page (with fictional numbers).

XYZ COMPANY	
Total annual revenues	$1,000,000
Total annual operating expenses	$500,000
Operating profit (or loss)	$500,000
Nonoperating expenses	$100,000
Profit (or loss) before taxes	$400,000
Income taxes	$120,000
Net profit (or loss)	$280,000

In effect, there are three types of expenses—operating, nonoperating and taxes.

Operating refers to the salaries, rent, marketing and promotion, materials, supplies and so on. *Nonoperating* expenses are those that are linked to the company's long-term investments, for instance depreciation and interest and any relationship with corporations, such as management fees. And *taxes*—well, everyone knows what they are. In case you don't however, taxes are payments imposed on persons or groups for government support.

Budgeting is nothing more than financial planning, and it isn't that difficult to evaluate, review or monitor a budget.

Everyone budgets, or at least should. Most people know their fixed monthly expenses and income. Reconciling the two, however, is sometimes a problem, especially for organizations (and often journalists) who seem to spend a great deal of time spending money and not so much time accounting for it.

But simply budgeting and analysis take only the ability to understand basic mathematical formulas and equations.

Budgets are generally composed for a year at a time, either on a calendar year (January through December) or fiscal year (July through June).

Although the major revenue producer is usually product sales (or tax and fee levies for governmental entities), the major expenses in a budget will generally include equipment and materials to produce and deliver products, facilities and operations, and employee salaries and benefits.

Budgetary analysis can also reveal prioritized goals, strategies and plans, as well as actual fiscal operations comparisons of past years.

There are many general terms of importance to understand in the budgetary process, such as the following:

- **Working capital:** This includes all assets—such as cash, accounts receivable and inventory—minus liabilities, such as accounts payable and accrued expenses.

- **Cash flow:** This is the money available to operate the business.

- **Expenses:** This is the money needed to spend on effectively operating the business or a department of a business.

- **Profit and loss:** When revenues are greater than expenses, there is a profit. If expenses are greater than revenues, there is a problem—known as a loss.

- **Opportunities for improving profits:** *Opportunity* is a word that became popular many years ago, replacing the word *problem.* Managers like to say: "We don't have a problem here; we have an opportunity." So, *opportunities for improving profits* is another way to talk about strategies or plans for one of two things: increased revenues or eliminating expenses.

- **Return on investment:** This means making a profit on the investments spent on the business. For instance, if $100 is spent on the business, and you make $150, then the return on investment is $50, or, a 50 percent return on investment.

- **Payback:** This is the time it takes to recover an investment. Generally, the faster the payback, the greater return on investment. For instance, if $20,000 is spent on a sales training program and it can be documented as being responsible for an additional $20,000 in sales in one year's time, the payback period on this investment is one year. If the $20,000 spent results in $5,000 additional revenue each year, the payback would be four years.

- **Capital investment:** This is money that is invested in the plant or major equipment. Capital expenditures become nonoperating expenses as they are depreciated.

- **Depreciation:** This is the amount that wear and tear reduces the value of the plant and/or equipment on an annual basis. For instance, a company car is purchased for $25,000. The life of the car is ten years. Its value goes down $5,000 a year for the first three years. During each of those years, depreciation can be "written off" and less taxes will be paid as there is less value "on the books."

- **Current assets:** This is anything that can be turned into cash at a reasonably quick pace.

- **Fixed assets:** This is land, the physical facility, equipment and so on that has value but not immediate or quick cash value.

- **Current liabilities:** This includes all bills and accrued expenses for which the total payment is due in a short period of time.

- **Long-term liability:** This includes bills and expenses that are due over a long period of time, such as a mortgage or other payments.

CHAPTER EXERCISES

1. Obtain a budget from your city or university. Do an analysis, and come up with five story ideas.

2. Select one of the story ideas, and write a story with an assigned length from your professor.

3. Come up with three business/consumer story ideas focused around your college football team going to a bowl game. Provide a couple sentences of explanation on each story idea, giving the major theme of the story and how you would obtain the information (who you would need to talk to). Be prepared to write one of the stories if it is assigned by your professor.

4. Come up with three business/consumer story ideas focused around Thanksgiving Day. Provide a couple of sentences of explanation on each story idea, giving the major theme of the story and how you would obtain the information (who you would need to talk to). Be prepared to write one of the stories if it is assigned by your professor.

5. Come up with three business/consumer story ideas focused around Christmas. Provide a couple of sentences of explanation on each story idea, giving the major theme of the story and how you would obtain the information (who you would need to talk to). Be prepared to write one of the stories if it is assigned by your professor.

6. You have been assigned to write a story about Starbucks coming to your community. Go online to www.starbucks.com, and review the company's timeline and history, mission statement and awards and accolades. Write a news lead and a feature lead.

14 Local Government

BY KENTON BIRD

The activity of governments is one of the major public affairs beats. Citizens need information on what their elected leaders are doing and how they are spending money, possibly on costly community statues, sculptures and water fountains.

Surveys consistently identify local news as one of the main reasons people read newspapers. Coverage of city and county government is one of the strong suits of any newspaper's local content. Yet journalists too often fail to explain government's activities in terms the public can understand. At many news organizations, reporting of local government falls into predictable patterns that do little to make connections with readers.

"Too often we and our newsrooms consider it 'boring but important'—and sometimes not even important," Susan Deans of the *Myrtle Beach (Florida) Sun News* wrote in the *Local News Handbook* published by the American Society of Newspaper Editors (ASNE).

Because citizens have most frequent contact with units of government closest to them—and have the greatest potential to influence decisions at this level—readers have high interest in local government coverage.

If government coverage is so important, why isn't it better? One explanation might be that editors don't know their readers' needs. In their book, *The Two W's of Journalism,* Davis Merritt and Maxwell McCombs divide the audience for news into three segments: information seekers, monitors and onlookers. Information seekers, in many respects, are model citizens. They pay close attention to government coverage, constantly acquiring new knowledge to apply to their actions in the civic arena. The next category includes readers and viewers who scan the news for events and actions relevant to their lives but don't follow an issue closely unless it directly affects them. The third group is the most detached from government; its members make some use of the news media but don't follow current events or engage regularly in such civic activities as voting.

The challenge for news organizations is to reach all three groups, often simultaneously, through reporting that digs below the surface, brings home the actions of government in ways citizens can relate and tells compelling stories that demand to be read. "Journalists must be communicators who are concerned about the effects—and especially, the lack of civic effects—of their messages on the public," Merritt and McCombs write. This requires a commitment to understand a community in all of its complexities—by seeking nontraditional sources, framing stories in new ways and telling news from a citizens' perspective.

Getting Started on the Beat

At many small news organizations, city and county government are part of the same beat. At others, they are separate but include other components. The city beat also might include business or health care; the county beat might embrace agricultural issues or rural communities. And because the criminal justice system overlays both city and county government, law enforcement and the court system are often added. At larger news organizations, more specialization is possible and desirable. Because it's common for anyone in the newsroom to pinch-hit for an absent reporter, the skills learned on the city–county beat are never obsolete.

Regardless of whether one is new to the community or just new to the beat, solid coverage depends on understanding the "sense of place" of the town, county or region. Knowing something about the community's history, traditions and culture is as important as knowing the names of elected officials and the locations of their offices. What are the town's "creation myths"—the stories about why and where it was founded? What Native American tribes called the area home before the arrival of European American settlers? What historical sites are important to collective memory? What is the significance of place names? The county historical society, museum or public library is a good place to start. Find out if there is a newsletter or historical magazine, and get on the mailing list.

Then, view the community through a newcomer's eyes. Where does one go for information about jobs, schools and parks? Where are grocery stores located in relation to established and new neighborhoods? Does an independent hardware store compete successfully with large building supply chains? Why? Find out if the chamber of commerce has a schedule of community festivals: parades, picnics, founders' days, harvest celebrations. Each of these events provides an opportunity to discover how the community plays together—and reveals who has influence outside official circles.

At city hall or the county administration building, gather newsletters, reports, staff directories and notices of public hearings. Find out who keeps a master calendar of meetings of the governing board and advisory committees—or build your own. Explore the agency's Web site, and determine who keeps it up to date. Knowing where to find an agenda, a report or the minutes of a meeting online can save a phone call or a trip to the county clerk's office.

Then explore the community's so-called third places—a civic journalism term that refers to places where people gather to talk about issues and concerns. (The name comes from a report by the Harwood Institute for Public Innovation that describes five layers of civic life. *Third places* come midway between official institutions and private homes.) Examples are coffee shops, bookstores, neighborhood restaurants and fitness centers—places where people come together by choice. Where do downtown business owners meet for breakfast? Where do lawyers gather near the courthouse after work? Where do parents stop for coffee after dropping off young children at day care centers? These are good places to take a community's pulse and find ordinary people who will be good sources for future stories.

Begin to develop a network of sources. In the Harwood Institute's report, called "Tapping Civic Life," Richard Harwood and Jeff McCrehan listed five types of people useful to understanding the information flow in a community:

- **Official Leaders:** elected officials, agency directors, school board members, presidents of foundations, CEOs of major companies.
- **Civic Leaders:** clergy and other religious leaders, the head of the chamber of commerce, leaders of neighborhood associations.
- **Connectors:** People who move between different groups, spreading ideas, but have no official role.
- **Catalysts:** Coworkers, neighbors, members of a religious congregation—anyone who offers historical perspective or encourages others to get involved in the community.
- **Experts:** Anyone whose specialized knowledge causes reporters to seek them out. College professors, urban planners, scientists and lawyers are in this category.

Journalists traditionally have relied on official and expert sources because they're familiar, easy to find and comfortable with responding to media inquiries. The other three categories offer great potential to reporters seeking to broaden their network of sources. But because they're usually identified through word of mouth, they're tougher to track down.

Finally, ask your editors for guidance about covering the beat. If yours is the newspaper of record for a community, find out exactly what that means. How much detail is needed in routine reports? How much background must be included for the benefit of readers unfamiliar with a topic? How much discretion do you have in choosing which meetings to attend, which ones to follow up after the fact and which ones to ignore? Ask the editor for examples of stories by your predecessor that exemplify daily and enterprise reporting—and stories that, in hindsight, didn't justify the time spent on them. Bring in stories published in other communities, and discuss whether they're practical for you to emulate. Knowing the editors' expectations—for quantity, variety and depth—will avoid later misunderstandings.

City Government

The reporter's first stop at city hall is the office of the mayor, city manager or city supervisor—whoever oversees day-to-day operations and controls the agenda for the city council. Larger cities might have a public information officer or press secretary who issues news releases and responds to media inquiries. While these staff members can be helpful in tracking down routine information, the reporter needs a working relationship with someone responsible for setting policy who can speak on behalf of city government.

The International City-County Management Association estimates that nearly half of the cities in the United States employ a council–manager structure. Under this system, the council hires a professional manager who oversees day-to-day operations. More than 40 percent of U.S. cities have a mayor–council system, with executive authority (including the power to make appointments and dismiss department heads) vested in the mayor. Many of those cities, though, hire a city supervisor or administrative assistant to which the mayor can delegate some duties. The remaining cities, fewer than 10 percent of the total, use a commission system (in which commissioners have both legislative and administrative duties) or a variant of the town meeting, common in New England.

City councils typically have four to seven members; in some large cities, they might have a dozen or more assembly members or councilors. Many councils meet once a month; some meet every week. In between, council committees meet with department heads, discuss issues and review legislation. In some cities, the substantive policy debate occurs at the committee level; by the time a proposal reaches the full council, deals have been cut and differences smoothed over. The decision by the full council could be a foregone conclusion before the meeting is called to order. Some councils have workshops or "agenda sessions" before their formal meetings to serve the same purpose. While these sometimes serve a legitimate function of hammering out policy details, they also can become a means of avoiding public scrutiny of controversial decisions. When in doubt, consult your news organization's attorney, the state's press association or a nearby chapter of the Society of Professional Journalists (SPJ) to be sure the open meeting law is being followed.

Don't overlook meetings of boards and commissions, such as planning and zoning, health and environment, transportation and arts and culture. While advisory in nature, some have considerable influence over how the city council deals with issues in their areas. Members of these groups are often the catalysts and connectors who convey information from city hall to citizens—and are potential candidates for city council in future years. A mayor who wants to shape city government long after she leaves office will recruit like-minded citizens for boards and commissions. When a new mayor comes into office, compare campaign contributors to appointees to important boards, and see which names are on both lists.

Use a meeting as a source of story ideas, not as an end unto itself. Put decisions of the council, board or commission in context by talking to people who will be affected by the action. If a street will be torn up for a new sewer line or a park will receive new playground equipment, interview residents of the neighborhood for reactions. If the council is raising dog license fees to expand its animal shelter, drop by a pet store and visit with dog owners. In writing the story, though, be careful not to let the reaction eclipse the decision. Anecdotal leads are fine for some types of stories, but sometimes the action is so significant that it demands a summary lead.

Department managers are useful sources for stories in their areas: finance, engineering and public works, parks and recreation or the library. Department heads are especially eager to describe their services and project their needs as budget reviews approach. Don't stop with the administrators; take time to get to know the people who sweep the streets, find and fix leaking sewer pipes and measure traffic levels at busy intersections. Sometimes, a routine city function such as parking enforcement can produce a revealing and intriguing story. While at the *Idaho Statesman* in Boise, reporter David Cuillier analyzed the frequency and location of parking tickets to produce this story:

City Wants to Increase Crackdown on Scofflaws

Many People Don't Pay Fines, Avoid Punishment

Nearly every day, Boise parking enforcement manager Tana Wardle looks out her office window from City Hall and sees the car.

Buick Regal. Brown. License 1L 19164. Parking tickets on the windshield.

"That car is on our hot list," Wardle says. "We're going to collect."

That car belongs to Fred Yates, who cooks at a restaurant across the street from City Hall and parks his Buick Regal on the street. Yates has more outstanding parking tickets than anyone else in Boise, sometimes snagging two or three a day.

From September until April, he racked up 85 parking tickets, according to an *Idaho Statesman* computer-assisted analysis of parking records. Last week, Wardle said, Yates topped 100, with unpaid fines exceeding $1,000.

But it's not easy to find parking downtown, Yates said. And, he added, some parking enforcement officers have been a little too aggressive for his taste.

"I'm not going to let the city bother me," Yates said. "I've got to park somewhere. I can't always leave at the middle of lunch to plug the meter. What am I going to do, ask a customer to go put money in my meter? I'm tired of this."

So is Wardle. But the city can't do much about it under the current system.

One-fourth of people who get parking tickets thumb their noses at the city, cheating Boise coffers—and taxpayers—out of at least $60,000 a year in unpaid fines. That's enough money to hire a police officer or get the Ann Morrison Park fountain running again.

Wardle wants to hire someone to collect unpaid parking tickets. Also, she's pushing for changes to state law that would make it easier for the city to crack down on parking ticket scofflaws.

(continued)

(continued)

She's not talking about an average downtown shopper, who gets one or two tickets a year. She's talking about the chronic offenders who sometimes collect 30, 40 or 50 parking tickets in a six-month period. "Habituals," Wardle calls them.

Some people pay the fines. But others have figured out they can rack up bundles of tickets without shelling out a dime. And it wasn't until September, when parking tickets became computerized, that the city could easily identify the worst offenders.

County Government

In contrast to cities, the power structure in most U.S. counties is much more decentralized and, consequently, more difficult for the public to monitor and for reporters to cover. Imagine a meeting in which department directors, staff members and citizens with business before the county come and go at will, while the governing board deals with routine and consequential items in seemingly random order. Motions are made, seconded and passed before anyone in the audience recognizes what happens. That describes a typical county commission meeting in a rural county.

The United States has more than three thousand counties (known as boroughs in Alaska and parishes in Louisiana). They range in population from fewer than one thousand in remote parts of the West and Midwest to more than 9 million in Los Angeles County, and in size from forty-two square miles in Arlington, Virginia, to thousands of square miles in parts of the West and Alaska.

Counties are considered subdivisions of the state, and as such, depend on the state legislature for their authority. Counties are the primary custodians of records—property, marriages and divorces and often driver's and auto licenses. They also collect and disburse property taxes to other agencies—including cities and school districts within their boundaries. In most states, counties run jails—from a few cells behind the sheriff's office in rural counties to large correctional institutions in urban ones. Finally, counties might have some responsibilities for roads, public health, welfare programs and parks outside of cities.

County commissioners wear multiple hats—legislative, executive and judicial—and exchange them without notice. In most counties, commissioners can be in session whenever a quorum (usually two out of three, or three out of five) are present. Reporters are often frustrated by the difficulty of tracking agenda items and monitoring decisions. It's not uncommon for commissioners to be "in session" from 9 A.M. to 5 P.M. several days a week—and in those meetings deal with everything from hiring a dispatcher for the sheriff to courthouse maintenance to major budget decisions.

Other county officials, usually elected on a partisan ballot for four-year terms, include the county auditor, who acts as the chief financial officer or controller; the county recorder, who oversees record keeping (sometimes combined with the auditor); the assessor, responsible for appraising property; the treasurer, who collects and disburses tax money; the prosecuting attorney; the sheriff; and the coroner (sometimes combined with the sheriff or prosecutor). These officials might have offices in the courthouse, but because they're accountable directly to the voters and not the commissioners, they pursue independent agendas.

In rural counties, an important contact is the county agent's office. The office is supported by county government, the Cooperative Extension Service of the state's land-grant university and the U.S. Department of Agriculture. In addition to providing expert advice to farmers and ranchers, the office may coordinate consumer education and oversee youth programs such as 4-H. The office is usually a good insight into rural residents' issues and concerns.

Home rule or charter counties have more flexibility in choosing their structure of government. Popular in urban areas, these typically have an elected executive (the equivalent of a mayor), a county council of five to seven members with expanded legislative powers, and fewer elected officials. These counties pose different coverage challenges: authority is more centralized than in commissioner counties, so it might be easier to track decision making. But the number and complexity of issues can be much greater.

Special Districts

Created to fill gaps between city and county governments, these districts have their own elected boards, budgets and taxing authority. They might contain just a portion of a county, overlay a county's boundaries entirely or extend into another county. Because their boards meet at irregular times and in unusual places, these units might escape public scrutiny of their policy and spending decisions. Yet a reporter willing to dig into their operations will find important and interesting stories.

Some states have a network of good roads or highway districts, responsible for planning, constructing and maintaining roads outside incorporated towns. In fast-growing suburban areas, the location of roads influences where growth occurs—and determines which land owners can profit from subdividing farms and ranches for houses. In northern climates, deciding which roads are plowed first after a snowfall is important and controversial (check the home addresses of the road commissioners and see where they fall on the district's plowing schedule). Similarly, a decision to pave a gravel road might reflect political pressures more than traffic volumes.

Library districts are jurisdictions that enable city and county libraries to share books, buildings, staff and computer networks. A district might also have revenue options, such as a guaranteed property tax levy, that cities or counties lack. Particularly in small towns, a library is an important community gathering spot—a good place for reporters to learn citizens' interests and concerns. Library bulletin boards publicize events and groups not visible elsewhere.

Recreation districts are empowered to construct such facilities as swimming pools, gymnasiums, tennis courts and soccer fields. These are especially important in fast-growing communities that attract families with school-age children. But districts that overestimate demand and underestimate operating costs might find themselves with recreation centers, parks and athletic fields that don't pay their own way and require taxpayer subsidies.

Other kinds of special districts include those that fund fire departments, operate water and sewer systems, maintain cemeteries, oversee soil conservation efforts in agricultural counties and control mosquitoes in swampy areas. Even the smallest of these

PROFESSIONAL TIPS

Neil Modie

Neil Modie was a reporter for the Vancouver (Washington) *Columbian* and Tacoma *News Tribune* before joining the *Seattle Post-Intelligencer* in 1970. At the *P-I,* Modie has covered King County government, Seattle city hall, environmental issues, the Washington legislature and state, regional and national politics. He now covers politics and public policy issues. Modie has a journalism degree from the University of Idaho.

Question: How does a new reporter get started covering city hall or county government?

Go around and introduce yourself to the department heads and the elected officials and their staffs. Ask them what their current projects and problems are. Background yourself from files in your newspaper's morgue about the people and agencies you'll be dealing with.

Get to know people outside city hall and the courthouse who deal with local government—businesspeople, labor leaders, political party people, community activists, civic leaders, etc. Learn the alliances, rivalries and enmities. Be careful not to be too quick to believe one news source over another until you get to know them well enough to figure out who's the more reliable, credible, informed and tapped into things, and who has what axes to grind.

Be wary of getting socially chummy with any news source. Someday you might have to write a story that makes him look bad, and you don't want your friendship to get in the way. People might want to flatter you or become your buddy for nefarious reasons.

Question: Who are the beginning reporter's best human sources on this beat?

You need to meet the local government leaders, of course. But it's also critically important to get to know and to cultivate the below-the-radar people: receptionists, secretaries, administrative assistants and clerks.

If you cover the police, sheriff or the courts, that includes bailiffs, court clerks, dispatch officers, etc. Never think of them as the unimportant people you deal with in order to see the important people. The receptionists and clerks see things, hear the gossip and typically know what's going on. They can tip you to things that you might not pick up otherwise and that their bosses might not even want you to know.

And, depending on whether or not they like you, they can make it easier or harder to get in to see the boss. Some are more clued in than others, of course. Just be sure you protect such sources if one of their tips leads to a story.

Question: What types of documents help explain what's going on with the council, commissioners or governing board?

You'll need meeting agendas, of course, and sometimes minutes of past meetings for background information. Get copies of ordinances, resolutions and motions, and of written staff analyses if there are any, and any outside-agency reports dealing [with] what is on the agenda. Go to the governing body's Web site to look for explanatory and background information, and check it periodically to make sure you haven't missed something. The decent sites will give you access to ordinances, agendas and so on.

(continued)

PROFESSIONAL TIPS   Continued

Question: What types of stories might be overlooked by inexperienced reporters on this beat?

Inexperienced reporters need to be wary of writing stories that read like meeting minutes—who said what, and what the vote was. When covering, for example, a public hearing on an issue that has generated a lot of controversy, focus on someone who might have an interesting story to tell. If the city council raises the pet licensing fee and someone who owns five dogs shows up to testify against it, report what the council did by telling her story. Talk to her afterward rather than simply report on what she and two dozen other people said. If the city council increases the local utility tax, ask a shop owner how it will affect his profit margin. If the council raises the fine for overtime parking, try going through the municipal court records, finding someone who has gotten, say, a dozen overtime tickets in the past year, call him up and ask if having to pay $20 instead of $10 will make him more careful.

Question: What advice do you have for avoiding errors and improving the accuracy of coverage of local government?

Check and double-check your facts, and triple-check your numbers and statistics. If you're uncertain about the accuracy or the balance of information you've been given, and that can't be documented, don't rely on only one source.

If you're writing about a complex or technical matter, you might want to phone the source of your information or some other well-informed person to read back the relevant portion of what you've written. However, I try never to let anyone know exactly how I've written a story before it's in print; I don't want them trying to talk me into writing it in a way that might make them or their department or agency sound better. Don't read them any more of what you've written than you have to.

agencies probably deserves a story at least twice a year: when voters elect commissioners and when the board adopts a budget.

Budgets and Audits

Monitoring taxation and spending by local governments begins with an understanding of the budget cycle. Tracking budgets may be complicated if an agency's fiscal year does not coincide with the calendar year. Because many state legislatures convene in January and meet through the early spring, state fiscal years often begin July 1. However, the federal government's fiscal year begins October 1. Some cities and counties follow their state's calendar or the federal fiscal year. The budgeting process usually begins three to six months before the next spending plan takes effect. It typically includes requests from department heads; review by the mayor, city manager or county executive; and a public hearing by the council or commission. See Chapter 13 for more information about budgets.

The primary source of local government revenue is the property tax. Public officials like property taxes because they are relatively consistent and less subject to economic fluctuations than other taxes. But because they are paid in a lump sum, usually twice a year, property taxes prompt perennial public complaints—and, in some states, outright revolts that have limited tax rates or annual increases. California's Proposition 13, passed in 1978, inspired similar tax-cutting measures in other states whose effects are still being felt by local governments. Here is an example of a budget story by former *Columbian* reporter

Ken Olsen, which shows the relationship between a voter-passed tax initiative and local government spending:

County to Join Lawsuit against Initiative 722

Clark County is joining a lawsuit against Initiative 722 and will ask the courts to allow it to delay implementing the measure here until the legal challenges are resolved.

County commissioners voted unanimously Tuesday evening to join Pierce County in its lawsuit, citing the potential for harm to fire districts and other small, stand-alone agencies with tinier budgets. Simultaneously, commissioners passed a new budget that calls for only a 2 percent property tax hike—the limit set by the initiative.

The lawsuit may save the county time and money.

"It will cost the county taxpayers about $500,000 to comply, with the strong likelihood [Initiative] 722 will be ruled unconstitutional," Curt Wyrick of the Clark County Prosecuting Attorney's office told the commissioners Tuesday evening.

The county also is faced with competing legal directives. Last week, a Thurston County Superior Court judge issued an injunction against the initiative and limited it to cities and counties involved in the first lawsuit over I-722. Then the Washington Department of Revenue told all counties to ignore the initiative in light of the injunction. . . .

The county may be able to live with the 2 percent property tax cap the initiative requires, Commissioner Betty Sue Morris said. But smaller taxing districts—such as fire departments—will suffer far greater pain. And the county assessor will spend an estimated $500,000 rolling property taxes back to the 1999 level plus 2 percent, as the initiative requires.

"I think it's the responsible way to advance," Morris said.

Representatives from three fire districts told the commissioners that I-722 would dramatically affect their ability to respond to emergency calls.

"We don't have any fluff in our budget," Brad Lothspeich, chief of Clark Fire District 6, told the commissioners. I-722 will cost the fire district $250,000. And if the initiative is later ruled unconstitutional, the fire district cannot recover the lost tax revenue. If the initiative survives the court challenges, taxpayers still will get the property tax rollback credited on future tax bills.

A few minutes later, the commissioners approved a 2001–2002 budget that calls for spending $194.9 million in general fund money, about a 2.4 percent increase over 1999–2000. That includes money to cover a projected 30 percent increase in medical insurance costs for county employees in 2001 and 2002 as well as cost-of-living increases and other projects.

By the end of 2002, the county will have added 61 staff compared to the number of workers on board at the beginning of the 1999–2000 budget cycle. The commissioners dropped plans to add a storm-water manager position because of uncertainty about whether they can continue to collect storm-water fees under I-722.

Property taxes are perhaps the hardest aspect of local government financing for citizens to understand and reporters to explain. They typically involve at least four different county offices:

- **The assessor,** who appraises homes, businesses and other types of property
- **The auditor** (or budget officer), who prepares and administers the budget
- **The governing board,** which sets tax rates

■ **The treasurer,** who collects taxes and disburses them to other units of government (see sidebar for a description of how this process works)

The county assessor's office can usually help provide an estimate of how a budget increase or new tax will affect a prototypical residence, business, farm or industrial property. This information can be presented in a box that can run along with budget stories, following this format: "The bond for a new library would cost the owner of a $150,000 house an additional $6 per month or $72 per year for the next fifteen years. A two-thirds affirmative vote is required to pass the bond."

Not all property in a jurisdiction pays property taxes. Tax exemptions for churches, schools, public colleges and nonprofit hospitals shift the burden to home and business owners. Sometimes, large institutions such as universities negotiate annual payments in lieu of property taxes to cover the cost of maintaining streets and providing police and fire protection. When a home owner or business believes a piece of property has been appraised at too high a value, the figure can be appealed to a board of equalization (in smaller counties, the county commissioners fulfill this function).

Additional revenues for local government are sales tax (either a county tax or a rebate from the state tax), fees for services (such as building permits, marriage licenses and recording deeds or other documents), utility charges (water, sewer and garbage pickup), and intergovernmental transfers, which refer to money collected by one unit of government and passed onto another.

State and federal grants—particularly Community Development Block Grants administered by the U.S. Department of Housing and Urban Development—can be a major source for projects to improve a community's infrastructure, renovate substandard housing or build senior citizen centers.

To discover how well a local agency is performing its duties—and especially whether it is spending money in accordance with prescribed categories and state law—request copies of audits. Many state auditors conduct periodic audits of expenditures by all units of local government in the state. Some audits are a cursory review of balance sheets; others probe the agency's cash management and investment practices. Pay special attention to footnotes, which may offer criticisms of how the agency operates. Find out who conducted the audit, and ask for clarification of anything that's not clear. If an agency hasn't been audited in several years, find out why.

Planning and Zoning

Land-use planning is among the most tedious and perplexing issues to cover, but it has far-reaching consequences. Where development is allowed affects the location of streets and utilities, police and fire protection and the cost of providing services. Fast-growing cities and counties deal regularly with changing land uses, but even a municipality with a stable population faces development pressures.

With the exception of taxes, no other local government story has more potential to provoke citizen reaction than zoning. There's nothing like the prospect of a big-box retailer moving to a wheat field on the edge of town to stir up residents concerned about the impact on Main Street stores, traffic and sprawl.

UNDERSTANDING PROPERTY TAXES

1. Taxing districts decide how much property tax will be collected each year (say, $1 million).
2. County assessors estimate the total assessed value of all taxable property in the district (say, $100 million).
3. The county auditor calculates a tax rate by dividing the amount of tax to be raised by total assessed value: $1 million / $100 million = 1%.
4. If your home's assessed value is $100,000, your tax bill will be .01 × $100,000 = $1,000.
5. If total assessed value for the district doubles to $200 million, and the amount to be raised stays the same, the tax rate will be: $1 million / $200 million = .5%.
6. Your taxes, if your home doubles in value, will still be $1,000: .5% (.005) × $200,000 = $1,000.
7. If assessed value goes up, and the tax rate remains the same, taxes will rise. The taxing district is demanding more money, even though the county auditor has not changed the rate: .01 × $200,000 = $2,000.

—From "Understanding Our Property Tax System," published by the Idaho Association of Counties, www.idcounties.org.

Almost every state requires cities and counties to prepare a master plan, sometimes called a *comprehensive plan,* and update it on a regular basis, usually once every ten years. The plan articulates the community's vision for the future; suggests locations for streets, parks and schools; and describes compatible land uses. Zoning is one means to carry out the plan, by designating parcels of land for low- and high-density residential, commercial, industrial and agricultural purposes, and for special uses such as schools and hospitals.

Requests for zone changes usually follow a two-step process. They first come to a planning and zoning commission for a recommendation, then go to the governing board (city council or county commission) for a final decision. Public hearings are typically required at each level, and often, the proposal is modified in response to objections raised at the first hearing. As with other types of public hearings, the most useful coverage occurs in advance: spelling out the nature of the request, the location (accompanied by a map, if possible) and the types of uses that would be allowed if the request is approved. The city's planning staff typically assesses potential impacts on traffic, water consumption and demand for services in advance; such reports can provide reporters with useful background, including names of adjoining property owners.

Areas on the fringe of a city, ripe for development because of potential to be annexed in the future, sometimes fall under dual jurisdictions. This land, sometimes known as *buffer zones, urban growth areas* or *areas of city impact,* is often where the most heated conflicts arise, as rural residents try to hang onto large lots and agricultural uses against advancing urbanization.

Two recent influences on city planning are the antisprawl "smart growth" movement, which seeks to direct growth in ways that have less impact on the environment, and new urbanism, a design philosophy that calls for smaller lots, narrower streets, mixed residential and commercial uses and walkable neighborhoods. A nearby college's architecture or urban planning department is a good place to find an expert who can determine whether a proposed development is consistent with either of these principles.

In addition to covering planning and growth episodically, a news organization occasionally should step back and give a cumulative accounting of how population growth affects a community. In Fort Collins, Colorado, whose population more than doubled between 1970 and 1990, the news staff of the *Coloradoan* spent six months examining the causes, consequences and cost of growth. Early in the process, they convened a focus group of nearly thirty residents of the city—developers, city and county officials, business owners and citizen activists. Their observations and questions helped shape the newspaper's approach. The result was a ten-day series that addressed growth from multiple perspectives, including the economy, transportation, environment, landscapes, schools, social issues and law enforcement. Each day, readers were asked to submit letters responding to the articles, which were published at the end of the series. Here is an excerpt from a story by David Persons addressing transportation needs:

What's Driving the Future?

Fort Collins Is Moving Quickly into Tomorrow, but Officials Still Struggle with How We Are Going to Get There

The city's torrid growth over the past two decades has caused transportation to become a major headache for local residents.

And, officials agree, it will take more than a couple of aspirins and wider streets to make the pain go away.

The city's inventory of more than 400 miles of streets is already growing at an average rate of 10 miles a year—but it isn't keeping up with congestion.

The College Avenue/Prospect Road intersection (near Colorado State University) has almost 30 percent more traffic now—about 76,000 cars a day—than 10 years ago, despite the fact that the city has widened the intersection and added almost 100 miles of city streets.

Area highways, especially Interstate 25, don't fare any better, often suffering from near-gridlock conditions several times a day.

Alternative transportation—spelled *no cars*—is on the fast track with city and county officials. But there are problems getting on the entrance ramp.

Residents who ride bikes to work are now faced with having to get across ever-greater distances as they live farther from the workplace.

Would-be bus riders soon discover routes frequently don't go where their cars can, or aren't as time-efficient.

Ron Phillips, the city's transportation director, for one, believes there are some solutions to these growing transportation woes, and not all of them are costly. They do, however, involve lifestyle changes.

"The real challenge is to change our (transportation) habits somewhat," Phillips said. "I'm not proposing that people ride a bus or ride a bike all the time, but if they changed their habits just 10 percent of the time, it would make a tremendous difference."

The city's master transportation plan has a goal of shifting 10 percent of city residents to a different mode of transportation in the next 20 years, Phillips said.

Empowering Citizens

News organizations can contribute to the democratic process—and make themselves essential to their audiences—with thorough, timely and creative coverage of local government. A Knight Ridder editors' report about local government news noted that the best coverage "gives readers an opportunity to respond and a way for them to respond. It reports the government's response. It produces or contributes to solutions. It gives progress on problem-solving efforts."

Almost every city or county story lends itself to a sidebar or box telling how the public can get involved or what's next in the decision process. Regular features can list openings on citizen boards and commissions, give advance notice of public hearings and offer contact information for local officials. Editors and designers are eager to break up government stories with graphic elements—charts, tables and "empowerment boxes" that suggest ways to stay abreast of the stories. Some newspapers use these boxes to refer readers to background documents and previously published stories on the paper's Web site—a way to help the "information seekers" who demand additional details.

Dan Kemmis, the former mayor of Missoula, Montana, strongly believes that strong and engaged newspapers are essential to a healthy civic life. "If people decide that they need newspapers (and other forms of media that are joining the movement) to shape and direct their communities," Kemmis writes, "then newspapers that fill that need in a legitimate way will find themselves being read." His argument suggests that thorough coverage of public life is in newspapers' economic self-interest and might assure their survival in a rapidly changing media environment.

CHAPTER EXERCISES

1. Discover how and when your town or city was founded. Contact the county historical society and discover what primary sources are available about the town's early history: maps, deeds, diaries, letters and photographs of the founders. Find out how the town got its name, where the original settlers came from, what the original industries were, and major turning points such as the arrival of the first railroad. Then, determine how today's residents learn about the community's history—through museums, publications and outreach to the schools.

2. Go to the U.S. Census Bureau's Web site, www.census.gov, and click on "American Community Survey." Find "housing characteristics" for your town or a nearby city. Using the most recent data, assess the housing stock: the number of dwellings built since the last Census, the mix of single-family and multifamily units, population density per square mile and the number of persons living in each unit. Then talk to a real estate agent about his or her perception of housing trends, vacancy rates, popular subdivisions and factors driving supply and demand.

3. Contact the office that handles property tax payments, often called the County Treasurer or Tax Collector. Analyze the tax bill for a single-family residence, a downtown business

and a farm or industrial property. Determine how the tax is calculated, including any exemptions. Break down each bill by the percentage that goes to each local government entity (i.e., city, county, school districts, and special districts).

4. Find out when new laws go into effect in your state (usually July 1 or January 1). Discern which of them will change the ways in which cities or counties do business or provide services. Localize the story with comments from officials who will administer the change and from citizens who are served by that agency.

5. Attend a city council or county commission meeting, and write a coverage story.

6. Obtain information and write an advance story about an open government meeting in your community.

7. Find out what special districts have been established in your community or county, and write an informational story.

Politics and Elections

BY KENTON BIRD

Much has been learned over the years about covering politics and elections, and reporters should concentrate on issues and positions—and not personalities and sound bites.

In his provocative and lively book about political journalism, *The Boys on the Bus,* Timothy Crouse gave this description of the reporters covering the 1972 presidential campaign: "The feverish atmosphere was halfway between a high-school bus trip to Washington and a gambler's jet junket to Las Vegas, where small-time Mafiosi were lured into betting away their restaurants. There was giddy camaraderie mixed with fear and low-grade hysteria. To file a story late, or to make one glaring factual error, was to chance losing everything—one's job, one's expense account, one's drinking buddies, one's mad-dash existence and the methedrine buzz that comes from knowing stories the public would not know for hours and secrets that the public would never know."

Crouse's behind-the-scenes account of campaign coverage introduced readers to *pack journalism,* the practice by which major newspapers, wire services and TV networks assigned reporters to follow a candidate through primary elections, party conventions and the general election campaign. The book showed the reliance on formula stories, the pressure to match stories other news outlets reported and the difficulty of breaking away from the pack to provide unconventional angles or insights.

While major news organizations still compete for seats on presidential candidates' press planes and their reporters join the feeding frenzy of daily briefings, most journalists covering politics labor in isolation and obscurity. The herd mentality that Crouse described is usually limited to national reporters covering the White House, Congress and the U.S. Supreme Court. At the state and local levels, covering politics and government is usually a solitary pursuit without the star quality or competitive frenzy of presidential campaign coverage. The lack of glamour diminishes neither the rewards to reporters who cover politics nor the value of political journalism to readers, listeners and viewers. Indeed, of all the public affairs beats, coverage of campaigns and elections is one that speaks directly to the role of journalism in a democracy.

Journalism and Democracy

Jay Rosen, a journalism professor at New York University, asked the question "What are journalists for?" in his 1999 book by the same name. And the first chapter of Bill Kovach and Tom Rosenstiel's *The Elements of Journalism* (2001) has the same title: "What Are Journalists For?"

Exploring the philosophy and practice of public journalism, Rosen suggested that journalists have an obligation to go beyond simply reporting facts and chronicling events. Instead, they need to view themselves as dynamic participants in a democratic society.

"If citizens joined in the action where possible, kept an ear tuned to current debate, found a place for themselves in the drama of politics, got to exercise their skills and voice their concerns, then maybe democracy didn't have to be the desultory affair it seemed to have become," Rosen wrote. "And maybe journalism, by doing something to help, could improve itself and regain some of its lost authority."

Kovach and Rosenstiel wrote: "The primary purpose of journalism is to provide citizens with the information they need to be free and self-governing."

Scholars of the civic journalism movement see the 1988 presidential campaign between George H. W. Bush and Michael Dukakis as a turning point in efforts to reform journalism from within. Campaign coverage was criticized for its emphasis on style over substance; a helmeted Dukakis in the turret of a tank and Bush visiting a flag factory were dominant TV images.

Critics blamed news organizations for their superficial coverage: the reliance on horse-race polls, the scarcity of issues coverage and the failure to hold candidates accountable for their records. In a column after the 1988 election, Davis "Buzz" Merritt, then editor of the *Wichita Eagle,* wrote: "The campaign just concluded showed at its frustrating worst the mutual bond of expediency that has formed over the years between campaigns and the media, particularly television. Together they have learned that feeding the lowest common appetite among the voters is safer, cheaper and less demanding than running the risk, for the campaigns, and the expense, for the media of providing in-depth information."

Out of this self-examination arose a desire by journalists to rethink the ways in which campaigns were covered. Merritt invited citizens to help set the agenda for the paper's coverage of the 1990 governor's race in Kansas. Merritt wrote: "In the interest of disclosure . . . I announce that *The Eagle* has a strong bias. The bias is that we believe the voters are entitled to have the candidates talk about the issues in depth." To that end, the paper identified ten issues it would follow throughout the campaign: abortion, agriculture, crime, economic development, education, environment, health care, social services, state spending and taxes. *The Eagle* ran a box every Sunday during the campaign, detailing the candidates' positions on issues—and how they had changed. And if a candidate didn't mention the issues that week, that fact was noted, too. Reader surveys after the election indicated that voters liked the attention to issues and didn't miss the horse-race coverage.

Two years later, the Charlotte, North Carolina, *Observer* took a similar approach in covering a U.S. Senate race. Executive Editor Rich Oppel wrote: "We will seek to reduce the coverage of campaign strategy and candidates' manipulations, and increase the focus on voters' concerns. We will seek to distinguish between issues that merely influence an election's outcome, and those of governance that will be relevant after the election."

To determine what those issues were, the *Observer* commissioned a poll asking North Carolina citizens what they wanted the candidates to discuss. Six broad themes, such as economy/taxes and crime/drugs, became the basis for the paper's coverage. Citizens discussed those issues in a series of television programs produced by a Charlotte television station. Oppel is convinced that greater citizen participation shifted the way his newspaper approached campaign coverage and gave his reporters greater authority when they pressed candidates for answers.

Several characteristics distinguish political reporting by a news organization that practices civic journalism:

- **A belief that** citizens should help set the agenda for coverage, through suggesting questions for reporters to ask in interviews or press conferences
- **Sponsorship of debates,** public forums or call-in radio or television programs at which citizens can ask questions directly of the candidates
- **Partnerships with other** news organizations, as in North Carolina, or with civic groups such as the League of Women Voters in sponsoring these public events and in providing other means for citizens to engage the candidates
- **Alternative ways of** framing stories that seek to go beyond the candidates' agenda, and attempt to explain the motives or consequences of policy positions
- **Attention to issues** on which the candidates agree, not just those on which they clash
- **A commitment to** provide information that empowers citizens to become participants in the process, rather than just observers (The World Wide Web opens up additional ways to engage readers and viewers, through online forums, Q&A sessions with candidates and links to the candidates' Web sites.)

Getting Started on the Beat

A reporter new to the political beat needs to acquaint herself with process, personalities and the issues particular to a city, region or state. One place to start is the public library, where a librarian can direct a would-be reporter to sections containing political biographies and accounts of recent elections.

The Boys on the Bus, mentioned at the beginning of this chapter, is a good overview of the 1972 presidential campaign, though its almost all-male cast of journalists seems a bit anachronistic thirty-plus years later. A more contemporary overview of an election is *Storming the Gates: Protest Politics and the Republican Revival* (1996) by political reporters Don Balz and Ronald Brownstein, who analyze the Republican takeover of Congress in 1994 under the leadership of Georgia Representative Newt Gingrich, who became speaker of the House of Representatives. One of the best recent biographies of a congressional leader is *Tip O'Neill and the Democratic Century* by John A. Farrell (2001). O'Neill, speaker of the U.S. House of Representatives from 1977 to 1985, is best remembered for the phrase "All politics is local"—good advice for reporters as well as elected officials.

Political scientists, historians and political reporters often write biographies of long-serving senators or governors that place them in the context of a state's political currents. Other useful references include *The Almanac of American Politics,* published by National Journal; and *Politics in America,* published by Congressional Quarterly. Both are updated every two years with the results of congressional and presidential elections.

Next, find several longtime observers of politics in the state who can tell the stories missing from the public accounts. Retired reporters and columnists are usually eager to tell stories from their time on the beat; so are former legislators or state government workers. In a state capital, these resources can often be found in a coffee shop or watering hole near the statehouse when the legislature is in session.

"Don't be shy about saying you don't know much," advises Adam Wilson, a reporter for the *Olympian* in Olympia, Washington. "Sources like to teach reporters, and political sources love to tell old political war stories."

Sometimes, the best insights come from longtime party activists, who provide insights into cliffhangers and landslides of the past—and help put recent events in perspective.

A political scientist or historian at a state university can be a valuable source because he or she can offer neutral analysis of issues, which is especially useful when you are trying to sort out competing claims. Almost every major university has a bureau of public affairs research or government studies, which conducts surveys, produces reports and provides training to local officials. Find out who in your state is recognized for expertise and credibility.

A review of the newspaper's archives is essential. "My No. 1 piece of advice to anyone starting a new beat, politics or otherwise, is to look up the byline of the reporter who came before you," the *Olympian*'s Wilson says. "If you can, look up their stories for the same month . . . a year or two earlier. It is the same paper trail you are walking, and things don't change so much as to make it unrecognizable."

Look for the issues that dominated the headlines, what campaign promises the incumbents made and how interest groups and citizens interacted with the candidates. Ballot measures (initiatives or referendums) also give hints to the types of issues that might arise in the next election cycle.

Politics is a beat on which reporters often will be approached with tips from government officials and party insiders who don't wish to be publicly identified. As with any leads coming from anonymous sources, reporters should weigh the value of the information against the person's motive and credibility. Many newspapers are reconsidering the conditions under which they grant confidentiality to an unnamed source. In February 2004, the *Washington Post* issued new policies on sources, quotations, attributions and datelines.

"Editors have an obligation to know the identity of unnamed sources used in a story, so that editors and reporters can jointly assess the appropriateness of using them," the *Post*'s policy states. Observing that government officials are eager to spin a story to benefit themselves or their agencies, the policy warns against publishing *ad hominem* quotations. "Sources who want to take a shot at someone in our columns should do so in their own names," the *Post* advises reporters.

The policy also offers rules for conduct of interviews and the handling of information obtained from them, clarifying four commonly used categories:

- **On the record:** Anything said may be quoted and attributed to the source.

- **On background:** Sometimes called *not for attribution,* the source's exact words may be used, but information is attributed to someone in a department or agency who is not named. Vague identification is useless; the *Post* urges that reporters "press for maximum revelation in attribution."

- **Deep background:** Information is used in the story but not attributed to any person—a condition the *Post* discourages. "Deep Throat was the classic deep background source," *Post* Executive Editor Leonard Downie said, referring to the source used by Bob Woodward in reporting on Watergate in the 1970s. The source was finally identified in 2005 as former FBI agent Mark Felt.

- **Off the record:** In the *Post*'s understanding of this term, information cannot be used in any story or for further reporting. Beyond providing a reporter with background knowledge, information obtained on this basis has little value. In reality, many sources, especially those who don't deal regularly with reporters, use the term *off the record* when they really mean "Don't use my name" or "Don't tell anyone where you got this information." To avoid misunderstandings, reporters should make clear to the source what information may be published and how it will be attributed.

Preelection Stories

If the primary purpose of political coverage is to help citizens make informed decisions in the voting booth, the most important stories are those published before the election. Davis Merritt and Maxwell McCombs, in their book *The Two W's of Journalism,* pose the ultimate question this way: "Do I know enough about the candidates to make the decision to hire one of them to work for me at the job he or she is seeking?"

Preelection stories, which seek to provide that information, usually fall into these categories: profiles, events, issues, campaign finances and advertising. Additional stories can explain registration and voting procedures—the mechanics of the electoral process.

Profiles

These are a political reporter's stock in trade. Depending on their timing—beginning, middle or end of the campaign—they take different angles. At the time a candidate announces she is running for office, the focus is biography: who is this person, and why is she qualified for this office? During the campaign, the focus shifts to how a person's experience in the private sector or in a previous elected position applies to the office she is seeking. And as Election Day nears, profiles explore what the candidate has learned during the campaign and how her positions have evolved.

The first step to a comprehensive profile is a thorough public records search. Use this to verify information on a resume or biography: age, college degrees, military service and employment history. If there's a bankruptcy, pending civil suit or past criminal conviction on the record, the reporter will want to know that early in the campaign—and, with her editors, decide whether it's relevant to the current candidacy. (There's a good chance that the opposing candidate's staff or a hired consultant is doing the same thing—it's called *opposition research.*)

An interview or series of interviews is next. Some of the best interview questions address a candidate's motives: why are you running for this office? What led to your decision? What do you hope to accomplish? For an incumbent, the follow-ups are: what were your biggest accomplishments of your last term? What was your biggest frustration? For a challenger, the obvious questions are: why should we choose you instead of the incumbent? In what ways would you make a better mayor (or council member or legislator)? If the incumbent is retiring or prohibited by term limits from running again, both candidates should be asked how their vision for the city, county or state resembles or differs from that of the person holding office.

Political profiles can't rely just on the candidate's statements; they also need comments from supporters, detractors and neutral observers. People who have worked closely with the candidate in another context—business, nonprofit agency or advocacy group—can provide useful perspectives. Don't rely solely on the candidate's memories and quotes to establish his or her record. No matter what stage of the campaign it is when the story is published, a box or sidebar with basic biographical information should accompany the profile. Here's how Dan Popkey, a reporter for the *Idaho Statesman,* began a profile on Tracy Andrus, a candidate for mayor of Boise and the daughter of Idaho's then governor:

Beyond the Famous Last Name

Tracy Andrus Seeks Election as Boise Mayor on Her Own Merits

When Tracy Andrus first talked about running for mayor of Boise, her wise, old Dad tried to talk her out of it.

"Why would you want to put yourself through that?" asked Idaho Gov. Cecil Andrus.

Her answer: "Somebody has got to do some things or Boise is going to change dramatically from what it was when I grew up."

Father reminded daughter she might lose, as he did when he first ran for governor in 1966.

That didn't scare her off.

"Usually children of public officials are soured on running for public office," Andrus said. "But she never flinched from public scrutiny."

(continued)

(continued)

> Tracy Andrus, 37, understands the grimy side of politics.
>
> She remembers with discomfort riding in the 1966 Fourth of July parade in Boise. It was 105 degrees. Wearing a mint green ruffled dress, she sat in a yellow convertible with black interior.
>
> "You're trying to smile and I'm so hot and thinking, all I want to do is go back to the motel and get into the pool," she said.
>
> Though she grew up in the shadow of a famous father, Tracy Andrus has always wanted to be judged on her own.
>
> "I feel I have to prove myself twice," she said in a 1973 interview. "I just want to like people and have them like me."
>
> But she can't get away from the comparisons. Even campaign aides tease her about gestures that mimic Dad, like the time she knocked down the mike during a radio interview. "I talk with my hands," she admits, though she resists such parallels.
>
> "Tracy is the apple of Cecil's eye," said Dr. Dean Sorensen, who treated Tracy when she was diagnosed with cancer in 1975 and has become a family friend.
>
> "I see a lot of Cecil in Tracy," said Sorensen, a former Republican legislator. "They're very much alike. They're very astute. She has a feeling of where to be and what to say."

Popkey interviewed family members, friends, campaign workers and business owners—including one critical of Andrus's leadership of a business organization. He included firsthand observations of the candidate's interactions with volunteers and voters. And he wasn't afraid to ask tough questions about Andrus's divorce and her ex-husband's financial troubles.

In a tip sheet called "Making Politics Fun," prepared for reporters covering the 2000 election, the Poynter Institute suggested that stories address these questions:

- **What are the** candidates' core values?
- **What experiences shaped** them and their views?
- **Who are their** heroes, role models and people who made a difference, and why?
- **What do the** people who know them best say about them?
- **What do people** who have competed against them say about them?

Many newspapers sum up their campaign coverage in a voters' guide, a special section containing profiles of all the candidates running in their circulation area.

"Your audience has probably not been reading your paper every day of the campaign," David Yepsen, political editor of the *Des Moines Register,* said on a Web site compiled by the Project for Excellence in Journalism. "For them it is not rehashing; it is news they may have missed. Published the week before the election, these are a helpful tool, especially for voters who don't regularly follow politics and may have missed daily stories covering the same topics."

Yepsen recommends including updated versions of previously published stories, ratings of candidates, tables and graphs to give voters a summary of the campaign just before they need to make decisions.

Events

These include press conferences, debates, forums and rallies. In many parts of the country, Labor Day is the traditional opening of the campaign for the November general election. But summer picnics, parades and community festivals often give candidates early exposure to voters. These stories usually don't provide much opportunity to go into depth about a candidate, but they do give glimpses into how comfortable a candidate is with meeting the voters, as well as names of potential contacts for later stories.

Rarely does one see a true debate—in which the candidates directly ask each other questions—at the local level. Most of the forums sponsored by such groups as the League of Women Voters more closely resemble a joint press conference. These are frustrating for reporters, because of the large number of candidates, tight time limits and lack of follow-up questions. But they are useful because the questions show the types of issues that concern voters. And audiences at such events consist of volunteers, partisans and citizens who closely follow campaigns—and are in a position to assess the candidates' strengths and weaknesses.

Journalists who cover these events usually resort to overly generic leads and, in the interest of balance, try to give each candidate a paragraph or two of comments. A better approach is to focus on the audience: were the answers helpful in differentiating among the candidates' positions? What issues were sidestepped or ignored? Did the responses change any voters' minds? What follow-up questions might have been asked?

Debates among candidates for state office and Congress are usually organized by civic groups or news organizations, often the public TV station in the state capital. These are more focused than the multiple-candidate local panels, but pose other challenges. Questions are usually posed by reporters who cover state government and politics; rarely do citizens have a chance to participate. Consequently, the most effective coverage might be in advance of the debate: finding out what questions the voters would like answered, previewing the issues likely to be raised and telling TV viewers what to watch for. After the debate, reporters can focus on local or regional issues raised, fact-check the claims and counterclaims and seek voter reaction. Sometimes, a high school or college debate coach or speech teacher can be recruited to score the debate on rhetorical and presentation points.

Closer to Election Day, candidates give stump speeches and hold rallies to energize supporters and attract television coverage. These usually have limited news value but are worth attending nonetheless, if only to see whether the candidate emphasizes different issues or uses sharper language when speaking to core supporters than when addressing a more general audience. Again, the opportunity to observe interaction with voters is probably the most valuable aspect.

Issues

Over the course of a campaign, candidates will choose to talk about issues they most care about or ones they think will attract voters or give an advantage over their opponent. Sometimes circumstances outside the candidates' control—natural disasters, budget shortfalls or unexpected scandals—add new issues to the mix. And voters will raise questions through letters to the editor, candidate forums and news organizations' Web sites that deserve a place on the agenda.

"Too often campaign coverage revolves around what candidates think about issues as opposed to what they intend to do about them, around how they talk about issues rather than whether they have firm plans to deal with them," McCombs and Merritt write. To avoid this syndrome, reporters need to push candidates for specific proposals and policies. Ask who is advising them on issues and which groups they have consulted with. A public lands policy recommended by a state's forest products council will have different goals and consequences than one recommended by an environmental group.

Bill Kovach, chairman of the Committee of Concerned Journalists, points out, "Issue coverage is about more than presenting two voices disagreeing with one another." He recommends examining root causes of problems as well as possible solutions. "For example, when you ask people about crime, they often respond by talking about education and opportunity," he writes on the Web site of the Project for Excellence in Journalism. "In the real world, issues are related to each other and not easily summed up in a position statement."

Stories that compare how all candidates for a particular office stand on a single issue can be more effective than those that conglomerate a gamut of issues into a single story. A grid showing candidates' positions on a handful of major issues can offer a good visual comparison, particularly if published in a preelection wrap-up or voters' guide.

When an interest group endorses a candidate, find out whether the endorsement comes with any money or is merely symbolic. If a teachers' union backs a candidate based on her support for higher appropriations for public schools, it can suggest an alliance that might cause other education groups to come forward. If the chamber of commerce or another business lobby supports the same candidate because she favors tax cuts, the office seeker's positions might need to be reconciled. The logical follow-up questions to the candidate are: how do you make up the lost revenues? Will school budgets need to be reduced? Where would you cut spending instead?

Campaign Finances

"Money is the mother's milk of politics," said Jesse Unruh, speaker of the California Assembly (the lower house of the legislature) from 1961 to 1968. His observation is as true today as it was in the 1960s. Money is a factor in politics from the smallest town council race to the 2004 presidential election, which saw incumbent President George W. Bush spend more than $300 million in private and government funds and Democratic challenger John Kerry spend $240 million. (These figures exclude spending by their political parties or advocacy groups, the so-called 527 committees, in the months leading up to the presidential election.)

Fortunately, campaign-finance legislation passed by Congress, state legislatures and city councils gives voters—and reporters—timely access to donation and spending records. Many of these records, formerly available only on paper at the agency that compiled them, can be viewed and easily downloaded through the World Wide Web. The challenge for journalists is to sort through records, discover trends and make meaningful comparisons among candidates.

States typically require candidates to report contributions and expenditures periodically during the election cycle. Small contributions are reported by number and total; those over a certain threshold (usually $50 or $100) are reported by name, address and occupation. A campaign-finance story might address these questions: what is the breakdown between contributions by individuals and those by political action committees? Who are the largest contributors in each category? Are there multiple contributions with the same last name and the same address? Are there any unusual names—other elected officials or prominent business leaders? Has the candidate made personal contributions with the expectation of being repaid after the election? Do contributions reflect an interest in the issues that an incumbent has voted on in the past, or a challenger is likely to in the future? If so, more sophisticated stories can make a connection between a candidate's voting record and the number and source of campaign contributions. Don't forget about post-election reports, typically filed a month after the election, which might show large infusions of cash to support a last-minute ad blitz.

Here's an example of an informative campaign finance story on a congressional race, written by Tom Hacker for the Fort Collins *Coloradoan:*

PACs Pony Up for Schaffer More Than Kirkpatrick

The difference between an office holder and an office seeker rings clear in campaign-finance numbers compiled by the two candidates in Colorado's 4th District congressional race.

Reports filed by the campaigns of Rep. Bob Schaffer, R-Colo., and his Democratic challenger, Susan Kirkpatrick, show a whopping edge to Schaffer in the number and amount of contributions from special interest groups.

Political action committees, or PACs, have chipped in a total of $152,852 to the Schaffer campaign, compared to $44,500 for Kirkpatrick.

Schaffer received contributions from 107 PACs. Kirkpatrick got money from 13.

"It's not just a matter of being an incumbent," Schaffer said. "My staff hustles. For instance, they called a couple of restaurant friends of ours to have them contact the National Restaurant Association. We've had doctor friends contact the AMA (American Medical Association). That's how it works."

A breakdown of the FEC reports by the independent Center for Responsive Politics shows Schaffer's biggest benefactors are agriculture PACs, with $28,648 in contributions, and conservative political groups, who added $21,530 to his campaign.

Kirkpatrick benefited most from labor unions that gave her campaign $14,000 and liberal political organizations, which chipped in another $4,982.

Kirkpatrick said at the onset of her campaign that "no candidate can run a credible campaign without PAC money."

But Schaffer, like other incumbents, has the advantage of nearly automatic PAC contributions to his campaign.

"Of course, money is going to come more easily to people whose records are known," he said.

Kirkpatrick was making several campaign appearances late Friday and could not be reached for comment on the PAC numbers.

Among other findings of the CRP report:

- Schaffer collected $104,977 from business PACs in all industries, while Kirkpatrick got just $1,750 from business groups.
- Schaffer has raised a total of $363,280 and spent $278,765 during the campaign, while Kirkpatrick has raised $240,004 and spent $231,860. Missing from

(continued)

(continued)

Kirkpatrick's PAC list were contributions from tobacco producers. Schaffer received five contributions from two tobacco PACs, totaling $2,500.

"Tobacco producers buy into my program." Schaffer said. "I don't buy into theirs. I'm no fan of tobacco."

Campaign spending patterns are newsworthy, too. Which forms of advertising does a candidate prefer, and why? Are there payments to political consultants or advertising agencies? Does the candidate patronize local businesses, such as printers, or out-of-state companies? Scrutinize expenditures for meals, mileage and lodging to see if they're consistent with a candidate's actual travel.

Advertising

Much of the money raised for political campaigns in the United States is spent on advertising: television is the dominant form for state and national races, but newspapers, billboards and direct mail are important in local races. Electronic communication with voters— through e-mail lists and Web sites—also might be considered forms of advertising.

Political reporters are paying more attention to the source and veracity of claims made in campaign commercials. Media outlets regularly treat advertising as news—sometimes giving more exposure to the message than the original commercial or print ad attracted. The attacks on Democratic candidate John Kerry by a group of Navy veterans—and the Kerry campaign's lackluster response to those ads—became a major issue in the 2004 presidential campaign.

News reports of the Swift Boat Veterans ads, which attacked Kerry for statements after he returned from Vietnam in the 1970s, reached millions of voters who never saw the original commercials.

One technique that both newspapers and TV stations have adopted is a regular feature scrutinizing commercials called *ad watch* or *reality check.* By presenting the text and images of the ad, comparing the statements to the public record and confronting the candidate (or his or her ad agency) about inconsistencies, the news organization can help voters assess the ads' truthfulness. Political science, marketing or advertising professors at a local university can help characterize an ad's persuasive strategy and analyze its effectiveness. Television segments that use slow-motion or stop-action editing can be especially strong ways to deconstruct a political commercial.

Polls and Surveys

Although news organizations, particularly those that advocate civic journalism, say they want to downplay the horse-race nature of politics, the public's appetite for poll results continues unabated. During the 2004 presidential campaign, newspapers, television networks and Web sites reported poll results almost daily. Many stories focused on why different polls taken at the same time showed different results.

Even with greater attention given to the accuracy of polling (and the importance of reporting the poll's sponsor and methodology), journalists continue to oversimplify and make assumptions that misstate poll results. Public opinion expert Priscilla Salant (see the "Professional Tips" section later in this chapter) identifies three common mistakes:

- **They report support** "for" a particular candidate, regardless of whether the support is strong or weakly held. Good polling organizations ask about the strength of support, allowing variations in the degree of support. They also report the opinions of likely voters rather than everyone who responds to the poll.

- **They often fail** to discuss sampling error, a condition that is inevitable because researchers survey only a sample of the population instead of conducting a census. Most national opinion polls involve no more than 1,200 respondents—a sample large enough to yield estimates plus or minus 3 percent of the opinions of the actual population. So if a preelection poll showed 51 percent of likely voters favored Democrat John Kerry and 48 percent favored Republican George W. Bush, the results are statistically a dead heat. (The actual popular vote was the reverse, about 51 percent for Bush and 48 percent for Kerry.)

- **They rarely report** the actual wording of questions. Responses vary enormously depending on how a question is asked and what background material the questioner provides before asking it. This is especially true for polling on issues such as the death penalty and abortion rights.

Fortunately, a number of journalism and public opinion organizations have raised awareness of polling techniques and offered suggestions for improving coverage of polls. The National Council on Public Polls (NCPP) presents "20 Questions a Journalist Should Ask about Poll Results" on its Web site, www.ncpp.org/qajsa.htm.

On the NCPP Web site, Shalden Gawiser, director of election coverage for *NBC News,* and Evans Witt, president of Princeton Survey Research Associates, offer insightful responses to such questions as the following:

- **"Who's on first?** (When is one candidate really ahead of the other?)"
- **"What other polls** have been done on this topic? Do they say the same thing? If they are different, why are they different?"
- **And finally,** "Is this poll worth reporting?"

Davis Merritt and Maxwell McCombs argue that even if all of the precautions are taken, news organizations still give too much time and attention to polls. "The rush to measure sophisticated concepts (of public opinion) with cheap, rough tools and report them as absolutes creates problems of polarization, pollution and diversion that further damages the news media's credibility and undermine its role in the democratic process," they write.

The search for solutions is harmed because public dialogue is difficult when the public perceives that an issue is settled, they assert. Rather than snapshots of candidate preferences and spontaneous reactions to news events, McCombs and Merritt suggest polling be used to determine citizens' needs, concerns and priorities.

Political reporters at organizations that practice civic journalism can push for more sophisticated use of polls that promote better understanding of public issues.

PROFESSIONAL TIPS

Priscilla Salant

Priscilla Salant is manager of rural policy and assessment for the Department of Agricultural Economics and Rural Sociology at the University of Idaho. She earned a bachelor's degree in economics from the University of California, Berkeley, and a master of science in agricultural economics from the University of Arizona. She is the coauthor with Don Dillman of *How to Conduct Your Own Survey* (John Wiley & Sons, 1994).

Question: How do news organizations commonly mishandle the presentation of poll results?

Too often, news organizations throw polling results at their readers without helping them interpret the numbers. Polling isn't rocket science. The basics are well within the reach of typical readers if reporters do a little more to help people be critical consumers of information.

For example, when reporting results of a telephone poll of likely voters, a newspaper might also report the questions asked to screen out people who are unlikely to vote. Or, in reporting that 45 percent of likely voters will vote for Candidate A, with a sampling error of "plus or minus 3 percent," the newspaper might also tell readers what such an error tells us about the reliability of the estimate.

The benefit of helping readers learn about the limits of polling data at election time is that these same readers will be better equipped to interpret the plethora of survey results reported during the rest of the year.

Question: What one essential fact or caveat should reporters include in every story about a poll?

Every story in which poll results are reported should explain how the poll was conducted so readers can judge its possible limitations. The explanation doesn't have to be long, but it should contain enough information so that interested readers know how to interpret the survey results.

For example, when the *New York Times* reports results of its own polls, the paper publishes a short sidebar called "How the Poll Was Conducted." The sidebar explains when the poll was conducted and by which method (usually telephone), how large the sample was, how it was selected, whether any weighting was done to adjust for disproportionate representation within the sample, how large the potential sampling error is and what it means and a link to complete results.

If a local newspaper conducted its own poll on a countywide race, for example, "How the Poll Was Conducted" might read like this:

> The latest Smith County Register poll is based on telephone interviews conducted October 10 through October 15 with 923 adults in Smith County. The sample of telephone numbers was selected randomly from the residential section of the phonebook. In theory, in nineteen cases out of twenty, results based on a sample of this size will differ by no more than 3 percentage points in either direction from what would have been obtained by interviewing all adults in Smith County. In addition to sampling error, these results are subject to possible errors related to question wording, unlisted phone numbers and households who either rely on cell phones only or don't have a phone at all.

(continued)

PROFESSIONAL TIPS   Continued

Question: How has the growing number of people who rely on cell phones (to the exclusion of home phones with listed numbers) affected the reliability of polling data?

By law, telemarketers and other organizations are prohibited from making unsolicited calls to cell phones. Since telephone calls made for the purpose of surveying people about their political preferences are all unsolicited, it is against the law for polling organizations to call cell phones. This is only a problem for poll reliability if three conditions are met. First, "cell phone–only" voters must make up a significant part of the population. Second, they must be different from other voters in a way that affects survey results. And third, they have to vote in relatively high proportions. If they are numerous, are different from other voters and turn out in high numbers, cell phone–only voters have the potential to introduce significant error into polling results.

As of the 2004 elections, the proliferation of cell phones has not affected reliability as much as many analysts had expected. Less than 10 percent of the population is cell only. While they tend to be younger and more affluent than the population as a whole, cell-only people don't seem to be voting in numbers high enough to affect polling results . . . *yet.* Keep an eye on this issue!

Question: Most political polls are simply a horse race: who's ahead, who is behind and who is gaining. In what other ways could news organizations use polls or surveys to provide greater depth to political reporting?

Undoubtedly, helping readers understand the characteristics and motivations of different voter groups would add greater depth to political reporting. One way to do this is to conduct focus groups, which are made up of people selected for their particular characteristics rather than at random. For example, to understand why a Republican candidate is doing better in the polls than would be expected based on the number of registered Republicans, a newspaper might interview a local group of ten to twelve voters who are registered Democrats but leaning toward voting for the Republican candidate.

A structured group process like this is exploratory and intended to help understand why people think the way they do. Needless to say, focus groups don't substitute for quantitative surveys because participants are not selected at random and don't comprise a large enough sample to yield reliable estimates.

Question: Do the daily opinion questions that newspapers and TV stations conduct on their Web sites have any value? How could self-selected Web polls be made more useful?

If a news organization's goal is to inform people about opinions held by the general public, daily polls conducted on the Web do far more harm than good. That's because too many readers don't distinguish between self-selected and random samples. Even when a reporter states clearly that the results are "not scientific," it's rare that people fully understand what this phrase means. It means this: the results of the poll pertain only to the respondents themselves and not to the general public. We have no way of knowing how representative the self-selected sample is, except that it consists of readers of this particular newspaper who have access to the Internet and chose to participate in the survey.

Web surveys can yield reliable estimates when conducted according to specific guidelines. For example, if a professor wants to know how students feel about the textbook being used in a class of 400 students, all of whom have Internet access, he can send each one a Web-based survey and offer a small number of bonus points for responding. Thus, everyone has an equal chance of being selected and also has a way (and an incentive) to respond. That is never the case for Web-based, general public opinion surveys. Not everyone has access to the Internet, and the sample is always nonrandom.

(continued)

PROFESSIONAL TIPS Continued

Question: If a small news organization is interested in doing its own survey, what's the best way to get started?

Get started by learning the basics of good survey research. Remember, it isn't rocket science! Even if you plan to contract out for the poll, be an informed consumer! In our book, *How to Conduct* *Your Own Survey* (John Wiley & Sons), we explain the ten basic steps in conducting a reliable survey. Other good references include the American Association of Public Opinion Researchers (www.aapor.org) and the American Statistical Association, which has published a good basic guide available at www.whatisasurvey.info.

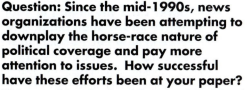

PROFESSIONAL TIPS

Dan Popkey

Dan Popkey has been a reporter for the *Idaho Statesman* of Boise since 1984 and a columnist since 1994. He has covered Boise City Hall, the statehouse and politics. He has a bachelor's degree in political science from Santa Clara University and a master's degree in journalism from Columbia University. As a congressional fellow of the American Political Science Association, he worked on Capitol Hill as a legislative assistant in 1989.

Question: Since the mid-1990s, news organizations have been attempting to downplay the horse-race nature of political coverage and pay more attention to issues. How successful have these efforts been at your paper?

We're searching for the right mix of traditional reporting on issues, the horserace, our watchdog responsibilities and putting readers' questions to candidates.

On balance, I think we've done a good job. We created a new "State" page that runs year-round. During the legislative session, it is heavy with coverage of lawmakers and the governor. During campaigns, we have a reliable spot for the issue statements of candidates. Our horse-race coverage is deeper and more nuanced. We write about the connection between money and candidates. That's a horse-race story—the winner typically has

more money—but an important one, measuring a candidate's loyalties and presaging how he or she will vote and lead. Our horse-race coverage also includes thorough profiles in the top races, though we have scaled back on the resources we devote in the printed paper to some down-ticket contests.

We've made up for that, and more, with an online feature. We put a series of questions to candidates and run their answers on our Web site, along with biographical information. A voter types in their address and compares candidates. Since few people know their legislative districts in the bigger counties, readers like this innovation. Candidates answer without the filter of a reporter (though there are strict length limits) and voters often see clear distinctions.

The online questionnaire is a branch of "civic journalism," an experiment that continues. We've tried focus groups, partnering with Public

(continued)

PROFESSIONAL TIPS   Continued

TV, sponsoring forums and debates, writing issue-rich stories based on the personal stories of one family, asking voters to tell us what they want to know, and more. We continue to look for ways to connect readers with candidates.

Question: Who are a political reporter's best sources? Who do you turn to for sorting out competing claims?

The best sources are the politicians themselves. In Idaho, we're fortunate, because I can almost always reach a state legislator and, if it's a significant story and I'm dogged about it, our congressional delegation and the governor. Of course, they are looking out for their own interests, but that's just another filter to consider.

Other good sources are well-informed bureaucrats, the staff of elected officials, lobbyists and interest groups. Finally, I never regret talking to ordinary people about the issues they care about. They often have questions that would never have occurred to me, and care about issues that we're missing. And, as with all reporting, talking to sources face-to-face is better than the phone.

I try to talk to the smartest, most up-to-speed sources on competing sides of an issue. I ask about other sources I should consult. I read what others have written. I use the Web to get grounded, helping me ask the best possible questions.

Question: How do you maintain your neutrality and prevent candidates from accusing you of favoritism?

I write a column, which is explicitly labeled as commentary. So, I have a point of view; otherwise it wouldn't be much use writing a column. Still, fairness matters. And after 20 years covering Idaho politics, my credibility continues to guarantee me access to the sources who know the scoop. I am sometimes accused of choosing sides and sometimes they're right. I've written often about human rights, including gay rights, because I think it's important that Idaho push back against the wrongheaded notion that we're a bunch of racists. I've advocated centrist approaches to environmental issues, because I think our natural wonders are central to our future. I've promoted public schools

and the people who work in them because I consider our system of free, thorough and common schools our most important institution. I've railed against the government when it wrongs ordinary people, wastes our money or conducts public business in secret. That's not neutral, but it is essential to our First Amendment responsibilities.

Sometimes, people charge that I'm anti-Republican. My answer is this: I'm a contrarian. My job is to hold public officials accountable. In the most Republican state in the nation, more often than not the officials I'm bird dogging are Republicans. If this were a Democratic state, my critiques would more often be aimed at Democrats.

Question: What are your three favorite questions to ask a candidate in an interview that might reveal something that's not in the press releases or stump speech?

How do you spend your free time?
Tell me about your kids?
What are you reading?

Question: How do you cover last-minute charges made against a candidate? Does the timing or source of negative information make any difference in how you handle the story?

Yes, timing matters. As campaigns have waged weekend-before-the-election smears, I've written columns warning people to be wary of the leaflets left on windshields in the church parking lots. I've also written stories in the final days, critical of false charges, explaining what they got wrong. And, when it's too late to do that—when I don't learn of the false attacks until too late—I've written about it anyway, as a check for the candidates and a caution to voters.

Question: What's the best post-election story to do after the ballots are counted, victory and concession speeches have been given, and the dust has settled?

What promises did the winners make, and how will they deliver now that they've got power.

Postelection Stories

Planning for Election Day begins at news organizations months before the polls open. Everyone in the newsroom—including reporters from sports and features—is often pressed into service. The larger a newspaper's circulation area or a broadcast station's reach, the more complicated it becomes to gather and present comprehensive and timely election results. Maps, tables and graphics need to be created, ready to insert vote totals. Photographs of candidates are retrieved from the file; past stories are consulted for background. Reporters need to know where candidates will be after the polls are closed and have a strategy to call for comments once the results are known.

The stories written in the first news cycle after the outcome is clear cover the basics: who won and who lost, the vote totals (and the percentage of precincts the totals represent), capsule biographies of the candidates and a recap of major issues that divided them. Victory speeches and concession statements typically are a source of good quotes. Reporters also can place the results in a state or national context, and provide any historical twists—a candidate wins a seat once held by her father, the first Republican elected for twenty years in a district that usually prefers Democrats or a political unknown topples an entrenched incumbent.

Later in the week after an election, stories can delve deeper into the raw numbers. In which precincts, districts or counties did a winning candidate draw most of her support? What issues, in hindsight, proved decisive? How did voter turnout affect the outcome? And how do the candidates themselves explain their victories or defeats?

Two days after the 2004 election, Erica Curless and Betsy Russell, reporters for the *Idaho Spokesman-Review,* offered this recap of legislative contests:

Democrats Get Out the Vote, but GOP Cements Statehouse Lock with North Idaho Wins

North Idaho Democrats can't get out from under the big Republican elephant that's keeping them down.

And they aren't alone under there. All of Idaho fervently voted Republican on Tuesday, squashing the Democrats' hopes of gaining more seats in the Idaho Legislature.

Idaho Democrats lost three seats in the state House, but kept even with seven seats in the state Senate. Two of the lost seats were in North Idaho, which just 15 years ago was largely Democrat.

"It was a grand victory for the Republicans," said a jubilant Lt. Gov. Jim Risch. "We're already the most Republican state in the union, but I guess now we're really, really the most Republican state."

Democrats were disappointed with their showing, but said it was to be expected in a presidential year.

"The Bush win had pretty large coattails," said state Democratic Party Chairwoman Carolyn Boyce. "2000 was really much more devastating and we picked ourselves up, we found great candidates, and we doubled our numbers in 2002. We seem to have two steps forward, one step back, but as long as we have those two steps forward, we'll keep slowly building."

(continued)

(continued)

One of the lost Democratic seats is in Coeur d'Alene, where voters opted for Republican Marge Chadderdon, a longtime party activist, over Democrat Mike Gridley, Coeur d'Alene city attorney.

Chadderdon, who got 54 percent of the vote, kept an edge over Gridley all night. She said that support from the national and state party helped secure the win, taking back a seat that is currently held by Democrat Rep. Bonnie Douglas. Gridley beat Douglas in the May primary.

"The Republican Party was with me all the way," said Chadderdon, who appeared on campaign fliers with both U.S. Sen. Mike Crapo and U.S. Rep. Butch Otter. "They needed to be there."

Gridley agrees that those GOP endorsements helped Chadderdon, along with Bush's victory. "I don't know another explanation," said Gridley, who had lots of money, even a few endorsements by local Republicans, and spent months door-knocking.

Politics between Elections

A political reporter's job doesn't end once the dust settles after an election. Just as the winning candidates need to prepare for the business of governing, the journalist changes her focus.

Adam Wilson, a reporter for the Olympia, Washington, *Olympian,* described the contradiction of being assigned to cover a campaign—and then to report on local or state government afterwards.

"You have to be a watchdog during the campaign, pointing out discrepancies and contradictions, but then have good relations with the winner for the next two years."

To do that, he reassures candidates that he's not just reporting on the election—he's "in it for the long haul," and will continue to pay attention to them—and their issues—after the votes are counted.

At the same time, the political process doesn't stop after elections—it just moves behind the scenes. Among the stories that emerge during nonelection years are the election's effect on party organization and leadership, reexamination of positions and platforms and jockeying for position for the next election.

Because seats in Congress and state legislatures are reapportioned every ten years to reflect population changes, demographic stories are important. Which areas of a state are growing, and which are losing population? Are rural communities losing traditional clout to suburbs? How do national patterns, such as declining union membership and demographic changes, affect state and county politics?

Magazines that cater to elected officials and candidates, such as *National Journal, Governing* and *Campaigns and Elections,* are full of trend stories ripe for local spin-offs. A reporter whose curiosity about politics never diminishes can discover rich and rewarding stories between election cycles.

Conclusion

Civic journalism's influence has been felt more deeply in political reporting than in any other area of journalism. The belief that journalism can enhance deliberation and counteract cynicism about politics is reflected in the approaches described in this chapter.

Jay Rosen writes: "Journalists make it their business to be knowledgeable and alert. They come to work ready to play a part in a public drama, even as they fill a job in a private business. Through this steady work they stand for something: the argument that democracy and civic life are everyone's business."

Through attention to these principles, reporters can make news about campaigns, elections and governing not only interesting but also relevant to the lives of citizens.

CHAPTER EXERCISES

1. Ask the county clerk or election supervisor's office for voter registration and turnout figures for your city, legislative district or precinct that includes your campus for the last four general elections. Find out what procedures the office uses to purge names of voters who move away. What generalizations can you make about student turnout for local, nonpresidential and presidential elections?

2. What voting method does your county use—punch cards, optical-scan sheets, touch-screen monitors or a combination? What safeguards are in place to assure that every vote is counted? Have there been problems in the recent past with inaccurate tallies or fewer votes cast than the number of voters who participated? Ask the county clerk or chief elections officer about preparations for the next election: what changes, if any, will be made in response to state and federal election laws aimed at reducing errors and streamlining the process?

3. Identify the closest race for the state legislature in the district that includes your college or university for the most recent election. Use the Web site of your secretary of state, public disclosure commission or state elections commission and download campaign finance reports for the two major-party candidates. Summarize contributions and spending for each candidate, find the largest contributor for each and determine which media outlet received the most money for advertising from each candidate.

4. During an election year, videotape commercials for an incumbent member of Congress and his or her opponent. What themes do they raise? Do they reflect local concerns, national issues or both? Ask each candidate's campaign headquarters for the source of any factual material quoted or cited; fact-check the ad with independent sources. Give the commercial a report card for accuracy, impact and effectiveness. (During a nonelection year, you might be able to get copies of past commercials from state political parties or former candidates.)

5. Find the name of the longest-serving political reporter in your state capital. (She or he probably works for the Associated Press or a newspaper with a year-round statehouse bureau.) Interview him or her in person, or by telephone or e-mail. Ask about the following:

      a. Favorite and least favorite politicians to cover
      b. Most helpful unelected official
      c. Biggest scoop of the past two years
      d. Greatest frustration about covering politics in your state

  6. Choose a candidate for city council, county commission or state legislature. From past news stories and public records, prepare a biographical box to accompany a profile. Include education, occupation, family, positions on key issues and something novel or offbeat (hobby, political heroes, musical tastes, etc.).

  7. Prepare a plan to cover one contested race on Election Day. Contact the candidates in advance to determine their whereabouts and activities; obtain cell phone numbers, if possible. Write at least five questions that seek to explain the election's outcome, and discover the candidates' reactions. After the election, write four paragraphs designed to be incorporated in a roundup of election results.

CHAPTER

16 Law Enforcement

BY KENTON BIRD

Sneak Peek

Getting Started on
the Beat
Useful Sources and
Documents
Covering Crimes
versus Crime
Professional Tips
Crime on Campus
Holding Agencies
Accountable
Disasters and
Tragedies
Chapter Exercises

Editors and reporters have thought and changed their approach to covering crime over the years, looking more at patterns and trends than individual criminal acts. For instance, in Pullman, Washington, common complaints are party noise and lost, roaming and loud dogs.

Dan Weaver, the police chief in Moscow, Idaho (population 25,000), believes journalists and police officers have a lot in common: they work long hours, evenings and weekends; they frequently face stressful situations; and they deal with people who are angry or in trouble. Both fields rely on interviewing and investigative skills to do their jobs. In small towns, both police officers and reporters are underpaid and realize that to advance their career or land a pay raise, they must move to a larger city.

In fact, Weaver believes there should be more affinity between the two occupations than there is. He makes clear in his department's news media guidelines the importance of

215

having good relations with reporters. "The public's perception of how the police are serving them often comes from the media," the policy states. "What citizens hear, read and see about the police is perhaps as important to their perception as is direct contact."

Moscow's policy is a model for law enforcement agencies seeking a productive and positive relationship with the reporters and photographers that cover them. Not all police departments are as cooperative. Some departments withhold information or release it selectively—out of misguided attempts to assure conviction of criminal defendants, or simply to make themselves look better. Other agencies mean well but organize their records for the benefit of their officers and the court system, not for access by the public and press.

To provide accurate and complete coverage of public safety issues, news organizations need a thorough understanding of how those agencies work—and a commitment to devote sufficient resources to the beat. They also must recognize that stories about violence, disasters and tragedies have great potential to provoke emotional responses from readers, even when handled with compassion and care.

Getting Started on the Beat

A beginning reporter is often assigned to the law enforcement beat, which when combined with coverage of the judicial system is nicknamed *cops and courts.* The label understates the complexity of the beat, which often includes stories about jails and prisons, fire departments, emergency services, disaster planning, police budgets and personnel issues. The larger the news organization's coverage area, the more agencies to cover—and the less time a reporter can spend with any one of them.

"Many editors and producers still use the crime beat as a sink-or-swim test," writes Dave Karajicek, a former police bureau chief for the New York *Daily News.* Reporters who can handle the pressure are "promoted" to other beats (a term that diminishes the value of skilled police coverage), while those who don't move to softer assignments or leave journalism altogether. "Unfortunately, too many news organizations use sink-or-swim as an excuse for failing to provide training and support when an inexperienced reporter is assigned to crime," he writes. To remedy that, Karajicek and other reporters founded Criminal Justice Journalists, a group devoted to sharing information and story ideas. Their online guide, *Covering Crime and Justice,* is designed to help reporters learn the beat quickly.

Karajicek, who taught journalism at Columbia University, notes that the police beat relies on breaking news—from traffic accidents to airplane crashes, from fires to homicides, even weather stories. At the same time, reporters are expected to produce enterprise stories and investigative pieces that require weeks, if not months, of reporting.

"Crime reporters are often the busiest journalists in any newsroom," he observes. Balancing daily stories with long-range pieces is one of the toughest parts of any beat, but it is especially difficult for police reporters because of the nonstop nature of crime and court news.

A police reporter's shift usually begins and ends with a series of checks—in person, by telephone or a combination—with all police, fire and emergency agencies in the news organization's coverage area. An up-to-date contact list—with names, positions and listed and unlisted phone numbers—is essential. A reporter who walks the beat might visit briefly with desk sergeants, clerks, dispatchers and others authorized to release information. Use these contacts as a way to build a relationship so that when a big story breaks, you are the first reporter to be called. Telephone checks are cursory: a quick identification of the reporter and news outlet, a request for an update on a running story or continuing investigation or a query about crimes, fires or unusual events. The outcome of initial checks sets the coverage agenda for the day; if there are no major crimes, accidents or fires, the reporter can resume work on her backlog of continuing stories. Follow-up calls are typically made just before deadline to make sure no significant stories have broken during the day.

Here are additional suggestions for getting started on the beat from experienced police reporters, who shared their tips at conferences sponsored by Investigative Reporters and Editors:

> **John Solomon, Associated Press:** "Get ahead by thinking like the cops, prosecutors and defense lawyers. Don't wait for the court papers, press releases or interviews. Anticipate the next move in an investigation and try to nail it down before the formal announcement."

> **Tom Spaulding, *Indianapolis Star:*** "You should be as familiar with the channels on your police radio as you are [with] a TV. Information passes by quickly, but a key is to get addresses of crimes or incidents as they are broadcast over the radio. . . . Also, scanner chitchat is 'legal' and unfiltered, and usually provides at least two to three paragraphs of good 'color' for an article, or at least tips to find more color."

> **Cheryl Thompson, *Washington Post:*** "When searching for stories, look for patterns— patterns in crime, certain neighborhoods, etc. . . . Look at the stories you've written for the daily paper. How many times have you written about a specific issue? There's usually a bigger story there."

> **Steve Mills, *Chicago Tribune:*** "Get to know the police department's critics. Some of them—lawyers, for instance—will be able to get documents that you might not have access to."

Useful Sources and Documents

A reporter assigned to the police beat needs to know as much as possible about the departments he or she will cover: its history, command structure, budget and personnel. Ask procedural questions: is someone designated as the public information officer? Who should you call if a story breaks after regular business hours or on weekends? What type of identification do you need to cross police lines in the event of a major crime? What kinds of records does the department keep, and who is the best guide to the paper trail?

As with all beats, reporters have to walk a narrow line between earning the trust of their sources and getting too friendly with them. The nature of police work sometimes creates situations where reporters and officers swap information informally. Make sure that if a police officer tells you something, you know the conditions under which that information is given: can it be reported? Is it for your background only? Many reporters make it clear from the beginning that anything they hear is on the record—and pull out their notebooks or audio recorders as a reminder. Good law enforcement officers recognize that journalists have jobs to do and treat them with professional respect.

Captain Robert Chaffee, longtime public information officer for the Colorado State University police department, offered this advice to reporters:

- **Don't expect police** officers to do a reporter's job. "Don't ask us to go spoon-feed you information that you can get yourself."

- **Recognize that police** officers, even those assigned to deal with media relations, have other duties.

- **If you make** an honest mistake, let the officer know what happened so it doesn't jeopardize future contacts.

- **Know state law** governing police records. Understand the constraints placed on the release of information by police.

- **If police refuse** a request, keep your cool. Don't become adversarial or confrontational.

Chaffee believes in recognizing the initiative of reporters, particularly those who have done their homework. "I will reward reporters who have motivation to ask the questions first," rather than waiting for the information to come out in a press release, he said.

Reporters need to be familiar with state laws governing access to police records, as well as departmental policies for release of information. The following types of records might prove useful: offense or incident reports, which often include the name and address of the person who complained; the dispatcher's log, which lists all routine and 911 calls received and the agency's response; and arrest reports, which show anyone detained or jailed by the department.

Generally, the following facts about someone who has been arrested are considered public: name, age, occupation, charge, residence, length of the investigation and basic circumstances of the arrest (including whether weapons were used and whether there was any resistance to the request). The following information is generally not public: the names of juvenile suspects, victims of sex offenses, names of witnesses and names of victims (until family members have been notified). In addition, information that might jeopardize prosecution of a criminal case, such as the existence of a confession or an officer's opinion as to the guilt of the suspect, is not usually released.

Dianna Hunt, a reporter for the *Fort Worth Star-Telegram,* calls search warrants "a treasure trove" of information. To obtain a search warrant, police must present to a judge an affidavit that describes in detail the reason of the search and what information suggests that evidence might be found on the premises. After the search, the warrant is filed at the courthouse and a copy is often retained by the police agency. "Always ask for the warrant, the affidavit and the list of items seized," Hunt suggests.

Covering Crimes versus Crime

When the American Society of Newspaper Editors set out in the late 1990s to assess why newspapers had a credibility problem, its research found that crime news, especially episodic reports of random crimes, was one explanation. The *Oregonian* of Portland, one of eight newspapers that tested ways to improve credibility, spent two months examining its coverage of crime and talking to readers. One conclusion, wrote public editor Michelle McClellan, was that the paper needed to provide more context. "The Oregonian should increase its emphasis on trends, crimes that directly affect the public and information about how to stay safe," she wrote.

Susan Gage, the *Oregonian*'s crime team leader, said beats were reorganized to cover higher-interest stories, including white-collar crime. "We still cover breaking news but put it in context and play it at a volume that is less alarmist," Gage said. Another change was the addition of weekly logs of all types of crimes, broken down by neighborhood. McClellan, who received and responded to reader complaints in her role as a public editor, said complaints that the paper sensationalized crime news dropped after the changes took effect.

Here is an excerpt of a story by reporter Maxine Bernstein, who has covered crime for the paper since 1998, and four colleagues. Instead of simply recapping the annual homicide count, the reporters put human faces on the deaths:

"Senseless" Homicides Stand Out

There Were 34 Killings in Portland in 2004, and Many a Result of Perceived Slights, Police Report

Andre Andaur, 14, and two friends were walking to a bus stop down a darkened Portland street, heading home after a 15-year-old girl's birthday party in May.

Andaur called his mother and told her he was on his way. Soon after, the occupants of a passing car locked eyes with Andaur and shouted something and made gang gestures at the three youngsters. As the car made a quick U-turn, Andaur and his friends ran back toward the party.

In front of the host's house, a passenger of the car got out and began arguing with Andaur when someone fired a gun. Andaur collapsed against a car on Northeast 106th Avenue, bleeding from his chest.

An 18-year-old attending the party, Alfonso Estrada Ortega, carried Andaur into the house and tried to revive the boy on a couch. But Andaur died from a single gunshot to the chest.

Estrada told detectives he accidentally shot Andaur. Estrada said he pulled a 9mm handgun and fired it in the direction of the car because he thought the occupants were rival gang members. Then he realized he had hit the boy.

The mid-May killing stood out among Portland's 34 homicides in 2004. During Estrada's bail hearing in July, Det. Jon Rhodes testified that Andaur was barely 5 feet tall and looked "like a little kid."

Andaur's death underscored the bravado of young gang members emerging in the city. And it exemplified several of the year's homicides that resulted from perceived slights or minor confrontations, including a downtown shooting two days before Christmas that resulted from one man slapping another in the head.

(continued)

(continued)

"There are some deaths where you can cite a motive and understand what led to it," said Portland Sgt. George Burke, a supervisor in the homicide division. "Then, there are some that are just so senseless and you just go, 'Why?'"

Portland's 34 homicides were up from 28 a year earlier and 23 in 2002. Four deaths resulted from officer-involved shootings. And although the number of homicides has spiked, it is still far shy of the city's peak of 70 in 1987.

Portland is among several U.S. cities that experienced an increase in gang-related homicides and youth violence the past two years. Compared to 2000, when Portland had no teenage victims of a homicide, there were six in 2003 and six in 2004.

Elsewhere in the metro area, another 34 people died of homicide, bringing the metro total to 68.

Vancouver and surrounding Clark County saw 17 homicides, a huge jump from an annual average of seven. More than half of the victims were women and most were killed by family members, but the homicides included a Clark County Sheriff's deputy, four children ages 17 months to 4 years, a motherly neighbor and two young men dumped in a field. Authorities could not explain the surge from eight murders in 2003 and four in 2002. . . .

Statewide figures show Oregon's homicide count has dropped slightly over the past three years. Preliminary numbers show 80 homicides in 2003, the latest figures available, down from 86 in 2002 and 94 in 2001, according to Jeff Boch of the state's Uniform Crime Reporting Program.

In addition to Andaur's death in Portland, two other brazen city killings suspected to be gang-related had families of two teenagers mourning.

On April 9, Marcus Mill, 16, was shot to death in the middle of the afternoon at a TriMet bus stop on North Killingsworth Street and Albina Avenue.

Mill had been riding a bus moments earlier with the alleged shooter. They had some type of dispute, which police said may have been over gang colors. Mill got off the bus and was shot about 2 P.M. in front of dozens of pedestrians, motorists, community college students and others.

"This was pretty tragic," Burke said. "Marcus did everything to avoid the confrontation."

On June 6, Alexx Alexander, 16, was found dead from a gunshot wound to the head inside a car near the entrance of the Portland International Raceway. Police suspect his shooting was gang-related. There has been no arrest.

"The younger kids are more flamboyant about their gang activity," Burke said. "We're seeing younger kids who want to show their allegiance to a gang. They're making their mark."

Portland's gang cases are not unique. Nationally, cities such as Boston are experiencing a rise in youth violence as well.

"There's no question that murders committed by gangs are vastly on the increase across the country," said Jack Levin, director of the Brudnick Center on Violence at Northeastern University. "We should really be taking it very seriously."

Among the factors driving the increase in youth violence are a growing juvenile population, budget cuts in after-school and outreach programs for teenagers, more gun violence and a complacency in communities where murder rates have fallen the past several years, experts said.

Yet, local law enforcement agencies caution that changes from year to year in Portland's homicide rate hardly reveal a significant trend. They said the drop in aggravated assaults, for example, is a better indicator of what's happening in the city.

Other newspapers have found ways to make crime coverage relevant. One of the earliest large-scale civic journalism projects was in Charlotte, North Carolina, where the *Charlotte Observer* and its partners examined high-crime neighborhoods through extended conversations with residents. The series, called "Taking back Our Neighborhoods," presented an overview of the city's crime problem before looking at several target areas. In each neighborhood, reporters met with church and civic leaders. The paper, along with a television station, several radio stations and the United Way, sponsored community meetings to give residents a chance to speak about the problem. The newspaper's facilitation of community forums was controversial but, in the view of public journalism advocates Davis Merritt and Maxwell McCombs, effective. "They demonstrated, in their reporting and through the forums the broad public interest that lay beneath the problem of dangerous neighborhoods," they wrote.

Another approach has been suggested by the Berkeley Media Studies Group: treating crime and violence as public health problems. "Violence is a difficult epidemic to understand [and] control because no one factor—elimination or redesign of guns, decrease in availability of alcohol or reduction of media violence—will prevent all violence," Jane Stevens wrote in the Berkeley group's handbook for journalists. Instead, she recommends, news reports should seek to explain the complex factors that cause violent crime—and include suggestions from community leaders about how to prevent it.

Stevens suggested that news stories address risk factors that contributed to the crime (the availability of a gun, relationship between suspect and victims and use of alcohol) and address consequences of the crime (such as hospitalization for victims and care for children in the household). Reporters who view themselves as public safety reporters instead of just the police reporter are more inclined to ask these kinds of questions. The responses can allow a more nuanced version of crime and its causes than the conventional crime story formula allows.

Crime on Campus

Crime at colleges and universities attracted national attention after the 1986 murder of Jeanne Ann Clery, a freshman at Lehigh University. Her parents, Connie and Howard Clery, were outraged that students were unaware about numerous reports of violence and had failed to take proper precautions. In 1986, the Clerys founded a group called Security on Campus to push for passage of state and federal laws requiring full disclosure of campus crime records. Congress passed the Campus Crime Security Act, sometimes called the Jeanne Clery Law, which compels colleges and universities to annually report certain categories of crime. Some states have similar laws. The U.S. Department of Education maintains a Web site with campus security statistics designed to help potential students and their parents know the safety records of colleges and universities they might attend.

Some higher education leaders have resisted full disclosure, fearing it will hurt recruiting and their school's image. Reporters need to assert their rights to examine not just the mandated annual reports but also daily police blotters, incident reports and information

PROFESSIONAL TIPS

Maxine Bernstein

Maxine Bernstein has been a reporter for the *Oregonian* since 1998, covering police and law enforcement. Prior to that, she spent seven years as a reporter at the *Hartford Courant* in Connecticut, covering everything from municipal news in a suburban bureau to business and legislative news to, ultimately, the Hartford Police Department. Bernstein is a graduate of Cornell University, where she majored in history.

Question: How does a reporter get started on the police beat?

First, the reporter should meet separately with the chief of police, the police public information officer [PIO] and the captains or officers who head each of the major police divisions, such as detectives, drugs and vice, traffic and internal affairs. These meetings should be informal, with the reporter trying to learn each officer's background and obtain general information about each division and its role in the department. In addition, the reporter should obtain public records on the department, including a roster of the police officers who are employed, the police department's budget and any police bureau policies or directives. Also, the reporter should begin to attend any oversight meetings, if there is a police commission that reviews the police department's work, and a citizens' review board that reviews complaints against police.

Question: Who are a reporter's best sources—public information officers, police chiefs and captains or cops on the beat?

Cops on the beat are the best sources for information on what is going on inside the department. Public information officers generally provide the barest information or details on a crime or police incident. Speak directly to the detectives who were at the scene of a crime, or the officers who were the first to respond to a police call—they will have the crucial details that you will want for your story.

Question: How do you get your sources to trust you without compromising your independence?

The best way to obtain a source's trust is to gain their respect over time, just as in any relationship. If you show that you are serious, and want to learn what really happened and find out as much as you can about a certain subject or incident, and report stories fairly and accurately, you will gain the trust of sources.

Question: What types of crime stories are often overlooked by inexperienced police reporters?

How victims are impacted by crimes, if there are any trends or patterns of crimes emerging. How police are attempting to prevent crimes from occurring. Police budget stories that might impact police enforcement. And, overall, putting a crime story in context: is it a rarity? Is there a serial problem? If there's a new policy adopted by a police department, check other police agencies and how it compares to what other departments do.

Question: What are the three most important things to remember about covering a major crime?

1. Try to speak directly to the detectives or officers who handled the crime scene or witnesses who were present.

(continued)

PROFESSIONAL TIPS   Continued

2. Check backgrounds of people you are writing about—i.e., a suspect may have a court record that could provide detailed information that would be appropriate for the story.
3. Verify police information and spelling of names and dates of birth. The PIO's information is not always accurate. Get phone numbers of witnesses you interview at the scene of a major crime so you can contact them later if you have follow-up questions.

Question: What advice do you have for avoiding errors and improving the accuracy of law enforcement and crime coverage?

Number 1, don't trust the police public information officer's spelling of names, dates of birth, etc.— verify the information through other means, i.e., public records, DMV, witnesses, court records. If there are conflicting accounts of what occurred, between cops and witnesses, report those conflicting accounts; don't simply report what police tell you.

---

about offenses handled through the student judicial system rather than criminal courts. The Student Press Law Center is a helpful resource for student journalists seeking access to records (see chapter 7 on access).

The following suggestions apply to coverage of all law enforcement agencies, but are especially applicable to campus police or security departments:

- **Get out of** the office. Make personal contacts with dispatchers, detectives and patrol officers so they can match a face to your name when you call later.

- **Make sure the** chief or public information officer knows when you need a response. Don't miss a comment or explanation because of a misunderstanding over a deadline.

- **Develop good working** relationships before a crisis, so that whoever is in charge of releasing information knows you can be trusted to report facts reliably.

- **If you make** a mistake, inform the source before she or he sees it in print or on the air, and run a correction promptly.

- **Do stories about** department operations—training, new vehicles or equipment, awards—not just about crimes.

- **Choose your battles.** Don't file an open-records request or threaten to sue if waiting a day and talking to someone else will produce the information you seek.

The best campus crime stories do more than present statistics; they place those numbers in context through comparisons to previous years and other colleges. A reporter can add depth by showing high-crime locations, offering explanations for changes in certain crime categories and suggesting ways that students can protect themselves against crime. Here is an example by Jim Foster of the *Coloradoan* about crime at Colorado State University that uses an anecdotal lead to introduce the annual summary of crimes:

CSU Sees Drop in Crime

But Campus Police Say Don't Let Down Your Guard

Jason Garcia feels so safe on the Colorado State University campus, he is willing to leave his backpack sitting in a hall for hours, knowing it will be there when he gets back.

Campus police, obviously, don't recommend that. And computer database research done by the *Coloradoan* shows why.

When a crime is committed on campus it is usually a theft. And most thefts, CSU Police Chief Donn Hopkins said, are books and backpacks taken from the library or Lory Student Center.

"I grew up in Denver, and the crime here is nothing compared to what happens in Denver," Garcia said. "I don't even hear other students talking about crime, or the campus not being safe. I don't see it as a problem at all."

The numbers support his assumption. The total number of crimes reported in 1997 dropped 18 percent to 2,587, down from 3,142 in 1996. The most reported crimes were thefts, vandalism and liquor violations.

But students shouldn't let their guard down, Hopkins warns. Drug use is up 25 percent from this time last year.

"It's difficult to say exactly what will happen," Hopkins said. "But the amount of crime, usually property crimes and assaults, can be correlated to the amount of drug use and alcohol abuse."

Hopkins said drugs and alcohol are involved in about 80 percent of the crimes reported at CSU.

That could be one reason the number of forcible rapes has increased 167 percent since 1997. In 1997, eight rapes were reported, up from three in 1995.

Other reasons for the increase in rapes could be better coordination with Women's Programs and Studies on campus.

"We are encouraging the victims to report these crimes," Hopkins said. "And if a victim approaches the Women's Studies program, they now contact us, and we contact them. We are working together to prevent this."

Ruth Carrothers, assistant director of Women's Programs and Studies at CSU, agreed better education programs are resulting in more rapes being reported. . . .

"On campus, the perpetrator is usually under the influence of drugs or alcohol," Hopkins said. "And it is an acquaintance scenario. It isn't when someone is waiting in the shadows to attack someone. We don't have those kinds of assaults here." . . .

CSU breaks police reports into 27 categories. From 1996 to 1997, seven of the 27 categories, including forcible rapes, showed increases. The others were harassment, burglary, theft from auto, bicycle theft, fraud and embezzlement.

Holding Agencies Accountable

A major part of a police reporter's job is to serve as a watchdog of law enforcement agencies, assessing performance and determining whether taxpayers are getting the services they pay for and deserve. Reporters have a responsibility to seek out, uncover and document police abuses. Because law enforcement agencies have the power to employ deadly force to carry out their duties, stories that examine training, use of weapons and high-speed automobile chases are always in the public interest.

These stories, of course, also might jeopardize a reporter's relationship with not only the agency that becomes the target of the investigation but other departments on the beat. For that reason, editors must be prepared to back up a reporter who is subject to retaliation through withholding information or refusal to respond to inquiries. Top editors or executives shouldn't hesitate to go directly to the sheriff or police chief. News organizations must stand up to complaints and assert their right to fully cover internal investigations, disciplinary hearings and penalties. Police officials need to be reminded that the public has a legitimate interest in how the agency operates.

Disasters and Tragedies

The law enforcement beat includes coverage of human tragedies—violent crimes, automobile accidents, tornadoes, floods and fires. Yet these events also have great potential for stories of courage and heroism that show the power of the human spirit to cope with adversity.

"The best of journalism takes people to places and events where they need to be," writes Bob Steele, the former director of the ethics program at the Poynter Institute. "It gives people information and insight needed to process what is happening, even if it produces more questions than answers in the short run, even if it upsets us and shakes our foundations."

One of the most difficult parts of a reporter's job is approaching family members of victims of a crime or disaster. The public's perception that journalists are callous and insensitive comes in part from the image of a television reporter confronting grieving relatives with the absurd question of "How do you feel?" Fortunately, such episodes occur with less frequency as broadcast journalists become more aware that other types of questions are more likely to produce better responses.

Experts, such as Roger Simpson of the Dart Center for Journalism and Trauma at the University of Washington, recommend patience, compassion and tact in dealing with such situations. If approached carefully, family members can provide telling details about the lives of loved ones that enrich and make meaningful stories of tragedy (for additional tips, see sidebar).

Because of their stoic approach to these stories, police reporters earn a reputation for being aloof and dispassionate—regardless of the magnitude of the events they cover. In fact, these seemingly hard-shelled reporters are often at risk of developing the journalistic equivalent of posttraumatic stress syndrome. Events such as the Oklahoma City bombing in 1995, the Columbine High School shootings in 1999 and the attacks on the World Trade Center and Pentagon in 2001 have heightened awareness of how coming face-to-face with catastrophe affects reporters, editors and photographers.

"Journalists' symptoms of traumatic stress are remarkably similar to those of police officers and firefighters who work in the immediate aftermath of tragedy, yet journalists typically receive little support after they file their stories," Al Tompkins of the Poynter Institute wrote four days after the 9/11 attacks. "While public-safety workers are

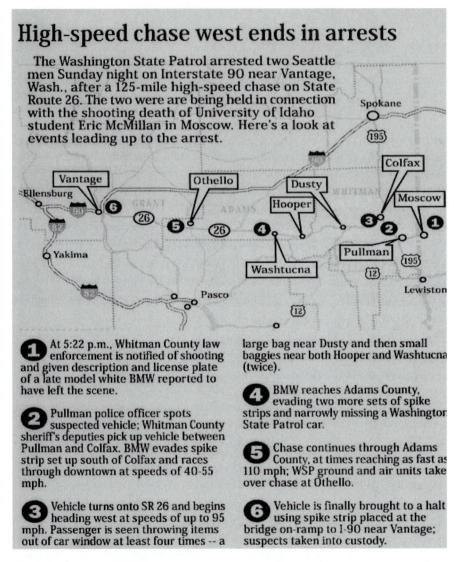

High-speed chase west ends in arrests

The Washington State Patrol arrested two Seattle men Sunday night on Interstate 90 near Vantage, Wash., after a 125-mile high-speed chase on State Route 26. The two were are being held in connection with the shooting death of University of Idaho student Eric McMillan in Moscow. Here's a look at events leading up to the arrest.

1 At 5:22 p.m., Whitman County law enforcement is notified of shooting and given description and license plate of a late model white BMW reported to have left the scene.

2 Pullman police officer spots suspected vehicle; Whitman County sheriff's deputies pick up vehicle between Pullman and Colfax. BMW evades spike strip set up south of Colfax and races through downtown at speeds of 40-55 mph.

3 Vehicle turns onto SR 26 and begins heading west at speeds of up to 95 mph. Passenger is seen throwing items out of car window at least four times -- a large bag near Dusty and then small baggies near both Hooper and Washtucna (twice).

4 BMW reaches Adams County, evading two more sets of spike strips and narrowly missing a Washington State Patrol car.

5 Chase continues through Adams County, at times reaching as fast as 110 mph; WSP ground and air units take over chase at Othello.

6 Vehicle is finally brought to a halt using spike strip placed at the bridge on-ramp to I-90 near Vantage; suspects taken into custody.

FIGURE 16.1   Graphics using chronology, like the one above from the *Lewiston Tribune,* have human applications and are often effective in developing ongoing or breaking crime coverage.

The Lewiston Tribune

offered debriefings and counseling after a trauma, journalists are merely assigned another story."

The Dart Center is one of several groups studying ways in which tragedies are covered—and how that coverage affects journalists. Through seminars, publications and its Web site, the Dart Center offers suggestions for presenting news in ways that informs

TIPS FOR INTERVIEWING VICTIMS AND FAMILIES

- Journalists can help victims and survivors tell their stories in ways that are constructive and in ways that make for great journalism.
- Sometimes you can't avoid intruding upon someone in grief. If you can't postpone your contact, remember to be sensitive and respectful in your approach.
- "I'm sorry for your loss" is a good way to start the conversation.
- Don't assume a victim or family member won't want to talk; often they are eager to share their story and memories with a journalist.
- If someone doesn't want to talk to you, be respectful and polite. And don't forget to leave your business card; at some point, the person may decide to talk to a reporter, and they will likely call the one that made the best impression.
- Make sure the person understands the terms of the interview. Tell them: "This is an interview for a story I'm writing. Your quotes will appear in the newspaper along with your name."
- Pay attention to your own emotions during the interview, and let your reactions inform your reporting (while remaining professional).

—Dart Center for Journalism and Trauma, www.dartcenter.org.

without exploiting tragedy and, perhaps most valuable, for how journalists can take care of themselves—both physically and emotionally.

One obvious issue is personal safety. Reporters and photographers often arrive at the scene of a crime, accident or fire before emergency response personnel. Not only must the journalists ascertain the danger at the scene, but they must stay out of the way of those whose job is to restore order and help victims. In some cases, reporters must consider whether to put down their cameras and notebooks to offer first aid or help rescue workers. News photographers, in particular, often find themselves in a situation where human imperatives take precedence over journalistic duties. In the process of reporting a disaster, they must take care not to put themselves at risk—no story is worth death or injury.

After the first- and second-day stories of the disaster are in print or on the air, reporters need a chance to reflect and debrief with a peer from the newsroom—ideally someone who has covered a traumatic event in the past. After the Oklahoma City bombing, Penny Cockerell, a staff writer for the *Oklahoman,* said: "What I really needed was time with fellow journalists . . . to talk through all the things that happened." But when work schedules allowed that sort of retrospective discussion, fatigue caused by overexposure had set in. "Everyone was so tired of the bombing that we never really got [to] have that big hashing out session," Cockerell said.

Reporters should be aware of symptoms of having covered one too many murder, child abuse or domestic violence case. They include fatigue, irritability and depression. Editors need to be aware when a reporter has spent too much time at crime scenes or in courtrooms. A reporter who's not her usual self might benefit from counseling, a temporary reassignment to another beat or some mental-health days away from the office. A change of scenery to pause and reflect may be all that a top-notch reporter needs to regain perspective.

CHAPTER EXERCISES

1. Invite a local police reporter and police chief into a class. Ask each to talk for fifteen minutes about their jobs. Open the session up to questions and answers.

2. After the tenth day of the month, go to your local police station or campus police/security office and ask to see the police log or incident report for the first three days of the month. Detail three good story ideas.

3. Check out your campus crime statistics online. Write an analysis-trend story of your findings for the past three years.

4. Interview a police officer about his or her beliefs on profiling, and write a story.

5. Arrange a ride-along with an officer and write a story, but be sure to clarify with your editor or adviser about potential legal risks if you witness a crime or arrest.

CHAPTER

17

Covering the Courts

BY SUSAN ENGLISH

Sneak Peek

The American judicial system provides a forum for all to speak and be heard. Because of its importance, it needs the watchdog protection of the press.

Journalists too often focus public affairs reporting on the executive and legislative branches of government. The orderly and proper functioning of those branches is, indeed, important to readers, citizens and democracy. Local, state and federal governmental agencies spend taxpayers' dollars in a very linear way. They collect taxes, write budgets and spend the money. The traditions of journalism demand that reporters and editors make this process as transparent to citizens as is possible.

However, the umbrella of public affairs reporting should also vigorously be extended over the judicial branch of the government. Journalists should demand as much transparency in the judicial systems as they do from city, county, state and federal officials and agencies.

Princeton University Professor of Religion Cornel West makes a case in his book *Democracy Matters* that it was the courts, or rather juries of citizens, that were the bedrock of democracy in its infancy in Athens, Greece.

West dates the birth of Athenian democracy to peasants revolting against abuse of power by the elite rulers who gathered all of the wealth into the ruling class. The crucial step toward what we might consider a crude democracy occurred with the formation of a new office of archon, which assumed much of the responsibilities of running the government and was separate from the king, according to West. He writes that in 594 B.C., Solon was elected archon and he began incorporating the excluded Athenians, the peasants, not only into the highest government bodies but also into the juries of the new courts.

"These reforms set in motion ideals of equality—of political and judicial equality—and notions of public life predicated on trust between conflicting classes and groups in Athenian society," West writes.

It is the idea that those with the least power in a society can turn to the courts with expectations that the decision rendered will be fair and just that makes democracy work for everyone in a society.

Journalism is inextricably bound to democracy and, while the ruling and lawmaking branches of other forms of government can serve their citizens well, it is in the courts system that a society exhibits its merits and mettle. For it is in the courts that society deals with the most vulnerable citizens, those who would otherwise not have a forum to speak and be heard, and also with its most vile citizens. The courts are charged with maintaining what we all agree is civil behavior and with doing it fairly and in a transparent environment.

Hence, the judicial system is the hallmark of democracy in that it exemplifies what democracy really means to the demos—as the ordinary or common people were called in the ancient Greek city-state democracy.

The Why of Courts Reporting

Journalists covering law enforcement and the court system should see their role as twofold. They should inform citizens that the judicial system is working as it is supposed to and report any instances in which it is not. They should also be a voice for those who are most vulnerable, both the victims and those accused of crimes against society.

If the true measure of a democracy is the way in which those who have committed offenses against the citizens are treated, then missteps and mistreatment harm the trust our society has that democracy is enduring and works well for all.

Many think this trust was badly abused when the U.S. military began detaining an unknown number of people at Guantanamo Bay, Cuba, during the military assault in Afghanistan, and again later in the prisoner abuse scandal at Abu Ghraib prison in Iraq in late 2004.

People asked how a country that exemplified democracy and was engaging in a war to spread democracy could engage in such cloaked activities within the judicial system.

These are questions that journalists should be asking, and they should be reporting to their readers what they learn from such inquiries.

We expect law enforcement officers to arrest and charge suspects with sufficient cause to do so. We expect the courts to uphold the demands of the U.S. Constitution that those charged are given a public trial within a reasonable time frame, with a jury selected from the community and a verdict that is issued publicly. We expect judges to adhere to sentencing guidelines that were debated and drawn publicly. We expect the prison system to treat inmates humanely and fairly.

Journalists act on behalf of the citizens in demanding these expectations be met and consistently followed.

The responsibility to watch and report on the judicial branch of the government is as great as it is to cover the legislative functions and executive actions. It may not seem so. After all, the courts do what they do, and if the inmates stay locked up when and where they should, what is there to report?

Plenty.

According to a story by Gail Russell Chaddock in the *Christian Science Monitor,* by the end of 2001, more than 1.3 million Americans were confined to state and federal prisons. Chaddock said that translates into one in thirty-seven adults living in the United States, the highest incarceration rate in the world. And the report by the Justice Department cited by Chaddock said more than 5.6 million Americans have had prison experience.

The *Christian Science Monitor* article notes if the trends continue, a black male in the United States would have a one-in-three chance of going to prison during his lifetime. In contrast, a Hispanic male would have a one-in-six chance, and a white male would have a one-in-seventeen chance of being incarcerated.

While this article, and many others since 2003, focused on the racial profiles of incarcerated Americans, journalists should also expand their coverage to the effects of such a significant prison population on society at large. This is where stories beyond trial and sentencing coverage can help give readers important context.

Allen Beck, chief of correction statistics at the Bureau of Justice Statistics, who was quoted in the *Christian Science Monitor* story, noted that the impact of incarceration does not end when the inmates are released. In many states, ex-felons are prohibited from voting, which was a hotly debated topic in the 2004 presidential election. In addition, former inmates can be excluded in some states from receiving public assistance, living in public housing or receiving financial aid for college, according to Beck. They could also be ineligible to work in professions such as education, child care, driving a bus or working in a nursing home.

Whose Story Is It?

As with many beats, the courts beat overlaps several others in ways that sometimes require several reporters and their editors to work as a team. Stories that land in the judicial system often begin somewhere in the law enforcement or, less often, military beats.

When the story is being discussed during a story conference, the reporters and editors must first decide who in the newsroom has jurisdiction over the story. It is easy when it comes to covering an individual trial or an escape from the local jail. But homeland security issues have blurred many lines when it comes to deciding whether a story falls to the city hall reporter, the law enforcement team or the courts reporter.

In most newsrooms, the traditional guidelines continue to be these: if the story involves a change in city budget, it goes to the city hall reporter; if the story is happening at the police department, the cops reporter swings into action. By the time it moves to the courtroom, the courts reporter should be on top of it. And in a team-reporting environment, all three reporters and their editors would be having discussions about how to frame the stories and who would do the bulk of the reporting and writing.

Ideally the cops and courts reporters work together toward a smooth handoff of stories from the law enforcement phase to the judicial end. Sometimes there is opportunity for cops and courts reporters to work together, which is especially helpful in complex stories.

The Judicial System

The courts system varies from state to state, especially in the naming of the courts. But the structure of the courts system is consistent in its essence throughout the jurisdictions.

The lowest court in the jurisdiction, whether it is at the municipal, state or federal level, is the trial court, the court of fact finding, juries and verdicts. The court system is divided by civil suits and criminal trials.

Civil suits are disputes between two parties, and the outcome will result in civil penalties rather than incarceration or other penalty determined by society. A civil suit could involve a dispute as minor as neighbors disagreeing over the responsibilities of a shared driveway. More commonly, though, a civil suit is filed by a person seeking to be awarded monetary damages, tangible and often punitive, resulting from car accidents, medical malpractice, breach of contract or some other perceived civil misstep. Civil courts also routinely handle divorces, issues of guardianship, bankruptcies and many property disputes.

Of all of the civil cases covered by reporters, arguably the most common are bankruptcies, for these cases sometimes affect the community in significant ways and hence are of great interest to readers.

Criminal trials can result in penalties imposed by the society in general, whether they are fines, community service or prison confinement. In criminal cases, the government makes charges of a crime against society.

Criminal courts are generally divided into state and federal systems. State courts hear cases involving state statutes or state constitutions; federal courts hear cases involving federal laws, regulations or the U.S. Constitution. Both state and federal systems begin with the trial courts, where the facts of the case are heard and verdicts rendered. Cases can be appealed to appellate courts and then on to the supreme courts, whether they are state high courts or the U.S. Supreme Court.

PROFESSIONAL TIPS

Sheila R. McCann

Sheila R. McCann has covered state and federal courts in Idaho, Washington and Utah. She is now coeditor of the social justice team, which includes court reporters, at the *Salt Lake Tribune* in Salt Lake City, Utah.

Question: Who are the best sources at the courthouse? What advice do you have for cultivating them?

Everyone—bailiffs who know the jury verdict just came in upstairs, court clerks who can help you track down that missing file, lawyers who can tip you to their interesting new filing, judges who can't talk to you about specific cases but can be invaluable mentors to help improve your writing about the law. The courthouse is a community. Be friendly and inquisitive; take the time to get to know it.

Civility and your good work will count—get a reputation for rudeness or for inaccurate stories, and no one will want to help you or talk with you. Be polite and you'll be a noticeable contrast to the brusque lawyers they often endure.

Help clerks help you by—when you can—knowing the case number of the file you want or the filing date of the document you're seeking. Having built good relationships will help on the occasions when you must be assertive about access to documents or hearings.

Question: What types of court stories are often overlooked by inexperienced court reporters?

Follow-up stories. Litigation is like a dance—know what step comes next, and watch for it. Civil and criminal court rules set the pace. When a lawsuit, charge or new document is filed, note how many days the other side has to respond. Keep a log of lawsuits you are covering, and check them regularly. Cultivate those great source relationships, but don't rely on them to do your job.

Electronic access to docket text, if your court offers it, can let you quickly check whether a document has been filed that you should go read. After a high-profile trial, interview jurors.

Learn the appeal process, and how to watch for appellate rulings in cases that you have covered.

Trend stories: what kind of statistics does your court or state keep? Many courts track cases by claim type; in federal courts, for example, you can identify and examine every lawsuit filed under the Americans with Disabilities Act (ADA) for the past five years and see how plaintiffs fared. Are the number of jury trials dropping? Has there been a surge in protection order requests?

Bigger-picture stories: it's not just court reporting, it's the third branch of government, with budgets, committees and annual reports. Check them out. Are judges in your courthouse helping your state study how to improve jury service? Do judges want raises? What will your state's judges be seeking from the next legislature?

Question: What about civil cases—which ones make the best stories?

Checking for new lawsuits can be overwhelming—so many disputes, so little time. To narrow the field: watch for claims against public agencies. Are police officers being accused of using excessive force? Do accident victims claim that a heavily traveled road is poorly designed?

(continued)

PROFESSIONAL TIPS   Continued

Look for lawsuits that raise broader social or consumer issues, such as claiming a commonly used product is unsafe, attacking a company or agency for allegedly unfair policies or challenging state laws. For example, we recently covered a lawsuit filed by a couple who used a surrogate to carry their biological twins, and sued the state when the biological mother was not allowed to put her name on the birth certificates. Or just look for the flat-out interesting. It seems like everything eventually ends up at the courthouse, and it's usually through civil lawsuits. One of the most intriguing trials I've covered was over a psychic's claim that a ski accident damaged her abilities.

You may choose to just make note of a case and let it develop before writing a story. Add it to your log and check periodically to see when to jump in.

Question: What are the three most important things to remember about covering a trial?

Logistics: arrive early to avoid disrupting court and to get a seat close enough to hear a soft-spoken attorney or emotional witness. Don't be shy—introduce yourself to the attorneys, the clerk and family members in the audience. Developing relationships inside this minicommunity can again be an immense help. An attorney who tells you that [a] crucial witness won't be on the stand until tomorrow can save you time and frustration.

While a judge, jurors—and maybe you—need to sit through hours of sometimes tedious testimony, your readers don't. You will likely need to boil a day of hearing evidence into a story that is under twenty inches. Be thinking of a structure for your story and adapt it as the day goes on. Get the best quotes—but don't fill your notebook with technical or routine testimony you won't use, such as the details of the chain of evidence (how an item was transferred from a crime scene to a lab to the courtroom).

The jury is hearing one side at a time, but you can strive to balance your reporting. Try talking to the lawyers and reading pretrial filings. In a story reporting damning expert testimony, for example, you can include a sentence telling read-

ers the defense will call Professor Z to attack the theory of Professor A.

Question: What advice do you have for avoiding errors and improving the accuracy of court coverage?

The best court reporters have learned the culture and language of the courthouse. They can capture the drama but also explain what a case means—which can require your own legal education.

To get it: read. Don't rely on an attorney's sound bite to tell you what a case is about—check what he or she has filed with the court, the judge's ruling, the other side's brief. Is that quote spin? Or an accurate assessment of what the judge said?

When you are covering courts, you are covering conflict—don't trust any one source to give you the full story. If an attorney refuses to comment, keep digging—read his or her filings, check out the exhibits.

Find a mentor (or many) who is willing to help you learn not only the mechanics of the legal system but how to translate legalese for readers. A judge or attorney who is willing to talk with you—not to be quoted, but to explain a term or critique your translation—can be invaluable, especially on deadline.

Also seek sources outside the courthouse—law professors, retired judges, attorneys with expertise on an issue you are covering—who can give you an independent point of view.

Question: How can a reporter produce in-depth stories about the working of the justice system without sacrificing daily coverage? Any tips on balancing the two?

This is a classic problem on any beat. A court reporter, however, might have days when no hearings are scheduled or newsworthy filings are due. If a day like that is looming in your week—and nothing breaks—try to use it for enterprise work. A big sentencing in the morning? Try turning [in] that daily promptly and using a few hours of the afternoon for research.

(continued)

PROFESSIONAL TIPS   Continued

Use the trapped-in-the-courthouse times you'll have. (Waiting on a jury? Check a file.)

If you want to pull off something big, try pairing up with another reporter. Some of my favorite court reporting and editing has involved database projects, a powerful way to cover what is happening in your courthouse. But they often take more spadework than one reporter, still turning dailies, can accomplish alone.

Here's a relatively quick one: in 1995, fallout from the Anita Hill testimony at the confirmation hearings of U.S. Supreme Court Justice Clarence

Thomas had some people muttering that women could just head to the courthouse and cash in. That didn't sound correct to fellow court reporter Ted Cilwick and me, so we created a database of all sexual harassment claims filed at Utah's federal courthouse between 1988 and 1995. With just two reporters, the research, our main story showing conventional wisdom was wrong, graphics and sidebars came together swiftly. Besides having fun, we gave readers original research and a story they couldn't get anywhere else.

The trial courts in the federal system are called U.S. District Courts, and there is at least one in every state, and more in states with greater populations where more cases are tried.

Federal appeals are heard in the U.S. Circuit Court of Appeals, of which there are thirteen. Courts have jurisdiction over a geographic area, so cases within one area cannot be appealed to a court in a different jurisdiction.

Appeals from circuit courts are made to the U.S. Supreme Court; however, the highest court does not have to hear all appeals. In fact, only a small number of the appeals are heard every year by the U.S. Supreme Court. The U.S. Supreme Court is in session from October through June, and it alternates between two weeks of hearing arguments and two weeks of recess during which decisions are written.

In addition to the cases that are appealed to the U.S. Supreme Court from the circuit courts, cases that come through the state systems to the state supreme courts can also be appealed to the U.S. Supreme Court.

The decisions made by the higher courts are called *precedents.* In future cases, the lower courts might look to these precedents for guidance in the rulings. State courts are not bound to follow the precedents set by federal courts on state matters, nor do the U.S. District and Circuit Courts have to abide by state law or the precedents set in the state in which they are located. U.S. District Courts, however, must abide by the rulings of the circuit court in whose jurisdiction they are located, but the rulings of the various circuit courts do not have to be followed by courts in other jurisdictions. All courts must follow the rulings made by the U.S. Supreme Court.

Unless reporters have a U.S. District or Circuit Court in their area, most courts reporters cover local and state trials.

Generally the first time a courts reporter gets involved in a story is when criminal charges are filed against a person through an indictment or the filing of "an information," presented by a public officer, such as a prosecuting attorney.

An indictment can come from a grand jury, which looks at the evidence and determines there is sufficient cause for binding the accused over for trial.

The first court appearance is an arraignment where the charges are read and, typically, the accused enters a plea. If the plea is not guilty, then the defense and prosecuting attorneys might engage in plea bargaining, during which the defense attorney and his client might agree to plead guilty to a lesser charge. Many criminal cases end through plea bargaining.

If the case proceeds, a preliminary hearing is called to review probable cause for moving the case to trial.

The trial begins with jury selection from a jury pool. The prosecutor, then the defense, make opening statements, then they present evidence in that order.

Both attorneys make final motions and closing statements, and the judge reads the instructions to the jury. Following deliberation, the jury returns with a verdict, and if the accused is found guilty, the judge sets a date for sentencing.

In most states, death penalties are appealed automatically.

Of course, not all trials are covered by the news media. Reporters generally select those that have some inherent news value, whether it is a particularly egregious crime that was committed, the person accused has some notoriety or the crime or case is part of a larger trend in the community.

Few newspapers have the resources to cover all trials. In deciding the merits of a particular case, sometimes it is also helpful to talk to the attorney prosecuting the case. Usually the defense attorney is also willing to talk to reporters about his or her client.

Because trials can last for days and sometimes weeks, covering a trial can be challenging. The events seem to unfold incrementally, and sometimes readers who do not understand the trial procedures accuse journalists of being biased. They say trial coverage is telling only one side at a time and that stories are not balanced. This is a challenge for reporters since the prosecution makes its case against the accused, calling its witnesses.

Even though the defense attorney can question these witnesses, days of testimony can appear to the uninformed reader as though the coverage is weighted against the accused. Then the defense takes over, and stories can look as though they are focused only on the story of the accused.

For this reason, courts reporters should take care to provide context in every story. It seems repetitive, but not all readers understand the trial process.

When deciding which trials to cover, and during the stories about the trial itself, journalists should keep in mind the reasons for covering the courts. Readers need to know that the judicial system works and that it renders verdicts that are fair and just; and what goes on in the courts in a community is the news of the day.

It might seem easier to wait until the trial is over before reporting the outcome, but what is said about the accused and who said it is news. The best courts reporters view trials as a serial story, feeding out each day's drama in the courtroom. Trials can be great narratives, which should have fully developed characters, plots, context and back stories.

Reporters may handle the early developments of a court case in the local briefs column of the newspaper. When the accused is arraigned, for example, the charges against him or her are read and an initial plea of guilt or innocence is entered.

The cases that will be heard in each courtroom at the county, state and federal courthouses will be posted on dockets. The court clerks keep track of the dockets, so reporters new to the beat or the community should introduce themselves to the court clerks, who can be very helpful. Courts reporters often check daily with the court clerks to see what cases have been put on the docket, and which cases were delayed that were scheduled to be heard.

When actually covering a trial, the journalist each day must be able to take what amounts to hundreds of pages of testimony and accurately summarize what happened that day in court in a few hundred words. It requires great narrative ability to move the story along and continue to keep it in context.

Cases and precedents can be tracked via legal citations, which are like addresses. The citation lists the name of the plaintiff first, then the defendant, the volume number and court record books in which the case is filed, the page on which it can be found, the court in which the case was tried and the year of the decision. If the case is appealed, the plaintiff's and defendant's names could be reversed depending on which filed the appeal. Subsequent appeals are listed after the initial citation, and the outcome of the appeal is indicated.

Journalists should familiarize themselves with local and state court systems and the restrictions particular to their jurisdiction. Rules regarding coverage of juveniles vary between jurisdictions, but tend to be the most restrictive. Generally, the names of juveniles arrested are not released, media coverage of the trials may be restricted and sometimes the court proceedings are not public record, as they are for all adult courts. Even when juveniles are tried as adults, there might be some restrictions as to what journalists can obtain and report.

Many of the issues such as the availability of information about juvenile defendants are discussed during meetings of local bench–bar–press groups. Often these groups begin meeting at the initiative of the newspaper editor, who sees them as an opportunity for the courts, law enforcement and media to work toward agreements that serve all these parties well. The discussions can range from when information is made available to the media by law enforcement agencies to the effectiveness of judicial gag orders.

If such a group is not meeting in your community, suggest starting such a discussion to your editor. Often the courts and cops reporters accompany the newspaper editor or city editor at these meetings. Seldom are the agreements between interests legally binding, but the discussion facilitates a better working arrangement. Models of bench–bar–press committees are available from several national journalism groups.

Students who aspire to courts reporting should consider also taking courses in American government and criminal justice, as well as the journalism history and mass media law courses usually required of journalism majors.

Resources

A great resource for students learning about the judicial system is the Student Press Law Center (www.splc.org). The center, headquartered in Arlington, Virginia, opened in 1974 with support of the Robert F. Kennedy Memorial and the Reporters Committee for Freedom of the Press.

The SPLC is an independent, not-for-profit corporation that provides free legal advice, information and assistance to high school and college journalists.

A number of publications are available from the SPLC, including "Law of the Student Press," a handbook to legal decisions that affect student journalists and their publications;

and "Covering Campus Crime: A Handbook for Journalists." Both publications should be among the resources that student journalists at all levels have access to and use regularly.

When student journalists join the professional ranks, they should be familiar with and use the many resources available through the Reporters Committee for Freedom of the Press (www.rcfp.org).

CHAPTER EXERCISES

1. Make a list of courts in your community. Invite a prosecuting attorney and a public defense attorney to class to talk about their experiences in interacting with journalists.

2. Spend a day shadowing the courts reporter from the local newspaper.

3. Invite a judge from one of the criminal courts in your community to talk to the class about trial procedures and restrictions on the press in his or her courtroom.

4. If time and class schedules allow, sit in on a trial from the opening arguments to the reading of the verdict, and list which developments would warrant a daily story. Write at least one daily story from the trial.

5. Access the archives from a local newspaper, and assemble the articles that were published on a single trial, from the arraignment to the reading of the verdict. Lead a class discussion about whether the scope of each article was encompassing enough to fulfill the imperatives of watching the function of the court system and capturing the news of the day.

18 Education

BY JOHN IRBY

There are numerous stories that can be found from the halls of educational institutions. While access is sometimes difficult because of student rights and privacy issues, education is one of the most important public affairs beats.

One of the roles of newspapers, large and small, is to foster or encourage discussion, or to create community dialog. Covering education is an area of public affairs reporting where a journalist can foster or spur a great deal of discussion.

Most beat reporters will swear the beat they cover is the most compelling and necessary topic for their newspaper. But the education beat might actually be, especially at smaller dailies and even weeklies.

That might likely be the case at a newspaper such as the *Moscow-Pullman Daily News*, which circulates in two communities eight miles apart. One reason is a 12,000-student population at the University of Idaho in Moscow, Idaho, and a 19,000-student population at Washington State University in Pullman, Washington.

On top of serving more than 30,000 college students, the newspaper also covers K–12 school districts in both communities, as well as those in outlying areas.

The Importance of Coverage

Education coverage is important for many reasons, but one is paramount: people realize education will shape the lives of their children, and many parents are eager to be in on as much of the shaping as possible.

Education is a lifelong process, an integral part of everyone's life. Take, for instance, my household. As I began this book project, I had a son in day care, one in elementary school, one in middle school and one in high school. My wife was a student working on her MBA. And I learn many new things daily.

Most also realize their property taxes go to pay for schools, so they have a vested interest in the education process. And because of the amount of money generated from taxes and other government funds, there is potential for mismanagement and misuse.

In a survey by the Education Writers of America, 40 percent of those surveyed said they were most interested in news about public schools, ahead of 36 percent who said they were interested in crime and 22 percent in economic news.

The same survey showed that readers want more education stories about substance, and less about conflict. More than three-quarters wanted news about standards, curriculum, safety, innovative programs and quality of teachers.

It isn't uncommon for parents to consider four things about their child's education, and all of these are areas reporters need to consider.

- **Is my child attending a school with good facilities?**
- **Is my child safe at school?**
- **What is my child learning?**
- **Is my child challenged?**

There are other reasons why education is an important coverage topic. While parents, celebrities, entertainers and famous people have influential opportunities, teachers and professors are often selected as the individual who made the most difference in a person's life.

The quality of what is being taught—and how it is being taught—therefore need to be closely monitored and reviewed. Public school systems are often the largest entity in a town or city, affect the most lives and employ the most people. Subject matter is also usually more readable because of its pleasant and positive nature than, say, the sometimes gruesome police beat; nor is it often as complicated as medicine, science or health.

Beat Sources and Stories

Like in all reporting, familiarity with the subject matter, and cultivating and developing sources, are critical. As an education reporter, you will need to develop working relationships with the key people in the schools you cover; teachers, principals, aides, union representatives, cooks, nurses, librarians, custodians, clerks, and so on.

If a university, community school district or individual school has a public information officer (PIO), you must also utilize them as a source as they will be the official source of much information.

But the PIO, who is loyal to her school or district or university employer, will often only provide information approved for release by someone higher up the food chain.

When you know "Bob" the custodian, or "Mary" the librarian, or "Sally" the cook, you have expanded your source network and will often be given tips that will not come from officials.

To develop sources, as in other beats, it is necessary to get out of the office, meet and work with people and use documents as a supplement; don't get stuck behind a desk and gather all your facts on the phone. And remember, complete reporting includes seeking undercovered voices and not simply getting too close to the bureaucrats or too familiar with their jargon—the easy way out.

Another caution in working with education sources is learning their attitude or mindset. There can be, and often is, an ivory tower mentality, especially as coverage escalates up the educational ladder.

Many administrators, faculty members and teachers seem to have an attitude that not much is happening in society unless it happens here—in their own world—first. To put it nicely, there is a bit of arrogance.

Too many in the field of education tend to talk down to reporters and aren't always responsive to questions, not only in providing a response but also in timeliness of a response. Things don't always move quickly in academia.

Educators and administrators are also apt to use long and confusing terms and language, or jargon. For instance, buildings without stairs can be "barrier-free modifications."

The best sources, however, are students and parents, even though they are the most difficult to utilize, often because of the protective nature of school administrators who hide behind laws, or at least interpret them to their advantage, in an effort to keep information private.

People in education, most often parents, students and teachers, are the key to fascinating stories, and they don't always have to be related to traditional educational facilities.

Consider alternative sources and stories: a homemaker learning computer skills at a job-training center, a refugee learning a new language, an older/reentry student, a special student.

Too many education stories are generated from official meetings and sources, but that doesn't mean they can be avoided. There is nothing wrong—and everything right—with just dropping by a board member's office to talk. Not to interview her for a story, but just to talk. Find out what is on her mind. Find out what issues she believes are important in education. Develop a relationship with her outside officialdom.

Staff and teachers should be treated the same. Sure, you will have official contact with them, and getting into a classroom is a great way to get story ideas through general observation, but getting together in other areas—often not even as an official reporter—will help build relationships and bring quality stories.

Students are a gold mine of stories. They have varied interests from art, to music, to computers, to sports, to business/stocks, to gambling, to volunteerism, to whatever. But when using them as a source, be cautious.

Ask questions they can answer. For instance, it wouldn't be advisable to ask elementary students why terrorists attacked the United States on September 11, 2001. How could they answer? The brightest minds in the country might have several ideas (which could be wrong), but how would an 11-year-old be able to answer that question?

Allow plenty of time for interviews. Give students an opportunity to answer. It is difficult, but oftentimes as the person asking the questions, you need to keep silent, waiting for the student to form his or her thoughts.

Don't print everything students say. There should be different standards for preteens, teens, college students and adults. Up to the age of 18, many feel reporters shouldn't include comments that could hurt a student.

Consider parental permission for controversial interviews. This obviously won't always be possible, especially in breaking news. But when possible, such as for a feature story on teen contraceptives, seek parents out to find how they feel about their juvenile son or daughter going on the record.

Don't ask leading questions. Students will sometimes want to please adults or just go with the flow, so it is likely you will get different answers to questions that are phrased differently. For instance, "I've heard a high percentage of high school students use drugs or alcohol," might get agreement, but a question like "Tell me the extent of alcohol and drug use" might get a different and more realistic response.

There are several additional learning sources—or areas where story ideas can be obtained: educational research organizations, trade or professional organizations, accrediting bodies (those that set standards), magazines such as the *Chronicle of Higher Education,* newsletters (PTA), school board minutes, Internet resources (such as a school district Web site or the Web site of the Education Writers Association) and even other newspapers.

Some might claim that the following list of stories is a list of conflict stories, but a strong case can also be made that they are interesting ideas that have been undercovered.

- **An after-school Bible class**
- **A graduation prayer**
- **Teen sex values**
- **Library Internet filters that block Web sites**

Performance stories are another area to consider: are there student or parental concerns with standardized tests? How many students are graduating and finding jobs? Numbers, however, can overwhelm a story or can be spun in many different ways, so be careful.

In performance stories concentrate on people, getting behind and beyond the raw numbers to explain why students are doing well or poorly.

Money stories are another area of interest. How are legislative budget cuts affecting schools? How much money actually goes to teaching? How much do administrators make? Will raises be cut or eliminated? What impacts will less money have on students?

Other areas to consider are teaching methods and curriculum. Clearly this is critical to what and how students learn. In writing these stories, reporters need to use examples, anecdotes and dialogue. Compare and contrast methods. Get student voices into the discussion, not just the administrator or teacher behind the efforts. Access the cost, time and effort involved.

Legalities

The Family Educational Rights and Privacy Act (FERPA) of 1974, also known as the Buckley Amendment after its principal sponsor, Senator James Buckley of New York, guards the privacy of student education records.

All schools receiving U.S. Department of Education funds fall under the act, which generally provides that schools must have written permission from an eligible parent or student before information from the student's education record can be released.

The general nature of the law presents a great deal of interpretational latitude. The law, however, allows for release under certain other nebulous conditions, including the following:

- **School officials with** legitimate educational interest
- **Other schools to** which a student is transferring
- **Specified officials for** audit or evaluation purposes
- **Appropriate parties in** connection with financial aid to a student
- **Organizations conducting certain** studies for or on behalf of the school
- **Accrediting organizations**
- **To comply with** a judicial order or lawfully issued subpoena
- **Appropriate officials in** cases of health and safety emergencies

Questions abound. What is a legitimate educational interest? Who are specified officials? What are the audit or evaluation purposes? Who are appropriate parties? What are certain studies? What constitutes a health or safety emergency?

FERPA does allow disclosure without consent, in most cases, of "directory" information such as a student's name, address, telephone number, date and place of birth, honors and awards and dates of attendance.

The penalty or punishment for a violation of FERPA can be the loss of federal funding, something most universities absolutely can't afford, thus the secrecy and/or caution with the release of information.

Many colleges and universities have used FERPA to keep from reporting campus crime information, and even today many claim that campus disciplinary proceedings can't be released because of FERPA, something that is strongly debated by many.

The Student Right to Know and Campus Security Act, however, requires the reporting of campus crime statistics. Still, that isn't always the case, even though the Clery Act contains amendments allowing postsecondary institutions to disclose to the alleged victim of a violent crime the results of any disciplinary proceeding conducted by the institution against the alleged perpetrator of the crime, regardless of the outcome of the proceeding.

Jeanne Ann Clery was tortured, raped, sodomized and murdered in her dormitory room at Lehigh University during the early morning hours of April 5, 1986. Her killer was a drug and alcohol abuser, a Lehigh student whom Clery had never met. He gained access to her room by proceeding, unopposed, through three propped-open doors, each of which should have been locked. He was convicted and sentenced to death.

Security on Campus, Inc. suggests that some colleges circumvent open records laws by channeling campus crime through student judicial procedures.

Many schools have clear policies on what can and can't be released: releasable or directory information includes the following:

- **Student name**
- **Local and permanent addresses**
- **Local telephone number**
- **Date and place of birth**
- **Citizenship**
- **Degrees and awards received**
- **Residency status**
- **Academic level**
- **Major**
- **College**
- **Dates of attendance**
- **Participation in officially recognized activities and sports**
- **Weight/height of members of athletic teams**
- **Most recent previous educational institution attended**

Nonreleasable or personal information includes the following:

- **All other information**
- **Any information,** including directory information that the student has indicated will not be released

The *all other* category of nonreleasable information, however, is often challenged. Some records held by universities do not fall under FERPA, even though universities claim that the information is protected or exempt from being released. That information includes the following:

- **Records in the** sole possession of school officials
- **Records maintained by** a law enforcement unit of the educational institution
- **Records of an** educational institution's nonstudent employees
- **Records on a** student who is 18 years of age or older or who attends a postsecondary institution that are maintained by a health professional

As an example, in 1992 FERPA was amended to exempt records created for law enforcement purposes and maintained by law enforcement units of educational institutions from the definition of education records. This means law enforcement records, such as police crime logs, are not protected from disclosure by FERPA. In fact, the Clery Act requires any educational institution receiving federal funds to keep its police logs available for public inspection during normal business hours.

Furthermore, in 1998 Congress amended FERPA to clarify that schools may disclose to the public the final results of any disciplinary proceeding in which a student has been found responsible for a crime of violence or nonforcible sex offense. Although it is not a requirement, many public schools might have to release it under state open-records laws.

Final results of disciplinary proceedings is defined as the name of the student who was found responsible for the offense, the violation committed and the sanction imposed by the school.

Also, buried within the No Child Left Behind Act is a provision requiring public secondary schools to provide military recruiters not only with access to facilities but also with contact information for every student—or face a loss of federal aid.

The Ames, Iowa, *Tribune* had the following to say about the Buckley Amendment in an editorial titled "An Absurd Policy."

> It seems like only yesterday—in fact it was only yesterday—that we were talking about the Buckley Amendment.
>
> That's the federal law that bans schools and colleges from disclosing information about individual students—grade points, disciplinary actions and other student records. The law, passed in 1974, says a school can release only the kind of information found in a student directory or on an athletic roster—the name and address, the weight and the height of a student.
>
> That sort of thing. Even parents can be told no more.
>
> It's absurd, of course. It's absurd that it must be a secret when a student violates the rules of a taxpayer-supported university—during the annual Veishea celebration, say—while it's a public document if he violates the very same rule that is framed as a municipal ordinance. But that's what the law says: no disclosure of discipline, no disclosure of records, no disclosure of grades.
>
> How, then, can universities release the names and grade points of those "scholar-athletes" that they are so proud of? Iowa State has 124 athletes who had a grade point of 3.0 or better in the last two semesters, and last month it released that list—with names and grade points. How could it do that?
>
> Curious, we asked the university for the grade points of all the other athletes—figuring if it could tell us that basketball player Paul Shirley had a 3.78 grade point in pre-engineering it could also tell us the grade point of, say, his teammate Tony Rampton. But Athletic Director Gene Smith politely declined. "The Athletic Department and Iowa State University are prohibited from releasing this information without the permission of the student-athletes," he said. "The information is protected by the Family Educational Rights and Privacy Act of 1974." That's the Buckley Amendment.
>
> Suspecting that that might be the answer, we had asked, at the same time, for a copy of the document that the smart athletes signed voluntarily giving permission to have their good grades announced. Smith enclosed a copy—it's NCAA Form 97-3a, in case you want a copy—and assured us that all athletes had signed it. Indeed, the form says every athlete must sign "to participate in intercollegiate competition."
>
> So much for voluntary consents.
>
> That left us even more confused. If every athlete must sign it, how come the university would release the grade points of only the smart athletes? What's more, we could find no place on the form that gave anyone permission to release the grade point of any athlete, smart or not-so-smart. The form merely authorizes the release of grades to "authorized representatives" of the school and the conference and the NCAA. And it adds:
>
> > You agree to disclose these records only to determine your eligibility for intercollegiate athletics, your eligibility for athletically related financial aid, for purposes of

(continued)

(continued)

inclusion in summary institutional information reported to the NCAA (and which may be publicly released by it), for NCAA longitudinal research studies and for activities related to the NCAA athletics certification program and NCAA compliance reviews.

Names and grades of individual athletes constitute a lot more than "summary institutional information" (and, besides, the grade points were released by the school, not the NCAA), so we went back to Gene Smith and conceded we were more confused than ever. Where is the consent to release the grade points? we asked. Where is the distinction that allows Iowa State to release the grade points of some athletes but not others? we asked. And since there doesn't seem to be any such consent or any such distinction, once again could we have the grade points of those athletes with less than a 3.0 average.

Gene—who must be awfully busy dealing with an insurrection on the women's volleyball team and a volatile men's basketball coach who may or may not be heading off to the Chicago Bulls—was unbelievably patient with us. It turns out there had been an oversight, he said, and he thanked us for bringing it to his attention. But he still can't give us the grades of the not-so-smart athletes. For now there's a new form. He faxed it to us.

"I specifically authorize and permit the Director of Athletics to authorize the public release of specific information about my academic excellence (3.0 G.P.A. or higher) for purposes of academic recognition," it says. From now on, Smith said, Iowa State athletes will be signing this form as well as the NCAA form.

So that's that. It's wrong, of course. It's wrong to keep secret the grade points of all but the smartest athletes. That's like giving baseball box scores that don't say who committed the errors, or basketball statistics that don't list the missed free throws, or football results that give the passing statistics only of those quarterbacks with high completion rates.

You can make a case—at least we can—that it's every bit as important for the public to know how those junior-college recruits are doing in the classroom as it is to know how the very smartest are doing. You can make a case that if an athlete must sign any release form—such as the NCAA form—then the university could make any student involved in any extracurricular activity sign a form saying his grades could be released or, especially, any disciplinary proceeding against him could be released.

None of that will happen, of course, for Iowa State University is an institution built on secrecy—secrecy that lets it hide everything from the discipline (if any) of faculty plagiarizers to the names of student troublemakers. But it's happy to tell us the grade points of athletes who do well—even if it violates the law in doing so.

Now, of course, it no longer violates the law in doing that.

So smart athletes can bask in glory.

And not-so-smart ones can scrape by in secrecy.

Unfortunately, similar activities occur at universities and in public school systems across the nation.

Structure and Other Information

The structure of education is usually fairly simplistic. School districts are often established within city boundaries. They are usually independent of city government or officials, and are controlled by an elected school board of between five to seven members. The school

PROFESSIONAL TIPS

Hannelore Sudermann

Hannelore Sudermann is a senior writer/assistant editor of *Washington State* magazine at Washington State University. She began her job in late 2004 after ten years as a newspaper journalist, the last several as staff writer and Moscow-Pullman bureau chief for the *Spokesman-Review* in Spokane, Washington (a 120,000-circulation daily newspaper). In that position, Sudermann covered higher education.

Question: Why is education coverage important?

Big picture: the future of a society depends on the education of its citizens. It is important to remind the public of the crucial role education plays in not only providing a well-trained work force, but creating critical thinkers who take an interest and participate in their communities. Right now in our country, there is a trend of anti-intellectualism, where voices in politics and the media are claiming that education is a form of elitism and are demanding greater accountability. With public funding under tighter controls, schools are turning to sources outside the public domain for support, accepting money and in some cases making business agreements with private enterprise. It is an interesting time.

Still, education is a great public bureaucracy, a giant well for tax dollars as well as business investments. Schools need to be scrutinized for how that money is used and whether it is being spent in the best interest of the students and the public.

Question: What legalities or barriers are there in education coverage?

Know your laws. Sometimes a school official or district will use federal laws like the Family Educational Rights and Privacy Act (FERPA) and the Health Insurance Privacy and Portability Act (HIPPA) as reason for not releasing information about students. Know the details of these laws. For example, HIPPA applies to health care providers, not school officials. You may find yourself explaining these laws to your sources.

Even if the schools are private, there is some information, including accreditation and nonprofit income, that provides inroads into their general workings.

Also use common sense. For example, one university official told me the contract between a private bookseller and the private student-run nonprofit bookstore organization was not open to public scrutiny. I reasoned that since employees of the university who weren't serving as legal counsel to the student group had reviewed the contract, they would likely have a copy in their files and those files would likely be open to the public. I got to see the contract. Remember, there is more than one way to get the information.

Question: How do you develop and cultivate sources on the education beat?

Show up. Be interested. Ask questions. Most people in this line of work believe they are performing a public service. They care about their jobs, are excited about their efforts and are typically willing to be open. Know who they are and what they do before you meet with them. Look at what's happening in their field of study or in other districts and campuses.

(continued)

PROFESSIONAL TIPS   Continued

Spend time on your campuses, wander into buildings and talk to department chairs, technicians, facilities crews and the longtime secretaries. They know more about the university or district you're covering than the newly hired public relations team. And if they know you're interested and feel they can trust you, they'll call when big news is breaking.

Question: What differences are there between K–12 and higher education beats?

The most basic difference is that a K–12 education should be every person's right and higher education is an elective choice. The K–12 system is more straightforward and structured. But K–12 educators are charged with the most precious responsibility of guiding, teaching and protecting their charges and should be held closely accountable for their actions.

Higher education sprawls in many directions, including science, business, high-finance athletics, administrative hierarchies and major philanthropy. It can be a place of influence, but it also offers more opportunity for problems and corruption.

Question: How do you get past educational jargon and what sometimes appears to be the arrogance and/or secrecy of sources?

Educational jargon and scientific jargon are facts of life in this beat. Sometimes, the easiest thing to do is say you're just a simple reporter and could things be explained in simpler terms? But I often find the more jargon there is, the less substance.

Be polite, serious and insistent, and have a good reason for wanting the information. For example, this is being done with public money and your readers have a right to know what's happening on campus. Go to multiple sources. If one office or person won't answer your questions, someone else might. If something obviously is being kept secret, ask why and then print that. Talk to outside sources about why public education and its workings should be open and transparent.

Question: Is there anything else you would like to share about education coverage?

Look beyond the press releases. Often there's a good story behind the story the school or university wants you to tell. Linger in the back of the room, stay late, get there early, that's when real issues and points can bubble up, and where private personalities come out.

Remember, every day can be different. One day you could be writing a process story on how enrollment is changing, the next you're covering a groundbreaking scientific discovery and the third you could be following a shooting on campus. Be flexible and alert. Education has every kind of story, and you should be ready to write whatever comes your way.

---

board is primarily responsible for maintaining the quality of the schools and setting an annual budget.

A superintendent is usually hired to run the day-to-day business of the schools and carry out the decisions of the board. Each school in the district will usually have a principal and be staffed by teachers.

Each school district, however, isn't completely independent. The state department of education has final authority, but usually only establishes minimum standards such as the number of school days required each year, the subjects taught, the qualifications of teachers and the selection of options of textbooks.

School coverage has changed over the years, particularly over the past ten or so years, because society has changed. Many schools reflect the paradoxes of American society—strikes, unionization of teachers, crime and vandalism, drug use and gangs. In some schools students are found carrying weapons when they pass through metal detectors, which helps prevent assaults on teachers and other students. There is sometimes a strong police or paramilitary presence of authority.

Criticisms of public schools over the years have made newspapers rethink their coverage of education. While enrollment figures, bond issues, faculty changes and the fortunes and misfortunes of athletic teams still form the backbone of education coverage, there is an increased emphasis on stories that try to help the taxpayer understand what is happening in local schools and across the nation. These are trend stories, issues such as school financing, classroom teaching techniques and technological advancements, changes in curriculum and graduation requirements and increased standards.

Diversity has also had an impact on education coverage. It has been estimated that 40 percent of those attending public schools are students of color. While diversity is certainly valued, it has also increased awareness—which means coverage—on issues such as racism, poverty, language differences and cultural barriers. As an example, students in Los Angeles public schools speak more than 120 different languages, and many students do not speak English.

Coverage in any area of public affairs should include what can be defined as *positive news* and *negative news.* Education is no different. But there is much more in the middle; stories that are neither positive nor negative, but are interesting and important to tell. Unfortunately, board members, superintendents, principals, teachers and staff members seem to only want to accentuate what they believe is positive, and completely ignore the rest.

For instance, if you called your local high school and asked to interview and write a news feature about the fifteen Eagle Scouts attending school there—a very high number—you'd almost certainly be given the key to the school. You'd more than likely be given free rein to follow those fifteen students throughout their day, from class to class. All of their teachers would be told—or certainly asked—to cooperate.

But if you called the same high school looking for information about three star football players who were suspended, you'd get no cooperation. Finding out they were suspended for fighting, trashing the chemistry lab, showing up drunk on campus, shoplifting or whatever might take days of investigation.

Then there are the neutral requests. For instance, if you asked to come over and interview students to get their reaction on any number of topics, such as the impending presidential elections, you might be denied.

Most K–12 schools have policies like the following from the Pullman, Washington, School District, no. 267:

> All visitors must register at the school office upon arrival at a school.
>
> Visitors are to follow building procedures for visitors.
>
> Visitors whose purpose is to influence or solicit students shall not be permitted on the school grounds unless the visit furthers the educational program of the district.
>
> If the visitor wishes to observe a classroom, the time shall be arranged after the principal has conferred with the teacher.
>
> If the purpose of the classroom visitation is to observe learning and teaching activities, the visitor may be required to confer with the teacher before or after the observation to enhance understanding of the activities.

The principal may withhold approval if particular events, such as testing, would be adversely affected by a visit. Similarly, if a visitor's presence becomes disruptive, the principal may withdraw approval. In either case, the principal shall give reasons for his/her action.

Always get school permission when going on school grounds. Laws clearly state that reporters much check in at the office immediately on arrival. It is best also on school property to get permission concerning photos.

Final Thoughts

The education beat can be one of the most fun at a newspaper, as well as one of the most important and informative. It can also be one of the most adversarial.

It is critical to meet with sources on a regular basis to develop trust and open an avenue for story ideas and tips.

Reporters should visit the schools they cover—often. Talk with students and teachers. Visit classrooms.

Know state meeting laws, and hold school boards responsible for them.

Stretch for the unusual—take a student test from time to time, and attend nonathletic events and club meetings.

Follow the money, as it will often lead you to the best stories.

Focus on humanity.

CHAPTER EXERCISES

1. Go online to any university department—Police, School of Communication, College of Liberal Arts, Environmental Sciences, Biology, Athletics, Office of Student Programs, and so on—and provide five detailed education-focused story ideas.

2. Define the following educational terms, converting the jargon into simple, easy-to-understand English, and come up with a story idea for each item: *ability grouping, basal readers, character education, cooperative learning, creationism, magnet school, master teachers, charter school, outcomes-based education, performance-based assessment, Scholastic Assessment Test (SAT),* and *whole language.*

3. Go to www.schoolwisepress.com/smart/browse/browse.html, and review one story. Critique the story. How could it have been better? What did you like? What didn't you like? Can you think of other stories spurred by the one you reviewed?

4. Write a five hundred-word story after identifying a topic and spending time gathering information at a local K–12 school.

5. Come up with five detailed story ideas about your college or university. After approval from your professor, send the list to the student newspaper or university news bureau. Ask for a response concerning interest. Once received, provide a copy of the response to your professor.

CHAPTER

19 Arts, Entertainment, Sports and Other Interests

BY SUSAN ENGLISH

Sports and entertainment are often covered as events, or from celebrity perspectives, but they also deserve coverage as public affairs because stadiums and arenas are often built and expanded at the expense of taxpayers.

Traditionally, the journalists in the newsroom have called the sports department *the toy department.* Sportswriters spend their time watching games and writing about who won, who lost and how much fun the fans had. Generally, although sports fans take the games very seriously, there was a sense that serious journalists did serious journalism and that sports were merely an entertaining diversion from the rest of our lives.

Traditionally, print journalists covered arts and entertainment only in a cursory manner. They were uncomfortable with celebrity news, which seemed like gossip, and newspapers left entertainment to television. If a band or the circus came to town, or a large tea dance was to be staged, it might warrant a note in the society or women's section of the newspaper.

As the saying goes: that was then, this is now. And now, the space given to the sports and arts and entertainment (A&E) sections often eclipses the space given to what was once considered serious news. In many instances, sports and entertainment news is serious news, and stories are played on the front page or the metro section front alongside coverage of city council meetings and school board decisions. That also means that sports and A&E writers have converged with news reporters, and vice versa. Sports and entertainment have become part of our worldview, woven into the fabric of our lives along with education, health care, the economy and all of the other issues that affect us.

The old boundaries between sports and education or health care, for example, or between entertainment and the local economy, have crumbled. How did that happen? Sports and entertainment became big business. They became part of the economy, both on a local scale and internationally. And while public money has long been spent on sports, for example to fund athletic scholarships, and to a lesser degree on the arts and culture, until recently, it fell below the radar of the taxpayers.

Now, communities spend millions of dollars of tax revenue to build sports arenas and concert halls. In some cities, the bidding to attract or keep a professional sports franchise is as heated and expensive as efforts to seduce a new manufacturing plant or the headquarters of a multinational corporation to relocate and bring with it good jobs.

One of the central roles of a journalist is tracking how tax dollars are spent. That now includes watching how public money is used to build stadiums, arenas and opera houses and explaining the process to the readers. While news coverage of the building of a new public facility still falls within the venue of a metro reporter, increasingly sports and A&E writers are called upon to team up with the metro or business writer or report the stories themselves. No longer can sportswriters confine their duties to writing advances and covering game stories, with occasional player profiles and a column thrown into the mix.

Sports and entertainment writers must know their way around city hall and the budget process, and they should be filing Freedom of Information requests.

While athletes and entertainers have always had run-ins with law enforcement, it used to be that, as celebrities, they were winked at and sent on their way. Now, professional teams are peppered with ex-felons, and increasingly sports and A&E writers are called upon to cover the arrest of an athlete or celebrity, whether it is for driving while under the influence or for assault, domestic or otherwise.

Hence, for sports and entertainment journalists, public affairs reporting falls into two broad categories: tracking how public money is spent, and following athletes and celebrities into the judicial system. Sports journalists who cover collegiate athletics should also track compliance with NCAA regulations and be prepared to report violations and sanctions should they occur, which they do with increasing frequency.

Public Money, Private Profit

Most communities, whether they are sprawling metro areas or small towns on the plains of Texas, have struggled with questions of using tax dollars to build sports stadiums and arenas.

The arguments against such expenditures remain consistent. In the cases of football stadiums for schools, opponents argue for equity. They call for equal money to be allocated to the school band or science clubs as is spent on the football team. Some say if there is money available, it should be used to fund basic education programs so all students can benefit, rather than the select few on the football team.

In a commentary published in the *New York Times,* journalist Buzz Bissinger, the author of the best-selling book about high school football, *Friday Night Lights,* even questioned the use of private money to build high school stadiums. He cited an October 2004 *USA Today* report that included the following examples: in the Dallas area, $180 million is being spent on new or pending high school football stadium projects. In Valdosta, Georgia, $7.5 million was spent to renovate the high school football stadium, including building a museum for memorabilia. North Hills High, in Pittsburgh, spent $10 million to renovate the stadium and build a field house.

While Bissinger acknowledges that these projects and many others are privately funded, most often by the high school boosters, he says the projects should still be questioned.

"In an age where educational resources are dwindling, how can the building of a lavish new stadium or field house possibly be justified, much less needed?" Bissinger wrote. "What does it say to the rest of the student body, the giant-sized majority who do not play football, except that they are inferior, a sloppy second to the football stars who shine on Friday night? How can a community brag about its ability to get financing for a multimillion-dollar football stadium when it can't conjure up the money to hire more teachers that would lead to the nirvana of smaller class sizes?"

Critics of new professional football stadiums and baseball parks in cities raise similar questions. They argue that public dollars should instead go toward improving community health care, repairing roads and bridges or renovating city parks so the entire community can benefit, rather than the owners of professional sports franchises.

Community leaders, however, cite the presence of a sports franchise as a quality of life issue and justify the use of tax dollars to attract or retain a franchise by claiming that a football or baseball team raises the stature of the city. They say sports teams help attract new businesses or industries, and thus create new jobs in the community and become a vital part of economic growth.

The results of several major studies support the critics' claims. Reporters should be conversant enough with the major studies that support both sides of the issue to ask pointed questions about proposals that involve public funding. And stories about privately funded sports and entertainment projects should also be balanced with the viewpoints of those questioning such expenditures.

Many civic projects built for cultural groups such as symphony orchestras or sports franchises are done so with a public–private partnership. The community kicks in some tax dollars that come from a variety of sources, and the football team or arts organization ponies up some money. Journalists, though, should look at not only who contributes the money but also who benefits, for many of these deals also involve a complex formula of revenue sharing.

Money Spent, Money Earned

One of the most common forms of public financing for sports arenas is through the sale of bonds. The city council can vote to sell enough bonds on the municipal bond market to cover the city's share of the project. Often the bond issue is voted on by the city residents, who are agreeing to pay back the bond purchasers over twenty or thirty years through increased property taxes. Other means of repaying the bonds are through increases in the hotel–motel tax or sales tax. Sometimes, the tax base has been expanded to include counties or entire states, which proponents say will also benefit from the presence of a professional sports franchise in the state.

The partnership often includes the sports franchise owners kicking in significant money to furnish the building or make improvements to existing facilities. Some cities require the teams to sign long-term leases so the franchise owner cannot succumb to the lure of a better deal elsewhere and leave the city with an empty arena and decades of payments on the bonds sold to build it.

The public–private partnerships also usually call for some revenue sharing to create a win-win situation. Sometimes the teams sign rental agreements for the life of the bonds so the city can begin to repay the bonds with this income. Even the rental agreements can be complex, for often astute franchise owners tie the rental fee to attendance levels—the more the community turns out to buy tickets to the games, the higher the rent that will be paid back to the community. Sometimes these rental agreements look favorable to an enthusiastic sports town, but journalists should carefully examine the sections addressing the skyboxes or luxury suites. These are the private rooms, or in some cases clubs with a restaurant and bar, that franchise owners retain the right to outside of the regular ticket sales. The season tickets in these luxury boxes are sold for thousands of dollars to corporations or well-heeled fans, and they often include private catering and bartending services as well as private elevators, reserved parking spaces and an array of other privileges.

If the attendance at the games does not include these suites, the revenue from ticket sales or rental agreements can be seriously skewed.

Among other revenue streams that are negotiable are the fees from parking in the publicly owned lots surrounding the building, revenue from the concessions and taxes added to ticket prices.

The franchise owners are, of course, looking for a deal that will net them the greatest profit with the least financial risk. The town council or whichever public officials are crafting the deal should be looking out for the city's best interests while also minimizing financial risk. And journalists should ask enough questions and understand the process well enough that they can explain it to the readers, presenting a balanced picture of the benefits for and risks to taxpayers.

These agreements often look a little different when arts and cultural organizations are involved, because while groups such as symphonies are private, they are usually nonprofit. This does not mean they do not need to generate revenue to fund their efforts; they, too, will be looking for deals to maximize income and minimize risk. But as nonprofits, their finances are open to journalists in ways the financial dealings of private groups are not.

A&E reporters should request the reports filed annually with the IRS as well as the annual audits conducted on the organization's books for all nonprofit groups on their beats.

Cities negotiate on the same types of agreements with arts groups that perform in public buildings as they do with sports franchises. The parking revenue, concessions profits and taxes on tickets are all up for grabs, as are the rental agreements.

Deals that are too sweet for sports franchises or expensive buildings for cultural activities, whether they are museums or symphony halls, can bleed public money from a city's coffers and make the city a very expensive place to live. On the other hand, if the city cuts a deal that's too lean for the team, the franchise owners can be tempted to take their franchise elsewhere where the profit is greater, and the city will be left paying for a big, useless building. The risk cuts both ways, and astute journalists need to know enough about what transpires off the field or behind the curtains at the opera house to tell readers who is winning and who is losing in the public–private deals.

Winners and Losers

Unfortunately, even if the teams stay in town and the symphony or museum remains financially viable, often the stadiums, arenas and opera houses that are built for them do not last for the twenty or thirty years it takes to pay off the construction costs.

Why is this? Technology . . . rising expectations for entertainment events . . . spectator comfort . . . safety considerations . . . increasing demands for revenue.

Here are just a few things that can make a building obsolete:

- **Huge video screens** have replaced scoreboards in arenas, but the screens consume large sections of former seats that must be removed. Then, even a full house might not provide the attendance levels needed to generate the revenue to pay off the bonds.

- **The teams demand** state-of-the-art facilities, including custom locker rooms and training facilities tricked out with high-tech media equipment, whirlpools, steam and massage rooms and coaches' offices also with private steam rooms.

- **The teams demand** more skyboxes to generate more revenue, removing even more seats for individual ticket buyers and decreasing the city's revenue from ticket sales.

- **It is no** secret that Americans have grown larger in the last generation and continue to grow. Spectators need larger seats, and just as airlines have had to install larger seats on planes, arenas and opera houses have also had to install larger seats. This translates into fewer seats and, again, fewer tickets available to be sold.

- **Salaries continue to** rise, whether for high-priced professional athletes or the more modestly paid symphony musicians. A deal made now is not likely to cover increasing costs ten years from now unless additional streams of revenue are found.

- **Buildings that are** built to last thirty or fifty years just don't. For example, the Kingdome—built in Seattle, Washington, in the 1970s to house the Seahawks NFL franchise, the Mariners baseball team and, for a time, even the Seattle Sonics NBA team—was torn down and replaced in 2000, years before it will be paid for. The roof leaked repeatedly, ceiling tiles fell onto the field, and spectators for both sports complained about poor sight lines.

Now, through complex public–private deals that involved tax revenue from city and county sources, Seattle built a stadium for the Seahawks, a baseball park with a retractable roof for the Mariners and a renovated arena for the Sonics.

PROFESSIONAL TIPS

Dave Boling

Dave Boling is an award-winning sports columnist for the *Tacoma News Tribune*, in Tacoma, Washington. He has covered the Olympics, 10 Super Bowls, the NCAA Final Four basketball tournament and the NBA finals. He worked previously at the *Coeur d'Alene* (Idaho) *Press, Lewiston* (Idaho) *Tribune* and the *Spokesman-Review* in Spokane, Washington. Boling has written three sports books and has two more in the works. He played football for the University of Louisville, where he studied political science, and studied forestry at the University of Idaho.

Question – As a longtime sports reporter and columnist, what percentage of your time is spent working on stories that are investigative in nature—those stories that tell readers the how and why of, say, team finances, drug use, NCAA violations or how communities use public money to bid for and keep sports franchises?

As a reporter, I spent considerable time working on these in-depth, off-the-field stories. At most papers, the beat reporter is so loaded with daily duties—game coverage, advances, updates, etc.—that it almost precludes big-project work.

The metro papers tend to break these stories because they may have a general assignments writer or an investigative person who is free of daily responsibilities who can take the time to work on the very time-consuming research that these types of stories demand. Unfortunately, then, the beat reporter on the small- or medium-sized paper is left to do these things on his own time—or not do them at all.

As a columnist, now, I spend very little time working on investigations. If I get a tip that an investigation is required, I almost immediately feed that to the beat reporter, who is generally better-sourced. I may work with the beat reporter,

then, and end up doing a column to accompany his report when it's published. In those cases, I find that my background on the topic, having helped develop it, allows me to make a more informed commentary.

I couldn't guess at percentages of time spent on these stories, but I know it's extremely little as a columnist. When I was a beat reporter, it was probably not more than 10 to 15 percent. And I would say that I was one of the more aggressive sportswriters in that regard.

Question – Is it common for sportswriters to do investigative journalism in addition to covering sporting events? How often do sports reporters hand off stories to metro reporters? Who decides whether a story about an athlete being arrested, for example, goes to the metro desk or the sports section?

I never liked the idea of feeding stories to the news side. I think the beat person has better connections and has probably earned more trust over time with the people who are involved. Now, I think it's great to work *with* news-side reporters, especially if they're more "fluent" in the use of the cops-courts system.

Generally, it's up to the sports and news editors, and, frankly, it's probably decided by how much they trust the sports reporter to do it correctly.

(continued)

PROFESSIONAL TIPS   Continued

Question – What are the advantages of covering all aspects of your beat—action off the field as well as the competition? What are the disadvantages?

I believe it's absolutely crucial to be involved in all aspects of the beat. Again, the primary reason is source development. Of all the great investigative journalism done over time, I'd guess that almost none of it came solely from a reporter's instincts or observations. The vast, vast majority was triggered by the tip from a source. Somebody on the inside has to trust you or recognize you as someone who can adequately handle the matter. These contacts are built through a reporter's extensive involvement in all aspects of the beat.

Question – What types of ethical dilemmas have you encountered in the years of covering sports and athletes? Can a sportswriter also be a fan, in that he or she is silently rooting for the hometown team?

I've been a hard-liner regarding ethics. I know reporters who go out for beers with coaches and athletes, or who get close to them personally. I think there's a trap there. It might not color your reporting, but I think it's human nature that it would. The rules of journalism that apply to news reporters should apply equally to sports reporters. Accept nothing of value (tickets, etc.), and treat news sources professionally.

It doesn't take long for sports reporters to have the "fan" leeched out of them. No, you can't be a fan. There will be teams you like to cover; there will be players you enjoy watching. But if there's any hint that a reporter is getting cozy with his beat sources, it's probably better that he be shifted to another beat. That is not to say you can't be friendly or that you have to be entirely impersonal. You'll never develop sources that way. I mean only that a good reporter has to make it clear that all his dealings are going to be conducted in a professional manner.

Question – Do athletic directors or coaches ever think part of the role of sportswriters is to help them sell tickets? Do they express annoyance that you cover the legal missteps of athletes, or write stories about potential NCAA violations? How do you explain your role as a journalist to them?

Athletic directors tend to be savvy enough to know they're wasting their time if they're trying to use a writer in that way. Most understand that we have to cover legal issues. They are naturally defensive when confronting issues of cheating, etc. Most athletic directors at major schools have been through it and know the drill. They understand completely (at state schools) that they have certain legal disclosure rules they have to follow. But they're fairly adept at spin control. They know what our jobs are. That doesn't mean they like it, or that they're cooperative. In most cases, they're trying to cover their butts like everybody else.

Question – Should aspiring sportswriters also know something about government and courts reporting? Have you ever filed a Freedom of Information request and is this something sportswriters should do more often?

Cross-training in the newsroom is the best thing ever for a sports reporter. I found that I spent a lot of time doing this, informally, heading across the hall to ask the cops or court reporters questions about how best to sort through the resources. I know some sports reporters who have taken time to go over and work the news side just to get this kind of experience. I have not had to work up an FOI request, but always keep the paperwork and protocol handy in case I do. As a columnist, I'm a little out of that business these days. Beat reporters—especially those covering public entities—should be well-versed in the process.

Seattle's situation is typical of what public–private partnerships do for and to cities. Following is an article by reporters Jim Brunner and Bob Young, published in the *Seattle Times* in January 2005, that gives readers the context and perspectives they need to assess the situation:

> Seattle's three major professional sports franchises could benefit from future tax subsidies as part of a proposal by the Sonics to fund a $180 million expansion of KeyArena.
>
> The proposal being floated would extend indefinitely the life of several temporary taxes now used to pay off debt for the construction of Seattle's publicly owned football and baseball stadiums.
>
> Instead of expiring by 2020, as originally conceived, some or all of the taxes would remain in place to raise money for future renovations to Qwest Field and Safeco Field, as well as KeyArena, according to Sonics officials and others briefed on the plans.
>
> Sonics officials previously had disclosed plans to ask the state Legislature for funding to expand KeyArena. They now acknowledge that the legislation would go further, essentially establishing a permanent sports-stadium tax.
>
> The idea has drawn sharp criticism from at least one City Council member, who fears that arts groups that rely on the same source of revenue could lose out.
>
> But Terry McLaughlin, executive vice president of the Sonics, said of the proposal: "We've approached it as being a better idea, that it is more comprehensive than a single building or a single franchise."
>
> McLaughlin said the management of the Mariners and Seahawks were briefed on the proposal and seemed supportive. "It's in their interests as well," he said.
>
> But spokeswomen for the baseball and football teams were noncommittal yesterday.
>
> "What we really want to do is look at the specifics before we are able to take any kind of position," said Rebecca Hale, spokeswoman for the Mariners.
>
> Martha Fuller, chief financial officer for the Seahawks, which have played at Qwest Field since 2002, said the team is interested in the Sonics' idea but hasn't seen enough details to formally support it.
>
> "We're just wrapping up our third season here. We certainly have no immediate needs (for additional public subsidies). But who knows what the state of sports facilities might be in 15 years, what fans might demand, or what the technology is at that point," Fuller said.
>
> Asking the Legislature to extend the taxes for all three sports facilities may prove controversial, the Sonics' McLaughlin acknowledged.
>
> One critic of previous stadium deals was immediately skeptical when told of the Sonics' proposal yesterday. "Oh my God, that's worse than I thought," said Seattle City Councilman Nick Licata, who helped lead the opposition to taxpayer funding for the football and baseball stadiums.
>
> Licata said he wants to ensure that arts groups, which have received some of the tax money, don't get cut out by the sports teams.
>
> McLaughlin said the tax idea emerged in brainstorming sessions with Gerry Johnson and Jay Reich, both partners with the law firm Preston, Gates and Ellis, who have played roles in recent public–private partnerships, including the construction of Safeco and Qwest fields. Both have been hired by the Sonics to work on the KeyArena plan. Johnson declined to comment yesterday, and Reich could not be reached.

(continued)

(continued)

The Sonics' proposed expansion of KeyArena would nearly double the size of the facility to widen concourses, add space for restaurants and concessions and provide more parking and new team offices.

The expansion, which would take up to three years to complete, would be staged so the Sonics could continue to play all home games at KeyArena. But the Seattle Storm, the professional women's basketball team owned by the Sonics, likely would have to move for a season.

The last arena renovation was completed in 1995 and paid for with $74 million in public bonds. In a deal with the city of Seattle, the Sonics agreed to help pay the bonds off by giving the city a hefty slice of revenue from luxury suites and all the income from the naming rights to the arena.

The Sonics now say the market has changed and the team has not been able to fill its suites, due in part to competition from the new baseball and football stadiums. Sonics officials say the team has lost $50 million over the past five years.

The Sonics' losses, in turn, have been dragging down the finances of the city-owned Seattle Center, which has run up a budget deficit of $9.4 million.

About $60 million in debt remains from the 1995 renovation of KeyArena. The Sonics and Seattle Mayor Greg Nickels are backing the proposal to extend several taxes to retire that debt, as well as pay for the expansion.

The city hopes bonds can be sold to provide cash up front for the expansion. The bonds would be paid off later by the taxes. However, Nickels has not endorsed the broader idea of extending taxes to the other two sports arenas. "It's really too early to know what will fly with the Legislature," said Nickels' spokeswoman, Marianne Bichsel. "The Sonics are taking the lead on this. What we have agreed to do is to go to Olympia with them to explore different possibilities to do that."

Altogether, the taxes used to finance the construction of the stadiums and pay off the remaining debt from the Kingdome raised more than $50 million last year, according to the state Department of Revenue. They include a hotel–motel tax, [a] sales tax, a tax on restaurant meals and drinks, and a car-rental tax. All are levied only in King County. (A portion of the hotel–motel tax is also devoted to arts organizations.)

Licata said he isn't sure the Sonics are wise to link KeyArena to the controversial football and baseball stadiums. "I think they take on baggage because there is lingering public animosity to how those [stadium] decisions came down," Licata said.

Safeco Field, which opened in 1999, was built with taxpayer money despite voters' rejection of a tax increase to pay for the stadium four years earlier.

Public financing for Qwest Field, which opened in 2002 as Seahawks Stadium, was narrowly approved by voters in 1997 despite critics who objected to taxpayer subsidies for the Seahawks and their owner, billionaire Paul Allen.

The following information box accompanied the article. Some information, such as the revenue from specific taxes, is best handled by the graphics department.

Stories such as this one on the Seattle sports arena are increasingly common on the front pages and metro section fronts of newspapers. A story in the *New York Times* in mid-December 2004 reported the troubles in Washington, D.C., involving the city's plans to bring the former Montreal Expos baseball franchise to Washington.

SEATTLE STADIUM FUNDING

The Sonics want to ask state lawmakers to extend several taxes currently dedicated to paying off the debt from Safeco Field, Qwest Field and the Kingdome, which was demolished in 2000. The taxes, collected only in King County, are set to expire at various times through 2020. The taxes include:

Hotel/Motel Tax

A 2 percent tax on hotel- and motel-room rentals goes to pay for the Kingdome debt, and to arts and cultural organizations. When the Kingdome debt is retired, the money will pay for the debt on Qwest Field. Last year, the tax raised $14.2 million.

Sales Tax

A .017 percent sales tax is dedicated to paying off the Safeco Field debt. A separate .016 percent sales tax pays for the debt on Qwest Field. The taxes raised a combined $12.9 million last year.

Restaurant Food–Beverage Tax

A 0.5 percent tax on restaurant meals and drinks is devoted to paying the Safeco Field debt. It generated $16.6 million last year.

Car-Rental Tax

A 2 percent tax on automobile rentals goes to the Safeco Field debt; 1 percent goes to Qwest Field. The taxes generated $7 million last year.

Sources: State Department of Revenue and King County.

The move was contingent on Washington, D.C., providing a new baseball park for the team. The city council's plan required that half of the baseball park's projected $280 million construction costs be paid for privately. A previous deal between D.C. Mayor Anthony Williams and baseball officials called for financing the ballpark almost entirely with tax dollars.

The Expos, renamed the Nationals, played the 2005 season in Washington's Robert F. Kennedy Memorial Stadium and the new ballpark is being built.

Reporters in cities with National Hockey League franchises started looking at the bleak revenue picture in their communities after the NHL and the players' association failed to agree on a new contract for the 2004–2005 season. Hundreds of games were canceled, leaving cities without parking, concessions and rental revenue to pay the debt on the 15,000-seat (or larger) arenas many cities built to attract a team.

Context, Context, Context

Stories about the partnership between the public and private sectors are complex, filled with numbers and discussions of the bond market and bond ratings, and they unfold sometimes over twenty years or more. It is highly unusual for a reporter to follow such a story

PROFESSIONAL TIPS

Jim Kershner

Jim Kershner has worked as a journalist in the Northwest for thirty years, about twenty of those as an A&E writer and editor. He is now a columnist and theater critic for the *Spokesman-Review* in Spokane, Washington. He has won numerous national awards, including seven awards from the National Society of Newspaper Columnists. He is a member of the American Theatre Critics Association.

Question – As a longtime entertainment writer, what percentage of your time is spent reporting and writing stories that are investigative in nature, those stories that serve to tell readers the how and why of the finances and politics of groups and organizations you cover?

Only about a quarter of my time is spent doing nuts-and-bolts reporting about the business and funding of the arts. Yet that reporting is crucial to the beat, since ignoring the health of the organizations would mean covering only the aesthetics of an art form without covering the world in which it must exist. That wouldn't be fair to readers or to the art form.

Question – Is it common for entertainment writers to do investigative journalism in addition to writing previews and news of concerts, plays and other events?

Yes, it is not only common, but nearly universal. The main reason is purely practical: nobody else on the paper is going to do it. Investigative teams already have their hands full with government and the rest of the messy world. So if a story about an arts board scandal is going to be done, the A&E writer will be the one doing it. And that's how it should be: nobody outside the beat will know as much about that community anyway.

Question – What are the advantages of covering all aspects of your beat—the financial woes of nonprofit groups, the use and misuse of funds, the struggles of the arts? What are the disadvantages?

One advantage is that the arts writer will become more well rounded. The writer will understand all sides of the arts, from the aesthetic to the practical to the financial. Yet there is one serious disadvantage: the writer is plunged into the internal politics and personalities of the arts community. This can spell big trouble if that writer is also a critic. A critic has an obligation to ignore internal politics and personalities, and deal strictly with the quality of the work.

Question – What ethical dilemmas have you encountered in the years of covering entertainment and celebrities, and how did you handle them?

Here's one that I, and probably every A&E reporter, has dealt with: the singer who cancels a big concert due to "illness" or "laryngitis." Sure, that happens. But often this is just a cover for either poor ticket sales or a stint in rehab. Should you play along, or should you find out and print the real reason for the cancellation? Of course, you should pursue the truth and publish it. You owe it to

(continued)

PROFESSIONAL TIPS   Continued

the thousands of people caught holding tickets. Besides, that's part of the fun (and glory) of being a journalist. You get to tell people the *real* story.

One other common issue, while not strictly an ethical dilemma, is the question of accuracy of quotes. Every reporter deals with this, but an A&E reporter interviewing a celebrity sometimes has more at stake, since anything in your story can, and will, be picked up in celebrity news columns all over the country. The easy solution: record every interview with a celebrity. You will then be certain you are quoting him or her correctly. Most celebrities prefer that an interview is taped, and some insist on it. It's good for both of you.

Question – Do sources ever become angry that you are covering their financial woes when they think you should stick to previewing their concerts and helping them sell tickets? If so, how do you handle the anger, and how do you explain your role as a journalist?

Since many arts organizations are nonprofit groups and rely on donations from the public, we must treat them the same way we would a charity. It's our job to tell the public how their donations are being used.

A nonprofit's records are not usually covered by sunshine laws—those are for government entities. However, nonprofits must make available certain IRS records that show their basic financial situation and how much of their money is going to administrative costs, for instance. You just have to request them from the organization, and they must hand them over.

As for getting angry, sure, they do sometimes. All you can do is explain that people are giving them money, time and support, and those people have a right to know where that money goes.

Also, many of these organizations are long-time civic institutions, and what goes on in them matters to the community. If they get mad at you,

tough. If the head of the organization won't talk to you, usually you can find other concerned members of the organization who will.

Surprisingly, arts organizations are often happy to talk to you about their dire financial straits (if it doesn't involve malfeasance). Most of them are always on the edge of financial disaster, so stories of impending doom often rally supporters to their cause, such as saving the symphony orchestra.

Question – Is there a part of arts and entertainment coverage that also requires knowledge of government reporting?

Yes. Some arts organizations, such as a city arts commission, are funded with tax dollars. To cover those types of publicly funded organizations, entertainment reporters need to keep an eye on government budgets. Those organizations are government agencies, so sunshine laws and the Freedom of Information Act rules should apply.

Question – What advice would you give a young journalist aspiring to cover entertainment and the arts? What reporting skills do you find particularly vital to covering the public affairs aspects of local culture and entertainment?

My advice is to become as well rounded as you can about the world in general. The worst A&E reporter is the one who knows everything about, let's say, music, and little about everything else. You should know politics, history, pop culture, high culture, sports, business, economics, religion and science.

Reporting is one of the last refuges of the nonspecialist. Just because you cover theater doesn't mean you can get away with knowing nothing about physics. Someday you'll be reviewing a play about physics (yes, there is one), and you'll make a big fool of yourself.

as it develops, even over a few years. It is incumbent on journalists to maintain document files so a reporter picking up the story five years later can understand the evolution.

Newspaper archives, of course, are invaluable in this regard, and reporters should make it a practice to read the stories that have been published on the issue. The key to making each story easily understandable is context.

Newspapers can provide context and detail not possible in broadcast reports. Every story should offer, in some form, the background of the issue and possible outcomes of the current development.

Although space is limited on the news pages, when such stories are posted on the newspapers' Internet sites, they can be linked to archived stories and broken into bite-sized chunks with their own hyperlinks.

Conclusion

The expenditure of tax dollars reflects community values, and increasingly, those dollars are being spent on venues for entertainment, especially when athletic events are regarded as entertainment. No longer is reporting the building of arenas, high school stadiums or opera houses left to the city, county or education reporters. Sportswriters and entertainment reporters must be prepared to team with metro reporters in reports of public–private partnerships, or carry the reporting load themselves. And newsroom reporters will be expected to go to the "toy department" and team up with the symphony reporter to explain how and why the public's money is being spent.

CHAPTER EXERCISES

1. Invite the NCAA compliance officer from your college or university to class to talk about how he or she interacts with journalists. How often do violations occur at your school, and how does the compliance officer handle alleged violations? What training is given to the athletes and coaching staffs?

2. As a class, track the funding of the athletic and entertainment facilities at the school, filing the appropriate FOI requests and interviewing facilities managers and the school's budget officers.

3. Invite a financial expert, such as a stockbroker, to class to explain the bond market, bond ratings and municipal bonds.

4. If your school is in a town or city with a public ballpark or stadium, interview the city council members and write a story explaining the funding and revenue-sharing deals with teams or organizations that use the public facilities.

CHAPTER

20 Environment, Science, Health Care and Medicine

BY JOHN IRBY

Wild animals are a significant part of humans' environment, and there are several groups that have formed to protect them. Coverage of the environment, science, health care and medicine is sometimes ignored or covered only from the perspectives of the loudest voices.

They are relatively small, about three to five inches long, and have a leopard-like pattern of dark spots. During the mating process, males develop a salmon-colored blush on their sides and belly. After mating, females develop orange-red patches on their sides that remain until they lay eggs.

They are blunt-nosed leopard lizards—with a short, broad head and a blunt snout. They are also on the California and federal endangered species lists and have been involved in many environmental controversies over the years, including several in the central California San Joaquin Valley community of Bakersfield, in Kern County.

The Southern runner boa, giant garter snake and desert tortoise are also endangered reptiles in Kern County. Endangered plants include the Bakersfield smallscale, California jewel flower, Kern mallow, striped adobe lily, San Joaquin woolly threads, Bakersfield cactus and San Joaquin adobe sunburst. And endangered amphibians include the Kern Canyon slender salamander and Tehachapi slender salamander.

Your community will likely also have a list of endangered animals and plants. Reporting and writing about them are services that are often best performed by veteran reporters who are generally more aware of context and nuance.

It's very unlikely that newspapers other than the very largest will have a dedicated reporter to cover such topics as well as the other general topics of this chapter—environment, science, health care and medicine. While many newspapers might be hesitant to write about such issues or topics, especially on a local level, it is possible that one reporter might be assigned to cover a variety of these kinds of stories, but only as time permits.

At smaller newspapers, such information is often only published if it is from the Associated Press or some other major or supplemental wire service. Still, reporters of any size newspaper, who are interested in public affairs coverage, should have a basic understanding of the major possible impacts of the environment, health and science.

While the subject matter can be complex, requiring specialized training, there is a basic, beginning rule to follow: approach these stories from the standpoint of a layperson, and write these stories so other laypeople can understand them.

Environmental Reporting

For seven years, Dr. Lawrence Kutner wrote a syndicated "Parent and Child" column for the *New York Times.* He once said: "The family environment in which your children are growing up is different from that in which you grew up. The decisions our parents made and the strategies they used were developed in a different context from what we face today, even if the 'content' of the problem is the same. It is a mistake to think that our own experience as children and adolescents will give us all we need to help our children. The rules of the game have changed."

His statement has great application to environmental reporting if just a few words are changed or substituted: "The environment in which your children are growing up is different from that in which you grew up. The decisions our society made and the strategies they used were developed in a different context from what we face today, even if the 'content' of the problem is the same. It is a mistake to think that our own experience as children and adolescents will give us all we need to write about our environment. The rules of the game have changed."

While the rules of the game have changed dramatically, the "content" is very much the same. Environmental issues have for years focused on a variety of concerns such as air, disasters, energy, forests, land development and conservation, pollution, recycling, water, weather and wildlife—among others.

Defining the environment can be complex: "The totality of circumstances surrounding an organism or group of organisms, especially the combination of external physical

Worst of the West

Based on a report released this week by the Environmental Protection Agency, Potlatch Corp. ranked third in the Pacific Northwest in industrial air pollution in 2002. Here's a list of the top 10 air polluters in Idaho, Washington and Oregon.

1	Weyerhaeuser, Longview, Wash.; pulp and paper mill	2.08 million pounds
2	Weyerhaeuser, Springfield, Ore.; pulp and paper mill	1.19 million
3	Potlatch Corp., Lewiston; pulp and paper mill	1.00 million
4	Simpson Tacoma Kraft, Tacoma; pulp and paper mill	919,463
5	Boise Cascade, Walla Walla; pulp and paper mill	911,455
6	Georgia Pacific West, Toledo, Ore.; pulp and paper mill	893,980
7	Amalgamated Sugar, Paul, Idaho; sugar refinery	892,584
8	Fort James Camas, Camas, Ore.; pulp and paper mill	802,279
9	Boise Cascade, Saint Helens, Ore.; pulp and paper	749,555
10	Agrium Kennewick, Kennewick, Wash.; fertilizer plant	687,750

FIGURE 20.1   This tabled bar chart from the *Lewiston Tribune* showed that a local paper mill was ranked third in the Pacific Northwest in industrial air pollution, an interesting and important environmental fact.

The Lewiston Tribune

conditions that affect and influence the growth, development and survival of organisms" (from dictionary.com).

But remember the first rule discussed in the introduction: approach these stories from the standpoint of a layperson, and write these stories so other laypeople can understand them.

The environment can also be more simply defined as circumstances or conditions around us, or conditions that affect or influence the growth, development or survival of organisms.

Covering environmental issues often comes down to investigating and writing about what mankind does (or doesn't do) that helps or hurts the environment in which we live, or investigating and writing about nature and natural environmental developments.

Over the years, there have been several environmental concerns, or disasters, that have received significant coverage, concerning our air, water, land or soil, fish, wildlife and human lives. And there must be many others we don't even know about.

One of the most recent and recognizable would be the December 26, 2004, earthquake and tsunami that killed more than 150,000 people across southern Asia.

Changes in the environment from the disaster include legitimate concern of epidemics and serious disease. There will be almost as many possible environmental stories resulting from the disaster as the high number of lives that were tragically lost. For instance:

- **In Sri Lanka,** fears of an entire species being lost are real, most notably sea turtles.

- **As bodies were** being recovered on the beaches of Thailand, it became evident that possibly 500 to 600 Indo-Pacific humpback dolphins were endangered.

- **The United Nations** Environmental Programme (UNEP) reported that reefs, shorelines, vegetation and croplands suffered damage. Concerns included "solid and liquid waste, industrial chemicals, sewage treatment, salinization of drinking water and damage to ports and industrial infrastructure . . . all of which might require rehabilitating and protecting vital natural ecosystems, in particular mangrove forests and coral reefs."

Terrorism in general—and September 11, 2001, specifically—have brought about other major environmental concerns and stories in the new millennium. While Americans can't forget that day of infamy, a limited amount of significant reporting has reached the masses on lingering environmental concerns such as airborne hazards of asbestos, benzene, chromium, dioxin, lead, PCBs and other harmful materials. The environmental concerns of September 11 have yet to be fully considered or reported, and the environmental impacts of future terrorist attacks are frightening when considering acts that include anthrax and possibly other biological and chemical weapons—on humans as well as in the contamination of resources.

It appears that public affairs coverage of the environment will obviously focus in the future on outcomes brought about by enemies from abroad, be they in or out of the United States. Whether those terrorists base their actions on religious or ideological beliefs, there are also an increasing number of homegrown environmental terrorists and extremists who have surfaced in the United States.

One such area is animal rights, and there is a growing belief among many groups and organizations that messages can only be sent through violent acts, justified by a zealousness to "save the world" from itself.

Other areas of growing extremism as related to environmental issues include nuclear power, forest management and global warming. Reporters find themselves faced with covering issues including asbestos, ozone layer depletion, acid rain, recycling, landfill capacity, sewage treatment, clean water and air, toxic waste and the perils of pesticides and herbicides weighed against the advantages of pest management.

Today, there is no shortage of environmental stories to cover, but they should be looked at from two perspectives: current realities and long-term consequences.

Many environmental groups have formed to offer reporters their side of the story. Among the most recognizable are the following:

- **Earth First!** This movement, founded in 1979, claims it works to protect wilderness through radical means—"Today is the most critical moment in the three-and-a-half-billion-year history of life on Earth," its Web site reads. "Are you tired of namby-pamby environmental groups? Are you tired of overpaid corporate environmentalists who suck up to bureaucrats and industry? Have you become disempowered by the reductionist approach of environmental professionals and scientists? If you answered yes to any of these questions, then Earth First! is for you."

- **Greenpeace:** This group claims to use "non-violent, creative confrontation to expose global environmental problems and force solutions." It also claims: "Greenpeace exists because this fragile earth deserves a voice. It needs solutions. It needs change. It needs action."

- **National Audubon Society:** This organization claims it works through advocacy, policy, science, litigation, sanctuary management, grassroots outreach and education to protect birds and their habitats.

- **The Nature Conservancy:** It preserves habitats and species, it claims, by buying the lands and waters that need to survive.

- **Sierra Club:** The members of this group claim to promote environmental conservation by influencing public policy—legislative, administrative, legal and electoral.

These are only some of the groups that often warrant and deserve coverage because of the actions and positions they publicly take on environmental issues.

While the environmental stories of today can be extremely complex to unwind, many reporters learned their craft in earlier times on a few major stories that, while complex in nature, were clear environmental disasters.

In 1989, the Exxon *Valdez* oil tanker struck a reef at Prince William Sound in Alaska. Millions of gallons of crude oil gushed from the tanker at a rate of 200,000 gallons a minute and contaminated 1,090 miles of shoreline, killing 33,264 birds (138 eagles and 33,126 other birds) and 980 otters.

In 1984, eight thousand people were killed within three days after a Union Carbide chemical plant explosion in Bhopal, India. More than 500,000 others were exposed and have experienced varying degrees of sickness, as well as untold deaths, in the past twenty-plus years.

And in 1986, the Chernobyl nuclear power station reactor explosion initially killed thirty people, but as many as a million others were exposed to varying degrees of radiation. Many have died or suffered tremendous physical problems ever since.

Also, the U.S. Department of Energy (DOE) has made available public documents for fourteen defense nuclear facilities spread across the United States from Washington to Texas to South Carolina.

Aside from environmental concerns of radioactive waste, the DOE facilities could become larger environmental stories if they become the targets of terrorists.

For instance, U.S. military forces, according to President George W. Bush in his 2002 State of the Union address, found diagrams in Afghanistan of American nuclear plants that were listed as the best targets for spreading fear in the United States.

The Hanford nuclear complex in the state of Washington was established in 1943 as part of the Manhattan Project to build the atomic bomb. Plutonium was produced at the site until 1986. Today, Hanford contains the nation's largest volume of radioactive waste from nuclear weapons.

Not far from Hanford, close to the Columbia River are Hermiston and Umatilla, Oregon. The interstate highway takes travelers to and from Portland, alongside 220,000 rockets, bombs and projectiles—hidden in earthen hill-like shelters—loaded with the most lethal poisons on Earth. The collection makes up one of the largest chemical weapon stockpiles in the country, containing enough toxic agent (in terms of sheer volume) to kill tens of millions of people.

Your state, and possibly your community, is likely to have similar or dissimilar environmental stories waiting to be covered—or uncovered.

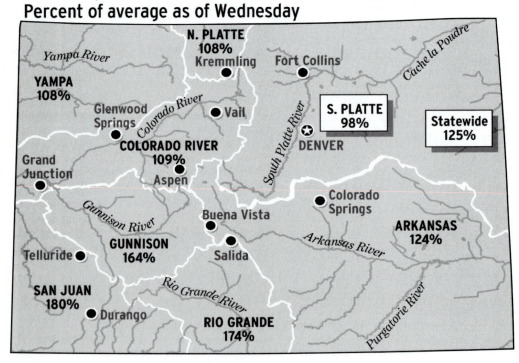

Snowpack in Colorado river basins
Percent of average as of Wednesday

FIGURE 20.2   This graphic from the Colorado Springs *Gazette* was used to illustrate how much snow had fallen in the state, which could have a significant environmental impact in terms of snowpack river runoff.

The Gazette

There is clearly a market for environmental reporting, as a *Wall Street Journal* poll revealed that eight in ten Americans consider themselves environmentalists. And more than 50 percent of them believe fundamental changes will be necessary in lifestyle—not scientific advances—to bring dramatic changes in the environment.

Science Reporting

While there is great interest in environmental reporting, there doesn't seem to be as much reader interest in science reporting, even though the topic is just as important in the scope of life.

The difficulties in coverage are similar to those of environmental reporting.

John Wilford, science and Pulitzer Prize–winning reporter for the *New York Times,* said: "The discovery is the most interesting aspect of science reporting. Some of it is the romantic in you. In many senses, science reporting is the frontier we are working on these days. There's no more Pacific Ocean or the interior of Africa to explore. Geographically, you have Antarctica and space. Intellectually, you have the frontier of trying to understand nature."

While science writing doesn't always rank high on the list of topics that interest readers, reporting new developments can be exciting and fascinating.

One of the chief problems, however, is similar to a problem in environmental reporting—writing the story so people can understand.

While scientists and journalists can often speak the same language, they don't always understand what the other means. The disconnect comes from two primary factors. First, the two don't usually hang out at the same bars or clubs, or think the same thoughts while on the job. Next, the words they use often have different meanings.

Bruce Murray, managing editor of FACSNET (the web site of the the Foundation for American Communications, or FACS), wrote an online article titled "The Methods of Science and Journalism." Murray explained it best when he wrote: "Common words such as force, theory, error, and energy are all used in strikingly different ways in the two fields." Dr. David Goodstein, academic adviser for the FACS Science Reporting Institute, was quoted as saying: "Force, as used in journalism and law, implies imposition of one person's will over another. In science, force is a technical word relating to the magnitude of velocity and carries no other baggage."

Science reporters have been a part of covering some of the most momentous events in history and will no doubt write about events that continue to change the world. The stories have included human organ transplants, space travel, atom splitting, drug development and therapy, DNA, the atomic bomb and genetic engineering.

Consider the number of vaccinations you've had. As a child, you were probably vaccinated for mumps and measles. As you eased into the preteen years, you might have been vaccinated for tetanus or hepatitis. As a teenager or young college student, you could have been vaccinated for any number of diseases, considering you lived in close quarters in college dorms or apartments and had a variety of friends and acquaintances. And if you served in the military, vaccinations are a way of life.

PROFESSIONAL TIPS

Anna King

Anna King grew up in the rural community of Roy, Washington. After graduating with honors from Washington State University in Pullman, she held a brief assignment at the *Nisqually Valley News* in Yelm, Washington. Then she lived and wrote in Italy for about two years and became fluent in Italian. Back in the Northwest, she worked at the *Puyallup Herald* as their lead city writer. She focused on travel, food, outdoor sports and entertainment writing as a freelancer for the *News Tribune* in Tacoma and several cities, including Puyallup and Enumclaw. She is writing for the *Tri-City Herald* as the agriculture, natural resource and water reporter.

Question: How does a reporter check his or her personal feelings when covering environmental issues?

Resources are scarce and the personalities are colorful when covering the environmental beat. Land, water and people always make an interesting mix, but I leave my personal values about the environment at home. As a journalist it's my job to inform people, not to sway readers one way or another. Reporters, to be credible, must include voices from all sides. The same few acres of land along a river might be an important refuge for wildlife, a farmer's sole livelihood and an ancient burial site for Native Americans. Reporters shouldn't decide what the best use of that land is, but tell a balanced, compelling story so the community will pay attention to what is going on there. If there is an issue you know you can't cover fairly, pull yourself off of the story.

Question: How can a reporter break through the jargon when covering scientific stories?

I often speak with eminent scientists, biologists and doctors. They are used to communicating within their world, where everyone knows exactly what they mean. When a scientist starts throwing unknown words or theories at me, I ask him or her to

"slow down," "tell me like you would explain it to your 5-year-old," or "I don't understand that." Then I have my notepad ready; that's usually when I capture the most colorful and easy-to-understand quotes.

It's easy to throw jargon into stories, especially the more familiar with the beat I become. I know the meaning of *nematodes* (a potato pest) and "cfs" (cubic feet per second, a measurement used to calculate water flow), but my audience doesn't. I do background research before I go out on a story. And if I still don't understand something when I am back at the office writing, I call my source again. It's much better to question your sources over and over to get the story right than to save face and get it wrong.

Question: How does a reporter know who is telling the truth when it comes to issues in health care such as the cost of drugs and insurance, particularly for the elderly?

It's often hard to tell when people are truthful or lying. Usually I ask myself these questions: why are they telling me this? What do they want? Did I contact them, or did they pursue the press?

Then check out their story: talk to other source references, check their name in public documents, do a second interview with them and see if their story changes. Then test your story: if it's about the cost of drugs, call up a pharmacy and ask

(continued)

PROFESSIONAL TIPS   Continued

them how much a particular prescription costs, call doctors, call other people that are in similar situations to your source. Also, find out if your story is part of a bigger trend. Try asking people across the state, country and border for their thoughts. I run anything questionable by my editor or fellow writers for ideas and opinions. Watch a source's body language, and try not to do phone interviews. Ultimately trust your gut.

Question: How can a reporter cultivate sources, such as doctors, when it comes to medical coverage?

With any source it's important to invest time with them. Doctors are busy people, but more than likely they are members of a local community club, they like to play sports or they drink coffee. Try and chat often with them in informal settings where they are relaxed and might provide you with good leads. Doctors know other doctors. Ask these professionals for new sources and an introduction. This is an excellent way to broaden your list of sources.

Question: You covered the "mad cow" issue in the state of Washington in 2004. What was the biggest surprise you found?

The biggest surprise of covering mad cow disease was covering such a huge international story about cattle right in the *Tri-City Herald*'s backyard. I was competing daily with National Public Radio, the *New York Times* and the *Seattle Times* for stories. I used my local knowledge of the area and ranching background to break fresh stories. The second biggest surprise is how much that one cow has changed international trade, beef prices and laws surrounding food safety. Mad cow disease has affected everyone from mid-Columbia alfalfa farmers and French fry processors to Canadian ranchers and McDonalds in Japan.

Question: Are there any additional tips you'd like to add for student reporters who have interest in a career covering these topics?

Do your homework. Know as much about the story as you can before you get to the site or speak with the first source. I learn way more about a story than ever appears on the page. The research that supports a story is similar to that portion of an iceberg that lies beneath the surface.

Go there. If you see it for yourself, the story will be better. There is no way to describe the sound of hundreds of elk running from a helicopter, a bull rider's prayer or the fresh smell of a pine forest if you weren't there to experience it. Phone interviews are always my last resort because those stories end up dry and stale. Get out on the boat, underneath the dam, in the mountains and to the scene of the fire anytime you can.

Focus on people. It's easy to get lost in the numbers, statistics, trends and controversy, but ultimately the most compelling stories are about how those things impact people's lives. Spend the time to find out.

For all of those shots, we can thank Louis Pasteur. Pasteur is most famous for his work in pasteurization, but he also discovered the basis of vaccination, and his method of sterilization aided surgery and obstetrics by helping to prevent contagion and infection.

Science reporting of historical facts and long-term implications—such as those that Pasteur was a part of—can make for interesting reading. Science reporting does not have to be boring or overly technical.

Another example is Jonas Salk, who stumbled upon the polio vaccine while working on an immunization against influenza. But equally interesting in Salk's life, which most people aren't aware of, was his dedication to finding a cure for war or, in his own words: "Finding a cure for the cancer of the world."

His scientific endeavors, great as they were, became a secondary factor in his life as he devoted most of his time speaking to world leaders about the imminence of peace before his death at age 80 in 1995.

Not all scientific breakthroughs, or scientific research efforts, appear on the surface to be that interesting, but there often is gold to be mined.

Take, for instance, a $2 million grant a university received to do scientific research to improve specific oils and fatty acid traits of soybeans, canola, sunflower and other crops.

Does anyone really care about such science?

They should, but they might not unless the story includes the fact that the research could lead to cheaper or better-performing oils for human consumption, such as cooking oils, margarine and other food products.

That is the human connection; science affects everyone, and a connection can be found in any scientific endeavor, even though some scientific stories might seem limited or focused in interest, such as the scientific interests of John Gorham.

Gorham is a longtime scientist and professor of veterinary microbiology and pathology at Washington State University. He is an international authority on slow-virus disease research in animals, and is probably best known for the codiscovery of the microorganism responsible for salmon poisoning in dogs and foxes. He has also developing a diagnostic test for scrapie in sheep; investigated the molecular biology, immunology and epidemiology of hemoparasitic diseases; and has studied bovine herpes viruses.

Who might be interested in Gorham's research? Possibly a local farmer, who notices that his prize-winning sheep and goats are twitching, excitable, intensely itching, excessively thirsty, emaciated, weak and, in some cases, paralyzed. That farmer might be very interested in a story on Gorham's world-class research on scrapie, which is usually a fatal disease.

But if that doesn't get your blood pumping, then how about the story of the sex life of a mollusk snail, or some other fascinating general scientific discovery? For instance, did you know there are nearly 100,000 species of mollusks and they have supplied humans with food, medicine and several other products since the beginning of time?

Science reporting has never—and probably never will—take precedence over other specialty areas of reporting, such as crime; there are two simple reasons. Crime reporting has more sex appeal (the sex life of a snail isn't really all that exciting), and it is easier to understand.

To compensate, some writers sometimes are ill-advised when they exaggerate or write sensationalized treatments of science. Not only does it backfire in the critical areas of credibility and accuracy, but also science writers will soon lose the respect of scientists, who often already have an issue with trust concerning many of those writing about their profession.

There are routine topics concerning scientific advancement that have been covered well over the years in areas such as radar, lasers, transistors, computers, processors and microchips, medical vaccines and breakthroughs and the space race.

The *Apollo 11* lunar module, also known as *Eagle,* was the first manned vehicle to land on the moon, in 1969; thus it received major coverage, including nearly four thousand accredited reporters covering the takeoff, flight, landing and return.

That, very likely, was a highlight of science reporting, as the number of science reporters has declined, as has this nation's space exploration.

Still, there have been (and still are) a wealth of topics in the space program to write about since *Apollo 11,* including the two tragic accidents, the most recent on February 1, 2004, when the space shuttle *Columbia* exploded upon reentry, killing the crew of seven. The other accident that set back the program was the 1986 *Challenger* explosion upon takeoff, which also killed a crew of seven astronauts.

The development of science—and thus reporting—is also hampered from time to time by other "failures" such as the faulty $1.5 billion Hubble telescope, which advanced space knowledge considerably but also became quite the controversy when it sent blurry images back to earth.

Coverage is also occasionally a given if activists sabotage scientific projects or go to court to prevent them. The focus of the coverage, however, is often on the protests and not the scientific developments.

John Franklin, formerly of the University of Oregon, said the following about science reporting in a lecture in Tennessee:

> I am aware that most Americans still tell pollsters they believe in science. But talk to those people; the so-called "science" they believe in includes astrology, yoga and ESP. They don't know what science IS. In one study of American science literacy, half did not understand that the earth travels around the sun. Only 6 percent of adults could be considered scientifically literate. More than half the students at Hollins College [Roanoke, Virginia] believe in ghosts and mental telepathy.
>
> If you believe in the power of the press, the most frightening poll was taken at the Columbia Graduate School of Journalism, one of my profession's most elite institutions. Fifty-seven percent of the student journalists believed in ESP, 57 percent believed in dousing, 47 percent in aura reading, and 25 percent in the lost continent of Atlantis. Another poll showed that two thirds of newspaper managing editors thought humans and dinosaurs lived at the same time, and that there was a "dark" side of the moon, upon which light never fell.

Franklin's comments underscore that science is not only difficult to report upon but also difficult for many Americans to understand—and an increase of quality coverage could help people better understand science.

Peter Gomer, a Pulitzer Prize–winning science reporter at the *Chicago Tribune,* gave a list of the nuts and bolts of science reporting at a FACS seminar. Here are some highlighted points:

- **When good reporters** call scientists or doctors, they are not ashamed to ask dumb questions.

- **Learn to greet** every extravagant claim by a scientist—any scientist—with polite skepticism.

- **Consider if the** scientist is university affiliated, in private practice or working for a commercial firm. Ask if he or she has any financial interest in the work being reported.

- **Consider where the** work was done. At a local hospital or Harvard? Was it peer reviewed? Were there enough animal or human subjects?

- **Were there proper** controls in the experiment?

Health Care and Medicine

Coverage of these topic areas has many of the same cautions as reporters need to heed in environmental and scientific stories. One is the difficulty in understanding medical terms. As there is jargon associated with most topic areas, it is advanced in the medical health field. A second difficulty is access to information—and the reluctance or refusal of some doctors to talk with the media.

There have been wonderful advancements made in health care and medicine over the years, partly from increased government funding for research and federal standards of enforcement, but there are still major diseases that result in limitation, severe debilitation and death, and a spotlight has been brightly focused on health care.

The number of people being treated for heart disease and cancer, the two leading causes of death in the United States, has gone up steadily, and another major disease—AIDS—has added to the stress. Individual insurance concerns and payment issues related to Medicare and other senior plans and providers have also caused controversy.

Millions of people don't have health insurance, and millions of others with insurance can't afford to go to a doctor unless it is an absolute necessity, as they can't afford the deductible.

Reporters covering medicine and health care can garner many story ideas from medical journals. There are hundreds of such publications, usually with poorly written stories of interesting and needed information ranging from the general to the specific, from microbiology, to tick-borne diseases, to psychology, to cardiology.

For instance, Nancy G. Westburg of the Department of Graduate Education and Human Services at Rider University in Lawrenceville, New Jersey, and Mary Guindon of the Department of Counseling and Human Services at Johns Hopkins University in Baltimore, Maryland, wrote a journal article in *AIDS and Behavior* titled "Hope, Attitudes, Emotions and Expectations in Healthcare Providers of Services to Patients Infected with HIV."

The abstract reads:

The results of this preliminary study of 94 healthcare providers show that they had high hope levels when working with patients infected with HIV. The providers named imparting hope during the counseling process as the most important intervention for increasing patients' treatment adherence. Although half of the respondents had uncertain expectations for the future of their patients, more than one third had hopeful expectations, with only a small minority having hopeless expectations. An overwhelming majority reported they did not have negative attitudes toward or uncomfortable feelings when working with patients who were infected with HIV, regardless of method of acquiring HIV, gender, or sexual orientation. Moreover, respondents seemed to have a balanced emotional state, with the majority reporting that they experienced more positive emotions than negative emotions when working with their patients over time. Implications for healthcare providers are discussed.

There are many story ideas that can come out of that journal article, many of which could be localized.

Other obvious sources for story ideas include hospital and health care news releases and medical meetings.

The following partial release from John Hopkins Medicine, a division of John Hopkins Hospital, Health Systems and University, would be a good start for several localized stories about the elderly and exercise:

Johns Hopkins Medicine
Office of Corporate Communications
MEDIA CONTACT: Name Here
Phone Number e-mail address
December 21, 2004

Exercise Combats Metabolic Syndrome in Older Adults

Researchers at Johns Hopkins have determined that in people age 55 to 75, a moderate program of physical exercise can significantly offset the potentially deadly mix of risk factors for heart disease and diabetes known as the metabolic syndrome. More specifically, the researchers found that exercise improved overall fitness, but the 23 percent fewer cases were more strongly linked to reductions in total and abdominal body fat and increases in muscle leanness, rather than improved fitness.

The researchers' findings raise the importance of physical exercise in treating both men and women with the metabolic syndrome, a clustering of three or more risk factors that make it more likely for a person to develop heart disease, diabetes and stroke— including high blood pressure, elevated blood glucose levels, excess abdominal fat and abnormal cholesterol levels.

The study, to be published in the *American Journal of Preventive Medicine* and available online Dec. 30, is believed to be the first to focus on the role of exercise training in treating metabolic syndrome in older persons, a group at high risk for heart disease and diabetes.

CHAPTER EXERCISES

1. Compile a list of departments, programs and colleges at your university that use environmentally sensitive chemicals, then make a list of five detailed story ideas.

2. Go to www.doomsdayguide.org/black_holes.htm, "Doomsday Guide: The Ultimate Guide to the Ultimate End!" Prepare a 2–3-minute oral presentation of an "environmental disaster," and provide a list of five local sources that could be used in writing a story about the disaster.

3. Select a scientific journal. Review an article, and come up with a detailed localized version of the story that could be written.

4. Write the above story.

5. Find a medical press release. Localize the release with a detailed story idea.

6. Write the above story.

7. Clip an environmental, medical or scientific story out of a major newspaper. Provide a one-page review and critique of the coverage—not the topic.

21 Social Services and Nonprofit Agencies

BY JOHN IRBY

From the beginning of time, people have needed help from social services and nonprofit agencies.

As a beginning reporter at a small daily newspaper in greater Los Angeles in 1971, I was offered a starting salary of $125 a week, or $6,500 a year. It was enough for one person to live on.

Today, a starting reporter at the *Moscow-Pullman Daily News* in Moscow, Idaho, would likely be offered about $350 a week, or just over $18,000 a year. The quality of life afforded by that salary is a small step above that of a "poor, starving college student."

But that $18,000 salary is well above the federal Department of Health and Human Services poverty guidelines. A single person living in the forty-eight contiguous states and District of Columbia is considered to be living in poverty if they make no more than $9,310 a year.

The federal minimum wage is $5.15 an hour. A single person working a forty-hour week for fifty-two weeks makes $10,618—and does not live in poverty, according to the government.

For a land of plenty, the United States has a growing gap between the rich and poor. In many cases it is based on education, skills and ability, something that can't always be controlled.

For instance, a basic accountant in the United States will make around $38,000 a year. Incidentally, if this person was the only source of income for a family of eight in Alaska, the government would consider them living in poverty. And, as a comparison, a chief financial officer's median salary in the United States is $260,785; a casino cocktail server's annual median salary is $15,759.

What does all this mean? It means that social services and nonprofit agencies are needed, and there is a need for fair and critical public affairs reporting of individuals and organizations who claim to be helping others.

One Woman's Story

There are many ways to write about and tell the stories of social service agencies. Those that are written with a focus on the agency, however, aren't as effective as the stories that focus on humanity. Here is how Katy Belokonny, a Washington State University senior public relations student taking a journalism news reporting and writing course, told a sad but true story about the many agencies that had an impact on one woman:

> Dry hands, bleach spots, splashing water, flying bubbles and crashing dishes: All day, everyday, the Washington State University dining centers are bombarded with dirty dishes. But, the competent dish crew behind the rotating carousel is constantly transforming dirty into clean. Lori L. Anderson has the art of dish washing perfected at the Wilmer Davis Dining Center.
>
> Anderson, 43, was an employee of WSU Dining Services from August 1990 until last spring when management decided to lay her off due to budget cuts. In those 14 years, she worked at many of the dining centers including Regents, the Compton Union Building and the Rotunda. However, soon after Anderson began, it became apparent Wilmer Davis would be her ideal dish destination. Although Anderson is mentally challenged, anyone who has worked with Anderson talks of her dedication, reliability and independence while working at the dining centers. Despite her qualifications, Anderson is experiencing difficulty finding adequate new employment. A similar scenario has been experienced repeatedly by millions of individuals with disabilities.
>
> In the past few decades many laws have been implemented to help individuals with disabilities, like Anderson, receive employment. In 1973, the Rehabilitation Act was passed in hopes of opening avenues of employment for people with disabilities. However, according to Louis Harris and Associates, Inc., reported in *World* magazine, two-thirds of people with disabilities seeking employment still could not find a job 13 years later. This prompted the passage of the Americans with Disabilities Act in 1990, which not only forbade companies from discriminating against the disabled, but also required them to create accommodating work environments.

(continued)

(continued)

Even with these advances, more than seven million individuals with disabilities elected not to work for fear of losing federal medical disability benefits, reported *Issues* magazine.

To encourage those with disabilities to become employed, the Work Incentive Improvement Act was approved in 1999 to expand Medicaid and Medicare benefits so individuals with disabilities could continue to receive health insurance coverage once they were employed.

Despite these legal provisions, the unemployment rate among people with disabilities is alarmingly high at 70 percent, according to the *Jewish Exponent* magazine. It appears stereotypes, attitudes, myths, fears, ignorance and misinformation on the part of employers are the biggest barriers to those with disabilities receiving employment.

Some of the most common misgivings include: employers thinking people with disabilities might not perform job duties as well as other employees, employers assuming those with disabilities do not want to work, employers worrying the cost of making the workplace accessible to individuals with disabilities will be too prohibitive, or employers worrying that insurance rates might greatly increase when people with disabilities are hired.

These employers' concerns have resulted in disability bias emerging as the second fastest growing type of on-the-job discrimination, according to the Equal Employment Opportunity Commission. The *Boston Globe* reported that the number of disability complaints filed with the federal agency soared from 1,048 in 1992 to 16,470 in 2001.

Research indicates not only are employers' fears unfounded, but there are numerous benefits of hiring those with disabilities. Given an appropriate opportunity, people with disabilities are productive, dependable and self-supporting in the work force. Individuals with disabilities, like everyone, vary in their abilities, interests and skills. Successful employment is dependant upon matching individual strengths with the appropriate type of job.

The dining centers were a perfect fit for Anderson. The repetitious nature of her job and interactions with accepting co-workers allowed Anderson to succeed at her duties as well as engage in activities she enjoyed. In addition to Anderson's daily four-hour shift at Wilmer Davis, her days were filled with walking, picture taking and coloring. Anderson would walk to work daily, partly resulting from her fear of vehicles, but mostly from her love for walking. Prior to her shift starting at 8 A.M., Anderson would snap photos on her Polaroid camera of Wilmer Davis and her favorite co-workers. The moment the clock ticked noon, Anderson began distributing her drawings to favorite managers and hungry students before she began her walk home. But, in between the picture taking and distribution of her drawings, Anderson diligently sorted the various dishware, wiped down tables and unloaded the clean dishes.

"Although Lori is mentally challenged, her near perfect attendance record, immediate compliance when completing tasks and endless enthusiasm for her job at Wilmer Davis, were equal to any of the other employees," Bill C. Prewett, food service supervisor, said.

Although many employers have various concerns that have resulted in discrimination, the reality is most workers with disabilities receive employee ratings similar to Anderson's.

The *Michigan Chronicle* newspaper reported that 90 percent of workers with disabilities have fewer absences than their coworkers and are considered good to excellent employees. In addition, only 30 percent of people with disabilities require special equipment to perform effectively.

(continued)

(continued)

The Internal Revenue Code also provides significant tax reductions to businesses that make their facilities accessible. Employers need not worry about rising insurance rates either, because statistics from the Equal Employment Opportunity Commission show insurance rates for businesses are not any higher when people with disabilities are hired.

Another benefit resulting from the employment of people with disabilities is an enhanced economy. When people with disabilities become employed, the economy is strengthened because they earn money, pay taxes and become contributing members of society, instead of being supported solely by government programs.

Statistics from the Senate Report No. 106-37, reported *Issues* magazine, reveal if only 1 percent, or 75,000, of the 7.5 million individuals with disabilities were to become employed, the government would save $3.5 billion over the work life of the beneficiaries. In contrast, employer stereotypes cost the nation combined losses of nearly a half trillion dollars a year. From the half trillion dollars, $230 billion is spent supporting people with disabilities who want jobs but cannot find them, and $195 billion is lost in earnings and taxes that are never realized, the *Michigan Chronicle* newspaper reported.

Anderson became one of the 75,000 people with disabilities needing employment when, unexpectedly, Wilmer Davis closed for remodeling in 2001.

When Anderson's Monday through Friday routine was dramatically altered management decided to move Anderson to the Compton Union Building (CUB). The transition to a less-structured environment was a difficult adjustment for Anderson. Part of Anderson's disability requires she have a set schedule because she has a difficult time adapting to situations apart from her routine. The decision was made to let Anderson go shortly after she began working at the CUB.

"Since I had worked with Lori for years and knew how reliable she was, I felt responsible to find a position for her," Manager of Dining Services Kim M. Finley said.

However, the opening of Hillside (the new Wilmer Davis) revealed Anderson's dish position had become extinct. Finley decided to create a job for Anderson performing janitorial duties at Regents. Receiving little support from Palouse Industries, who was responsible for acclimating Anderson to her new position, she again struggled with the new adjustment. When the labor budget was cut for dining services last spring, management decided to lay off Anderson.

"It is unfortunate, for Lori, that people are obsessed with getting more for their money," Jennifer L. Jenson, employment service coordinator at Palouse Industries, said. "That just does not seem right when you are talking about people."

In addition to the greater economic implications, those with disabilities suffer great financial losses personally without employment. The loss of employment has been devastating for Anderson financially. Due to Anderson's prior status as a temporary employee of dining services, she is unable to collect unemployment. Although Anderson is working for a program at Palouse Industries, she gets paid subminimum wage due to a special certificate under the Department of Labor. This has taken a tremendous toll on Anderson's ability to support herself.

Anderson is just one of the 7.5 million people with disabilities who are waiting to become employed. Like many people with disabilities, worry and false perceptions of limitations by employers prevent Anderson from job consideration.

"People with disabilities do not have an abundance of choice," explained Lorraine B. Fulfs, residential provider of Social and Health Services.

(continued)

(continued)

The emotional implications of Anderson's job loss have been equally profound. Anderson's excitement for her former job still wakes her up early each morning, and she quickly begins walking to WSU on the same route she has taken for the past 14 years. She makes her routine stops at the dining centers to deliver drawings, visit with friends and take pictures.

In all weather, Anderson is on campus with her headphones blaring, camera hanging from her shoulder and hands clutching newly created pictures. She refuses to take off her tattered employee name tag, which has a Polaroid picture of Wilmer Davis crookedly taped onto it, and she is occasionally seen wearing her red-and-white-striped work gown.

Anderson's dedication to WSU and the pleasure she derived from working at Wilmer Davis have not allowed her to accept that she is no longer a WSU employee.

"Washing dishes at a dining center might be the most trivial minimum-wage job to you or me, but it was a career to Lori," Jenson said.

False perceptions of Anderson's limitations by employers prevent her from job consideration. While the dining center has the luxury of replacing Anderson with a mechanical dishwasher, Anderson cannot as easily replace the financial or emotional gratification she has lost.

Although there has been much legal progress in the past 35 years for individuals with disabilities in the workplace, attitudes are not legislated by laws.

Social Services

If there is a need, it seems there is a social service available. Take, for instance, the Washington State Department of Social and Health Services, which in 2003 served about 1.5 million people in a state with just over 6 million residents. The high number of clients could be from the options of available services, as there are nearly 350 links of opportunity on the department's Web site (www1.dshs.wa.gov/wayswe.shtml)

The site is detailed in instruction on how to take advantage of services. For instance, the following tells how to report child abuse:

> We all have a responsibility, as neighbors and community members, to look out for one another and help keep each other safe. Preventing abuse of children and adults takes everyone. . . . Law enforcement and social service agencies cannot be everywhere. It takes all of us to help make sure that those who need protection are safe. For the first time, it's now easy, in Washington State, to know where to call if you suspect a child or a vulnerable adult is being abused or neglected. Anyone can call DSHS Toll-Free 1-866-ENDHARM. When you call, you will speak with a real person, who will connect you to the direct number to make your report. The answering service operates seven days per week, 24 hours per day.

Getting help or treatment for alcohol or drug abuse, general medical concerns, senior issues, financial hardship, juvenile rehabilitation, food/housing/clothing, unemployment, birth control, child care, domestic violence and dementia are only a click away, as are immigration–refugee assistance, job retraining, language translation, Medicaid/Medicare, pregnancy–abortion–adoption, nutrition, paternity and a mapping of sex offenders.

All social service agencies can't be covered all the time. Public affairs reporters, however, should challenge and investigate the patterns in the services offered and used.

How many seem necessary or add-ons? Which ones are being used most often? What are the reasons? How much do they cost the state? Is there internal or external abuse? Good public affairs reporters will write social services stories that inform and mediate debate.

Because of the patterns that often develop, journalists have an opportunity to provide deeper reporting. Many feel they have a responsibility to search for the reasons why something happens and then explain it to readers.

Searching for the "why" can involve techniques that aren't always used in day-to-day reporting, such as using data or surveys, field experiments, historical reviews, technical and environmental studies and human factors. And expanding the number of people interviewed about an issue or event concerning social services can enrich perspectives.

Writing about social services isn't always easy. Contextual information will not be obtained from an Internet Web site, short telephone interviews, rewriting government press releases or using only simple background documents or routine facts—all of which are the staples of day-to-day journalism.

Information from social service agencies, likewise, will be held tightly. Some—generally raw data—should be made public, but you might have to make public records act requests (see chapter 7) to obtain it. And, most of the time, individual personal information is private and will not be released.

While each state has endless opportunities for stories about social services, the federal government is also a wide-open landscape of story ideas that can come from agencies and resources such as the National Institutes of Health (NIH), Occupational Safety and Health Administration (OSHA), U.S. Census Bureau, U.S. Center for Disease Control (CDC), U.S. Department of Health and Human Services and U.S. Social Security Administration.

Nonprofits

After being promoted to managing editor of the 75,000-circulation *Bakersfield Californian,* I quickly learned about nonprofit organizations, those that are established for charitable, educational or humanitarian purposes, not for making money, and are most often funded through private donations.

They are similar to but different from social services, which are organized and most often funded by the public though taxes in the name of advancing human welfare and improving the condition of those who are disadvantaged or less fortunate in society.

The phone rang. I picked up the receiver and was asked after two minutes of pleasantries to become a board member of the Boys Club.

Like many citizens, I wanted to give back to society. But was it a conflict for a newspaper managing editor to serve as a board member of an organization that the newspaper covered? That's another issue worthy of discussion.

I accepted with one amendment to our verbal agreement. I would not be expected to flak for the organization in getting news releases into the newspaper, and I would be transparent in any situations in which the newspaper wrote about the organization.

The agreement lasted one day. At my first meeting, I was greeted with much glee. "We are so thankful you have joined the board," one longtime member said, adding, "Now maybe we can get some decent coverage in the paper."

PROFESSIONAL TIPS

Brent Champaco

Brent Champaco is an award-winning reporter who covered social services, education and city government for three years at the *Tri-City Herald* and *Moscow-Pullman Daily News*. He joined the *Tacoma News Tribune* as a suburban reporter in 2005. He graduated in journalism from Washington State University in 2001 and was a Chips Quinn Scholar at the *Marin Independent Journal* in California.

Question: Why is it sometimes difficult to get information from social service agencies?

Social service agencies are like any other public or government agency a young reporter will encounter. Most are skeptical of your ability to accurately tell a story. Some think they're not held to the same standards of accountability that government agencies must meet. Some have been burned in the past by previous reporters. Some agencies think the media is their public relations arm, so they'll talk all day about their fundraiser but pray the story about the director's misuse of funds slips through the cracks.

Question: What tips can you provide that would help journalists get information from social service agencies?

Get to know the agency inside and out. Talk to people, everyone from the assistant director to the front-desk secretary. Know the people it strives to serve. What challenges do they face? Why do they need help? Writing about people and their experiences is the best way to bring readers into a story.

Also, you need to know about an agency's finances. People donate millions of dollars to these groups and want to know how their money is spent. Is it struggling because it truly is serving the needs of its clients or because of mismanagement? Why does its board of directors conduct its annual retreat at five-star hotels? How much of the agency's budget consists of administrative costs? A lot of this stuff is available on the agency's 990 tax form (if they file one at all). You can get that from the IRS or Web sites like www.guidestar.org.

Question: How is coverage different for social service agencies and nonprofits?

The closest beat to social services is education. Agencies in both areas are supposed to help our society's most vulnerable people. The juicy, award-winning stories are there, but you've got to be willing to write the fluff piece. As stated earlier, social service reporting is often about people, not hard news or numbers.

Question: Can a reporter donate to a nonprofit—such as the Boys and Girls Club—and report on it?

I would avoid it. There are major ethical issues involved. Although most reporters are smart enough to distinguish their personal beliefs from their work, donating to the agency you cover cripples your credibility. Many media outlets prohibit their newsroom employees from donating for that reason. A reader likely would have serious reservations about investing in a story that possibly is too fair to the agency.

(continued)

PROFESSIONAL TIPS   Continued

Question: Do you have anything else to share with young reporters concerning nonprofits and social service agencies?

Many of the basic lessons you learned in college apply to the beat. Accuracy is vital and often opens doors to more in-depth stories. Be relentless. Don't give up on a story just because the nonprofit agency claims there isn't one. That usually means there's more you need to find out. Have fun with the beat. It isn't all doom and scandalous gloom. People have stories to tell, often funny ones. Write about the lives of the clients. They're people before they're poor and needy.

Give the reader a reason to spend ten minutes of his or her life reading your story. Convince the audience that social services might target a few people, but helping those individuals is in the best interests of everyone.

Another wanted to know if I was the person who would be the contact because they had some page 1 news about a fundraiser.

It was unfortunate, but I resigned.

Nonprofits, rightly so, are eager for publicity. Paid staff members and those who volunteer for nonprofit work are drilled in the importance of getting their name and message to the public—their lifeline of financial support.

Before covering nonprofits, reporters need to learn the basics.

There is much information available, including that found on the Bloodhound Network (www.bloodhoundnetwork.com), an encyclopedia of the Internet created by Bloodhound editors and, more importantly, the Internet community. Volunteers provide information about their professions, hobbies, sports and several other topic areas. Concerning nonprofits, it reports:

> Nonprofit organizations include a wide variety of activist, civic, religious, public service and public broadcasting organizations that work in the public interest rather than the goal of making money and may operate at the local, state, national or international level. To qualify for nonprofit status in the United States, an organization must be approved by the IRS. The organization is then exempt from paying taxes which would be levied for a for-profit business.
>
> Only specific types of organizations can qualify to be nonprofit. Nonprofits are recognized and authorized by Congress, which determined that certain types of enterprises should be free from the burden of having to pay income taxes. To accomplish these goals, it established a class of entity now known as a tax exempt corporation, or nonprofit corporations.
>
> In giving these corporations tax exempt status, however, Congress imposed specific requirements and limitations on their activities. The IRS tends to strictly enforce these rules, otherwise the organization will lose its tax exempt status.
>
> A nonprofit corporation is not prohibited from making a profit, but there are limitations on what it can do with its profits. There are also limitations on how it can make money—and it must make money in accordance with its nonprofit purposes.

There are any number of well-known nonprofit organizations, like the Red Cross and United Way, that collect millions of dollars and provide a great deal of help and assistance, especially in times of major disaster.

But for all the nonprofits that are doing very good or relatively good work, and are responsible in financial matters, there are others that need scrutiny.

Coverage of nonprofits should not focus only on the mishaps. Nor should it resemble chamber-of-commerce small-town boosterism.

Americans, however, followed closely the American Red Cross controversy over donations after the September 11, 2001, terrorists' attacks, which prompted organization President and CEO Bernadine Healy to resign amid disputes with the Red Cross board about how the millions raised would be used on behalf of the attacks' victims.

The charity was criticized for being slow to make clear to donors that their money might not make it to September 11 victims, as some money had tentatively been targeted for administrative and other efforts—and the future.

When donors respond to a disaster or emergency, it is safe to say that they are responding to that specific situation and that their expectations are their funds will be used for that specific situation.

That same situation occurred in late December 2004 and early January 2005, following the earthquake and tsunami in South Asia. Story after story was reported about nonprofit agencies soliciting aid, and about which ones could—or could not—be trusted to utilize donations most effectively.

Because of this, many organizations made public pronouncements concerning financial responsibility. Family Care Foundation (FCF), which provides humanitarian services in developing nations, makes grants and provides training for grassroots organizations in the Third World, assured its donors that 100 percent of all donations would be used for tsunami relief efforts in the disaster areas, bypassing all other overhead.

The Christian Children's Fund out of Richmond, Virginia, indicated on its Web page that, in general, 80.7 percent of its gifts—$128 million—went directly to children's program services. Just over 11 percent ($17.9 million) went to fundraising, and 8 percent ($12.7 million) went to management and general costs.

The American Red Cross collected $6,416,640 from 66,468 donors by mid-January 2005. It informed donors: "The American Red Cross is not a government agency and all Red Cross disaster assistance is free thanks to the generosity of people like you. The value of your donation is increased by the fact that the ratio of volunteer Red Cross workers to paid staff is almost 36 to one. Contributions to the American Red Cross, a tax-exempt organization under Section 501(c)(3) of the Internal Revenue Code, are deductible for computing income and estate taxes."

The Red Cross reported shortly before February 2005 it had raised more than $1 billion.

In covering nonprofits, especially in times of emergency, reporters must be conscious that frauds and scams will increase.

The *Washington Post* reported the following from the Philanthropy Code of Ethical Online Philanthropic Practices, which can serve as a guide for not only donors but also nonprofits reporters.

How to Give Charitably and Safely
- **Give only to** legitimate charities recognized by the appropriate governmental bodies in their countries.

- **Ask questions of** the charity, and check www.guidestar.org for information provided by certain charities to the IRS. Find out how the charity plans to use your money.

- **Make sure the** charity site uses encryption. The letters *https://,* rather than *http://,* should precede the page's URL, and/or an unbroken key or padlock symbol should be in the corner of the Web browser.

- **Try to give** directly to the charity. If the charity has no online giving opportunities, consider contributing to www.networkforgood.org, which provides all registered charities in the United States with the capability to receive online donations.

- **Check for a** privacy policy concerning the use of your name, e-mail address or other personal information. Don't disclose personal information unless you know who is collecting the information and how it will be used.

- **Print a copy** of the final confirmation page that appears on your computer screen when you have made your gift, and keep a copy of any e-mail confirming the gift for your records.

- **Look for contact** information, which reputable charities will provide.

- **Request regular information** from the charity on its Web site or in e-mail updates.

Stories about fraud during emergency situations serve as a public service. Fraudaid.com (www.fraudaid.com) provides a wealth of tips and story ideas, including sample fraud letters seeking aid.

CHAPTER EXERCISES

1. Write a story that analyzes the percentage of money raised that is spent on administrative and general costs compared to actual aid, support or programs. Select a well-known nonprofit.

2. Select a social service agency in your state. Review its Web site, and come up with a list of questions you have about the service.

3. Spend two hours at your local unemployment office. Do not act like a reporter, and resist the temptation to interview people. Do, however, discreetly take pertinent notes. Turn in a list of five detailed stories from your experience.

4. Interview the director of your local United Way, Red Cross, YMCA or YWCA (or some local charity or nonprofit), and write a news feature about that organization.

5. Interview the director of a social service agency in your community, and write a news feature about the agency.

6. Find a person who has benefitted from a social service agency or nonprofit, and tell his or her story in a news feature.

APPENDIX A

Obituaries

BY JOHN IRBY

Sneak Peek

Thinking before
Writing
Student Work
The Basics
Professional Tips
Celebration
Examples
The Checklists
Exercise

There can be beauty and celebration in all things, including death. When writing an obituary, remember that you are bringing the person back to life for the last time.

Do you ever read newspaper obituaries? If not, you probably will one day, as you get older. An aging comedian said a few years before his death that he reads them every day to make sure he is still alive. Newspaper researchers tell us that about half of all newspaper readers look at obituaries.

Still, despite a high readership, many newspapers will not write an obituary unless the person who has died is well known, or a public figure.

In 1897, a New York newspaper reported that humorist Mark Twain had died. Twain, who hadn't died, sent a cable saying: "Reports of my death have been greatly exaggerated."

There are two keys to remember in obituaries: first, make sure people are dead before you write an obituary. Accuracy is, after all, critical. Second, in writing an obituary, celebrate the life of the person; don't write about death.

The *Cabinet Press* in Milford, New Hampshire, learned the hard way in August 2003 when an obituary and photograph of a 44-year-old teacher were dropped off for publication. The woman, however, was still alive.

"It never occurred to us that someone would be sick enough to do this," said Michael Cleveland, editor of the *Cabinet Press.*

Cleveland said the obituary didn't raise any suspicions because it was well-written, laudatory and accompanied by a professional-looking photograph. He said the newspaper often prints obituaries submitted through the mail.

Thinking before Writing

Carolyn Milford Gilbert, founder of the International Association of Obituarists, editor of ObitPage.com and known as the "Obit Lady," says obituaries should be addressed with reverence and sincerity, but also with a "wicked sense of humor."

Years ago, beginning journalists at newspapers were assigned to write obituaries. That isn't always the case today. Beginning journalists, for the most part, no longer write obits. Many newspapers publish paid obituaries that are written by funeral homes or survivors such as a husband, wife, brother, sister, mother, father, son, daughter or other relative. And those that are written by newspapers are often done so by experienced or veteran wordsmiths.

Frankly, many obituaries of the past weren't all that interesting—unless the reader knew the dead person. They were written in form fashion with very little creativity.

Paid obituaries, however, have become the rage at many medium- to large-circulation newspapers, as it is a good source of income, and it also makes for some interesting reading, especially if the family or a friend of the deceased writes it. There is also often a public affairs angle in obituaries.

Student Work

Students in my classes routinely write their own obituaries. A few think it is morbid. But most understand it is easier to celebrate their own life and write a quality obituary, than to interview a neighbor or the professor and do an equally thorough job.

The lead, as always, is critical. The best ones are creative, show personality or celebrate life. They do not focus on death. Here are some examples of student leads:

- **He never met a bad habit he didn't enjoy.** The author, a 33-year-old reentry student, had a reputation of smoking, drinking and playing poker until all hours of the night.

- **She was a wild child who lived a wild life, but had her own rules and regulations.** This was written by a young woman whose blue-tinted hair overshadowed her facial piercing.

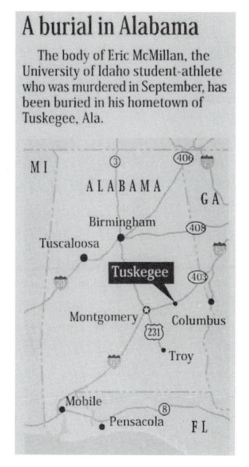

A burial in Alabama

The body of Eric McMillan, the University of Idaho student-athlete who was murdered in September, has been buried in his hometown of Tuskegee, Ala.

FIGURE A.1 Even though obituaries are celebrations of life, straight details in some situations need to be told, and simple maps or graphics can be the best way to handle such information.

Brian Beesley/Lewiston Tribune

- **She would want everyone to cry at her funeral, only because she would have bawled her eyes out at yours. She came out of the womb crying and was known in her family as "the crier." Unfortunately, her death was so unexpected she was not able to cry about it.** This student wrote a clever, fun and appropriately sad lead.

- **She had passion for theater, iced caramel coffee and politics. She loved taking naps on Sunday afternoons, jogging with friends and watching improvisational comedy. She disliked pancakes, cats and driving and preferred talking to her friends at her favorite coffeehouse instead of going to fraternity parties.** This student had many interests to write about.

The Basics

Even though celebrating life should be the main consideration, writing an obituary is like writing a news story—which it is—in that correct information is essential.

Misspelling a name in a sports or business story is a journalistic sin, but misspelling a name in an obituary is a journalistic deadly sin. Obituaries are often the last word(s) written about a person, and survivors cut copies out of newspapers, laminate them, place them in scrapbooks and/or mail them across the country to families and friends.

Obituaries will answer the same information as a news story—who (the name), what (died), where (a hospital), when (time, day), why (heart attack) and how (while running). But don't try to answer all of those questions in the lead; sometimes none or only one of those elements will be in the lead.

Celebration Examples

Jim Sheeler of the *Denver Rocky Mountain News* wrote the following about the life of refugee Ban Phu Tcheng:

> When Ban Phu Tcheng's family fled the bullets in China when she was a little girl, they left behind everything they ever had. When she fled war in Vietnam 15 years later, she carried with her all that would ever matter.
>
> When they ran from the wars, they were not allowed to take any material possessions—they were only able to take family. And that's all she cared about for the rest of her life: family, said Tcheng's son, his voice falling to a broken whisper Sunday as he spoke by telephone from his parent's home in Aurora.
>
> "She survived so much. She survived two wars," he said. "I just wish she could have gotten through this one."
>
> The 54-year-old mother of two was shot and killed for her car late Friday night as she left work at a restaurant supply company. . . .
>
> Early Saturday morning, her 1993 Ford Explorer was pulled over for a traffic violation. During questioning, two people inside the stolen car led police to an 18-year-old man who was arrested at a nearby hotel, police said.
>
> The suspect, Michael Wheeler, was booked into the Adams County Detention Facility at 2 A.M. Sunday and was being held for investigation of first-degree murder and aggravated robbery.
>
> "She was just a sweet little old lady," said her 23-year-old son, who asked to remain anonymous. "If you bumped into her, she would fall over. She was just a little old lady."
>
> She was born in China, but her family escaped to Vietnam in the 1950s. Fifteen years later, Tcheng fled the bullets again, making it from Vietnam to Colorado with her husband. The pair settled in Pueblo, where they helped run a restaurant, then moved to Denver to start a family.
>
> As her children grew up, their bedtime stories were the true tales of their parents' lives, and the moral to the story was always the same.
>
> "There was nothing more important to her than the family," her son said. "When you come from such war-torn areas, it's hard to keep in touch with family, so it was really just the four of us. We were the picture of a perfect family."
>
> She spent most of her life working in restaurants, usually as a waitress, trying to keep her children from having to work, trying to keep them safe. At home, she shared the kitchen with her husband, creating elaborate meals together, her son said. This year was to have been their 30th wedding anniversary.

(continued)

(continued)

> "She was always working, taking care of us," said her 21-year-old daughter. "But in two years, she was going to retire, and it was going to be her turn to relax. Then we were going to take care of her."
>
> After a long pause, Tcheng's son caught himself staring at his mother's indoor garden—a virtual nursery that he said consumes much of the home. Among it all, he eyed one of her favorite plants—one that everyone else had long ago given up on.
>
> "I never saw it (bloom) in four years," her son said. "I thought it was a weed."
>
> When the recent drought threatened the plant, his mother went into the backyard, dug it up and gave it another chance.
>
> "She made it grow," he said. "She made everything grow.
>
> "She made it flower."

Sheeler's story celebrates a life. Rather than getting bogged down in the details of the crime, shooting and death, he uses a suspense lead, and the reader is drawn into wanting to know more about this person who fled bullets and war.

The reader then starts to wonder what has happened—surely it must be serious—as we learn that family was the only really important thing in Tcheng's "life" (written as if it has indeed ended).

The nut graph follows, with just enough detail to know what has happened.

Scheeler then returns to the celebration of the victim's life. Tcheng was a "sweet little old lady." She escaped strife and tragedy, came to America, ran a restaurant, had a family and told her children bedtime stories. She deeply loved her picture-perfect family. She worked hard, fed her children well and loved her husband for 30 years. She would have soon retired to her passion, gardening, where she could turn sure death into life.

It isn't always easy to celebrate life. That doesn't mean, however, that it can't be done and that interesting stories can't be told through obituaries.

The Checklists

While there is much freedom in obituary writing, storytelling should be foremost in the author's mind, along with inclusion of basic checklist information:

- **Time and place of funeral and burial (and, often, who will officiate):** While some funerals are held at graveside, most are conducted at a funeral home or church. Not all people, however, are buried in a cemetery. Some are placed in above-ground vaults at a cemetery, and others are cremated with the ashes being stored or spread at various places. **Example:** Funeral services, officiated by the Rev. John Jones, will be held Monday, April 1, at 2 P.M. at Caldwell Funeral Home, 1111 S. First St. Burial will follow at Deep Slumber Memorial Park, 2222 N. Second St.

- **Visitation times (if any):** It is common, especially in closed-casket funeral services, for mortuaries to hold visitations, to view the body, often the afternoon or night before the funeral. **Example:** Visitation will be offered at 6 P.M. Sunday, March 31, at Caldwell Funeral Home. (*Note:* The use of an address would be included unless it has already been used earlier in the story.)

PROFESSIONAL TIPS

Ralph Pomnichowski

Ralph Pomnichowski, 61, is a freelance writer and photographer working out of Great Falls, Montana. He wrote obituaries and all other kinds of news for daily and weekly newspapers in Montana for many years. He also worked for the U.S. Senate and a statewide farm and ranch organization.

Question: Why do people read obituaries?

To find out what killed you. And how old you were when it happened. People who didn't like you, of course, just take glee in seeing that you're dead for sure.

After that, it's all just biography, unless you passed in spectacular fashion, maybe in a flaming wreck, or unusually, as in falling off a ladder, or feloniously at the hands of another. Maybe by your own hand.

After you're pushing up daisies, people will find in your obituary things about you that they never knew.

Many readers scan obituaries of unfamiliar names to determine if the departed are people they knew casually, recognizing them by occupation, address, or some other identifier.

Question: Is there a format to writing obituaries?

Sort of; as usual, it's a matter of putting exactly the right word in exactly the right place. The weaving of the information into a flowing account is the hard part.

If a reader has to reread something above, you've failed. The obit doesn't have to be purely chronological, but it had better not be confusing.

If a funeral home supplies data on a standard form for standard citizens, that's fine. But readers expect a lengthier epitaph for outstanding people, starting with one or two of that person's finest accomplishments.

Even a young person may have enjoyed popularity or notoriety in life, like an athlete or prom-

ising scholar killed in a car accident, but such an obituary has fewer life events to work with and must depend more on recollections by those who knew him or her.

Assembling the obituary of someone who was rich, philanthropic and thus fairly well documented is far less difficult than writing the life, for instance, of a priest or longtime volunteer for whom thanks and admiration were shown mostly with hugs and smiles.

It takes a lot more telephoning to assemble an obituary of a person less well known. You still use the info turned in by the family and the funeral home, but filling in the gaps and finding the gems take patient conversation.

There are exceptions. Transients with no known background, for example, will get relatively few lines in the newspaper. A short obit also can be the case for a person with no survivors. And in a few cases, relatives and friends of the dead person will not talk.

Question: Is it difficult to interview friends and family members? Any tips?

The woman's shriek at the other end of the line, then the phone bouncing off the floor, were the sounds telling me the highway patrolman really hadn't contacted the family just yet, as he'd told me. While he was momentarily summoning up the

(continued)

PROFESSIONAL TIPS   Continued

nerve to make another bad-news phone call, I was already dialing.

My call had been to round out the story of a girl's fatal highway accident earlier that day. So, there are surprises occasionally.

When I called families of soldiers killed in Vietnam to ask if I could stop by and pick up photos and information to fill out the brief military announcements, answering parents always cooperate. Occasionally, a protective relative who happened to answer at the house would try to stall in their behalf. Waiting a while and trying again almost always was successful.

Be courteous. It's not easy at either end of the phone.

Survivors of the combat dead usually offered information and recollections. The questioning was done with the same respect accorded any other grieving people.

In another case, I called a soft-spoken elderly woman for information and comments about a fellow widow who had died. They'd been lifelong friends, so my interview elicited church activities, travel, volunteering at the hospital and a number of other recollections.

Then I asked about the husband. Way out of character from the rest of the interview, she called him every kind of a son of a bitch. She repeatedly called the long-dead oil-patch worker a beast, one of her more timid descriptions. Alas, her colorful words couldn't be used in a family newspaper, so the guy got short shrift.

Obituary questions are the usual: date and place of birth, parents, siblings, education, sports, hobbies, accomplishments, honors/awards, elective office, club affiliations, military service, accidents, employments, how long they enjoyed retirement before drawing their last breath, philanthropy, pets, etc.

Question: How does a reporter go about celebrating someone's life?

It's not exactly straight reporting. You're recounting an existence in feature fashion, using quotes in places.

Key on accomplishments but mention any significant setbacks and how they may have been overcome. You're probably writing this person's last public biography.

If he or she was a churchgoing pillar of the community, it's easy to round out the litany of good works with amusing anecdotes from family and friends.

But if he was a rascal and every cop in town knew where he lived, it's a different situation. His victims would have views markedly different than those of his family and friends. In my experience, unless such persons committed heinous offenses with attendant wide publicity, the obituaries were competent and played straight.

Everybody has something to hide. Are you going to play ferret for an obit? Probably not, in most cases.

Question: Anything else you'd like to add about writing obituaries?

It's the last hurrah for the dearly departed, so I usually left in some facts, even when a story started running sort of long. After all, their morgue file is going away for good, unless he or she was someone whose photo might have occasional use in the future. The copy editor may shorten the story for you anyway.

There are different styles for obituary writing everywhere, but I always placed funeral arrangements near the top.

None of my personal interviews were done using a tape recorder. There's nothing worse to ruin an interview with most people.

■ **Survivors:** Most, if not all, obituaries include a list of survivors. They generally include parents, spouses, siblings and children. Grandchildren, aunts, uncles, cousins, other relatives, boyfriends, girlfriends, fiancées, live-in companions and friends can be included, depending upon the wishes of the surviving family, or at the prearranged request of the person who has died. Place of residence of survivors is often listed if they are from out of town. **Example:** Smith is survived by her husband,

Sam, and daughter, Sally, both of Anytown, USA; mother, Gladys Leach, of Atlanta, Ga.; sister, Dorothy Lewis, of Salem, Ore.; sons, James and John Smith, both of Grand Rapids, Mich.; and a lifelong friend, Lisa Louise, of New York, New York.

- **Date and place of birth:** The age of the person when he or she died is often included with the name at the top of the obituary. But it is also common to include the date and place of birth in the obituary. **Example:** Smith, 95, who spent most of her life living and working in Pontiac, Mich., was born Oct. 24, 1909, in Escanaba, Mich. She considered herself a "Yooper," the nickname given to those who live in, or are from, the Upper Peninsula of Michigan. (*Note:* Always make sure the age and year of birth add up.)

- **Achievements and occupation:** Many of the achievements of a person's life, and his or her occupation, should be included in the celebration aspects of the obituary. **Example:** Smith graduated from Harvard University and worked her way into a partnership at Baker, Smith, Yankel and Jones, one of the leading environmental law firms in the United States. For more than 20 years, she was known as the lawyer who won the largest groundwater pollution lawsuit against a major U.S. company. Smith also found time to volunteer more than 30,000 hours of service with the Young Women's Christian Association (YWCA) as a swimming instructor. She also donated more than $1 million over her life to care for homeless families.

- **Organizational memberships:** Again, much of this should be included in the celebration aspects of the obituary. **Example:** Smith was a 40-year member, and regional vice president, of Toastmasters International, a club dedicated to improving public speaking. She also belonged to the following organizations: Big Brothers and Sisters, Michigan Bar Association (MBA), YMCA, Rotary International and Mensa International, an international high-IQ society that welcomes people whose IQ is in the top 2 percent of the population.

Accuracy, as it is in all aspects of journalism, is critical. Many people are written about in the newspaper only three times in their life—birth, marriage and death. Always confirm spelling of names, check addresses, check birth date against the age, confirm information provided, make sure the obit is not a hoax, choose the correct words, avoid overworked and flowery terms and phrases, and refer to the *Associated Press Stylebook* (or approved style manual) when making religious references, as terms vary considerably among denominations and faiths.

The home address of the person who died was once standard information. Today, however, it is nearly always kept out of obituaries because of the possibility of burglary during visitation hours or funeral or burial services. When an approximate area can be provided (Northwest Escanaba, downtown, southeast part of town, etc.), it is a fact many readers can identify with as they might think they know the person because of the geographical information.

Cause of death was also once nearly always included in obituaries. It is a relevant fact of high interest. It, however, is routinely left out today because of privacy issues. Many people do not want to face the perceived embarrassment or stigma, oftentimes inappropriately so, of diseases such as AIDS, cirrhosis of the liver or suicide.

Other embarrassing information should generally be avoided, unless it is relevant to the celebration or life story. For instance, if a person was convicted of shoplifting when she or he was 24 years old, it would not be relevant in the obituary when she or he died at 95, unless the shoplifting charge changed the person's life, possibly resulting in a 40-year law enforcement career. That would be relevant information.

EXERCISE

1. It is common at some companies for executives to write the first draft of their own obituary. Newspapers across the country have obituary files with obituaries of people who are very alive. In this exercise, you will write your own obituary. So you don't get bogged down in some of the details, some basics are supplied (there also might be nonnecessary information to discard). You should concentrate on the celebration of your life, but *do not* make up facts (don't say you leave behind a 2-year-old daughter unless you have a 2-year-old daughter; don't say you were a star pitcher for the Los Angeles Dodgers or a U.S. senator unless you were).

Obituary Exercise Information Sheet

- *Funeral Home:* Campbell Funeral Home, 1111 W. First St., Escanaba, Mich., (800) 555–1555.
- *For More Information, Contact:* Funeral Director John Jones.
- *Name of Deceased:* Your name.
- *Address:* Your address.
- *Occupation:* Student (at your university). Include your major, date when you are expected to graduate, job(s), and so on.
- *Age:* Your age.
- *Birthdate and Birthplace:* Your birthday and birthplace.
- *Cause of Death:* A blood clot, five days after you had emergency surgery for a ruptured appendix. This is very unusual. You came home from the hospital the day before and were eating breakfast when you felt pain and dropped to the ground and died.
- *Date and Place of Death:* Date of the assignment. At home.
- *Time and Place of Funeral Services:* 10 A.M., five days after the assignment is made, Campbell Funeral Home.
- *Conducted By:* The Rev. Sam Smith.
- *Burial:* Deep Slumber and Rest Memorial Park, Escanaba, immediately following funeral.
- *Time and Place for Visitation:* 6–9 P.M., day before funeral, Campbell Funeral Home.
- *Biographical Information:* Be truthful.
- *Survivors:* Be truthful.
- *Celebration Information:* Be truthful.
- *Quote:* You can make up *one* quote (no more than two sentences) about yourself, attributed to a best friend and/or relative. Try to imagine exactly what that person might say about you and/or your life. Don't be overly dramatic, unless of course you actually believe those are the words the person would use.

APPENDIX B

Getting a Job

BY JOHN IRBY

Sneak Peek
What You'll Find
Self-Evaluation
Other Considerations
Professional Tips
Résumés
Cover Letters
Interviews
Exercises

After graduation, it is time to focus on getting a job. Hopefully you have learned your lessons well, including spelling.

You spent the last four (or more) years of your life scrimping to make ends meet. Your main food source was Top Ramen. You ate it crunchy and snack style (cold)—and as a gourmet dinner (hot). You dreamed (sometimes it is a nightmare) of the various types and flavors: Beef . . . Chicken . . . Pork . . . Shrimp . . . Cajun . . . Mushroom . . . Vegetable . . . Spicy . . . Creamy . . . Teriyaki.

Your grocery store beer runs included cases of Old Milwaukee, or Keystone Light, or Brew 102, or Mickey's Big Mouth. Let's just say that "the price was right."

You were nicknamed CD—not because of a large music collection, but because all you went on were cheap dates.

It was all necessary, as everyone knows that college students don't have much money.

But your life will change in just a few weeks. Your sacrifices will be rewarded as you become a college graduate and enter the workforce. No doubt you will have little trouble getting that first full-time job, or an internship, as a newspaper journalist. You will be gainfully employed. And with a bit of luck, you might even land that high-paying perfect investigative reporter gig at a major metro.

OK, so I lied.

Even if you get the major metro offer, shun it. You are better off starting at a smaller daily or community newspaper where your education will continue at a realistic pace and you will have a greater chance for long-term success.

If you have read this text, you know that *Reporting That Matters: Public Affairs Coverage* tells the truth in a personal and interactive way. This isn't the time to switch tone or tenor.

What You'll Find

The job market for entry-level reporters is like most other job markets—it is dependent upon the economy. Newspapers have a history of "boom" and what some would call "bust" periods of employment opportunities. We can't predict what the national economy and job market will be like when you graduate.

But journalism graduates in the early part of the decade were having little problem getting employed until the September 11, 2001, terrorist attack and aftermath. Not only did job openings dry up, but many newspapers also had major reductions in staff size and number of daily newspaper pages.

For instance, as recently as the end of 2005, layoffs and buyouts continued across the county. The *Spokesman-Review* in Spokane, Washington, for instance, cut 11 positions in June 2004—the third round of cutbacks since September 11.

The *Christian Science Monitor* cut its staff by 14 since the beginning of 2004. And there have been many more jobs lost.

Still, entry-level jobs were being found in 2005 by the best journalism graduates, even if many of the positions were at smaller or community newspapers paying "challenging" salaries. And there are many inquiries like the one below that arrived via e-mail in 2005:

John,

We have an immediate opening on our news staff. Do you have any sharp recent graduates (or anyone else!) looking for a full-time position on a quality weekly? Here's the info.

Immediate opening: General assignment reporter-photographer position with award-winning news team on one of eastern Washington's largest, liveliest weekly newspapers. Applicants should have solid reporting and writing skills; photography skills desired; page layout a plus. Journalism degree or one year's newspaper experience minimum. Apply in writing with résumé, work references and clippings.

Steve McClure, managing editor of the 8,000-circulation *Moscow-Pullman Daily News,* had the following openings, all at the same time in 2005:

- Sports editor
- Pullman city/bureau reporter
- County reporter
- Arts/business editor

Finding a job, however, isn't the only challenge for graduates. New journalists—often filled with passion and excitement about the prospects of changing the world—must sometimes face a newsroom culture that oftentimes can breed low morale.

A nationwide survey revealed that an overwhelming percentage of participating journalists (84 percent) believe that poor morale is a widespread problem among newspaper journalists.

Carol Stevens, deputy managing editor of the editorial pages at *USA Today,* said in the survey she'd like to see "increased direct interaction between superiors and reporters."

Lanny Larson, assistant feature editor at the *Fresno Bee,* suggested "more meaningful communication at all levels, and an atmosphere that encourages robust discussion of all issues, even difficult ones . . . [and] more praise from the top."

Communication is unfortunately lacking from day one at many newsrooms. While some groups and individual newspapers have made efforts at improving how we talk with each other, it isn't uncommon for a new reporter to be shown the restroom, her desk and computer and then be put to work.

These negatives, however, are balanced with many positives, including excitement, personal interaction, meeting unique-different-interesting sources, education, collegial colleagues, stimulating work and (in some cases) a decent or better wage and benefits.

Self-Evaluation

However you find the job market when you graduate, you can enhance your chances of meaningful employment by taking advantage of your education—so you can demonstrate the talents and skills you have been taught.

In beginning your job search, the best place to start is with a self-evaluation. What you find out about yourself can be invaluable when putting together a résumé, writing a cover letter or preparing for an interview.

A good place to begin is by making a list of your strengths. What do I do well? What can I offer a potential employer? Why would someone want to hire me? Make a list of your strengths with a short (one-paragraph) explanation. For instance:

- **Travel:** I spent a year studying in Italy and traveled extensively throughout Europe. The experience helped me understand different perspectives and will make me a better reporter.

- **Bilingual:** My minor in college was Spanish, and I took four years and am able to read, write and speak the language fluently. This makes me an asset in markets with large Spanish-speaking populations.

- **Political savvy:** My minor was political science, and my internship in Washington, D.C., at a news service helped prepare me for general as well as specific beat assignments.

Other strengths might include reporting, writing, interviewing, passion, a hard work ethic, dedication, having an ability to translate jargon, familiarity with topic or subject areas, ability to put people at ease, and so on.

In hiring hundreds of reporters and editors over a nearly 30-year career, I never hired a reporter who didn't have weaknesses, acknowledged them and discussed how he or she was overcoming those weaknesses (understanding your weaknesses is the first step to overcoming them). Weaknesses should not be stressed in interviews and cover letters, or on résumés, but they are an important part of your self-evaluation, and it is likely you will be asked to talk about any weaknesses if you are invited to an interview. The favorite question for many recruiters is "Tell me about your strengths and weaknesses."

Make a list of weaknesses in advance—and then stress how you are working through them. For instance:

- **Spelling:** I have a tendency to struggle with correct spelling of some words. I have, however, compensated by using a dictionary religiously and also spell-check.

- **Shyness:** I have a natural shyness when meeting new people. But I have learned to overcome this by starting my interviews with small talk, often complimenting the source or pointing out something we might have in common. This seems to help me relax—as well as my source.

Be realistic in your self-evaluation. You might someday want to be the editor of a major metro, but for now ask yourself what you can realistically expect in your first job. Are you set on one part of the country, or are you willing to go anywhere (which will expand your options)? While you might want to cover education, you might have to start as a general assignment, business or government reporter.

Clearly, the more options you are willing to consider, the better your chances of obtaining that first job.

Go ahead and think about that ultimate job in 5 to 10 years, and consider the best way to get there. But for now, know you might have to start with less.

Other Considerations

Editors are looking to hire graduates who, as indicated earlier, have taken full advantage of their educational opportunities. Being well-read can make a significant difference. If you haven't already, start reading not only newspapers but also magazines, trade and text books, and Internet sites.

Variety is critical.

The *Onion,* a satirical weekly online newspaper, uses "America's Finest News Source" as its trademark. But is it? Nope. It is extremely entertaining and can be included in the variety of reading that can enhance your knowledge and understanding of news events, but it is not the *New York Times* or *Dallas Morning News*—or even your local community newspaper.

Time, Newsweek and *U.S. News & World Report* are weekly newsmagazines that do a very good job in summarizing some weekly news events and also provide deeper context and background to major continuing events.

These are the type of publications that can pay dividends when an interviewer asks a question specific to the latest news about the Iraq War.

At the same time, while reading will keep you informed, when you read well-written stories, you will be exposed to the kind of writing that can help your own work.

All things being equal, who is most likely to be offered a job?

1. A candidate who had researched the company that is offering the job, as well as the community, region, state, and so on.

or

2. A candidate who informs the interviewer that he or she will learn about those things once on the job.

Research is critical when looking for a job, and you will have an opportunity to show your commitment and real interest in a cover letter or résumé.

Résumés

Résumés are certainly important, but the most important thing about a résumé is accuracy. Always remember to edit, edit and edit your résumé before sending it out, and have a friend and/or professional review and critique the résumé in advance.

Hiring editors who find spelling, syntax, grammar or other errors often dismiss the applicant with no further consideration, regardless of strengths or accomplishments (the same holds true for letters of application or cover letters).

Graduates applying for their first job should strongly consider keeping their resume to one page, as work experience and accomplishments are usually limited.

Concentrate on academic preparation for the career or job you are seeking. If you are looking for a reporter's position, list the specific or related courses you took—courses for news reporting and writing, ethics, public affairs reporting, editorial writing, media writing, law, history, and so on. Don't bother with scheduling numbers and initials, such as J–305, because they mean very little to a hiring editor. You might, however, want to distinguish between lower- and upper-division courses.

After highlighting your academic preparation, list any extracurricular activities or leadership accomplishments, such as serving as a reporter or editor of the student daily newspaper, or membership or offices in related organizations such as the Society of Professional Journalists or Women in Communication.

PROFESSIONAL TIPS

James P. Medina

James P. Medina is business editor of the *Ventura County Star* newspaper group. It has a combined circulation of more than 100,000 subscribers with editions in Ventura, Thousand Oaks and Simi Valley, California.

Question: In looking to hire an entry-level reporter, how important is it that they have student newspaper experience?

It's very important because they face deadlines, brainstorm and collaborate with peers, work with photographers and/or graphic artists, get their stories online and take direction from editors. This prepares them for what they will encounter in an actual newsroom. And it teaches them the multiple facets that go into publishing a story.

Question: For that same entry-level reporter, how important is it that they have had an internship?

It's a very valuable experience. Interns are exposed to how newsrooms operate, including the editing process, wacky hours, deadline demands, diverse news, beat calls. They also get to interact with a wide range of professionals. And they might be assigned a mentor—someone who could be a long-time ally in his/her career. An internship also could turn into a part-time or full-time job. It's an eye-opening experience that helps students determine if they want to pursue a career in journalism.

Question: How important is the applicant's résumé and cover letter in the application process?

A clear, concise résumé is essential. It's like the fact box that runs with a lengthy story. Editors routinely go back to it to check something as they consider various candidates. Make sure everything is accurate, and highlight special attributes, even workshops or conferences you attended outside normal class work. It shows ambition and initiative.

The cover letter is less important. It should be short, with no spelling errors. Many people try to be pithy or witty, which can sometimes fall flat. Above all, be genuine. And have someone proof it before you consider it done. A lot of editors often fly by the cover letter after two paragraphs, if that, and go directly to the résumé. With the surge of online job postings, the first thing an editor often sees is a short e-mail introduction with a résumé attached. So, the cover letter is quickly disappearing.

Question: How many clips, and what kind of clips, are you looking for?

Five to seven clips is generally the rule. They should show some diversity, such as hard news and features. And there should be some clips that really show off the person's writing. The biggest pitfall to avoid is poorly put together clips. People submit dark copies in tiny type that is illegible. Or stapled articles with dangling jumps folded up in a jumbled mess. This is the work an editor is going to judge you on. Make it a priority instead of the last thing you do before you mail a package. The clips should be submitted in a folder. This simple step will help get you noticed. And it shows you pay attention to details.

(continued)

PROFESSIONAL TIPS   Continued

Question: Is there anything else you'd like to share that can help young journalists get a job or internship?

Do your homework before talking to an editor. There are plenty of online resources to study an area and publication. It's a simple step many applicants never do. You can set yourself apart by demonstrating your reporting skills. It also helps you develop an instant rapport with an editor. If you're prepared for a job interview, an editor can surmise you'll be equally prepared when interviewing sources.

Next, list any work experience, including newspaper internships and part-time or freelance experience with community or hometown newspapers.

Other considerations include making information such as telephone numbers or addresses easy to find. Also, select your references carefully. Always know what a reference will say about you to avoid surprises, and get their approval before listing them as a reference.

Always include work samples; do not say "available upon request." When samples are not included, the hiring process can be delayed. But be careful in selecting work samples. Accuracy, again, is the key. If there are mistakes in the sample, even if caused by someone else, it reflects negatively on you. Make sure your samples show a variety and range of your work. Five clips are generally enough.

Following is a typical résumé:

Your Name
555 W. 5th St.
Anytown, USA 99999
(555) 555–5555
e-mail@address.com

Objective:	To find a job as a general assignment or specific beat reporter at a daily/community newspaper.
Education:	My State University, Bob Woodward School of Journalism, B.A., 2001–2004, graduated with honors. Specific journalism-related courses taken include: media writing, news reporting and writing, computer-assisted reporting, history, law, public affairs reporting and ethics.
Activities:	Worked five semesters (2003–2005) at The *Daily Blab* student newspaper. I served as a reporter, copy editor, news editor, managing editor and editor-in-chief. I was also elected president of the student chapters of the Society of Professional Journalists (2003) and Women in Communication (2004).

(continued)

(continued)

Work Experience:	2002–present, Starbucks, Anytown: Part-time barrista.
	2000–2002, Books R Us, Mytown: Part-time sales clerk.
	1998–2000, J.C. Penney, Yourtown: Part-time sales clerk.
References:	John Jones, *Daily Blab* adviser, My State University, Anytown, USA, (555) 555–5555, jjones@dailyblab.com
	Sally Smith, J.C. Penney supervisor, Your Town, USA, (555) 555–5555, ssmith@penney.org
	Jane Johnson, Bookstore manager, Mytown, USA, (555) 555–5555, jjohnson@books.org
Work Samples:	Attached.

Cover Letters

Far too many cover letters are not effective. It is because they are thrown together at the last moment without thought. Too many are self-serving. Hiring editors hate letters like the following example:

Date
Newspaper Employer
555 5th Ave.
Anytown, USA 99999

Dear Mr. Editor:

I am writing to you concerning the job you have offered. I really would like to be hired as I really need this job. I just graduated from college and I have lots of loans to pay off and I won't be able to start that process unless I get this job.

I did a lot of reporting and writing in college, working for my student newspaper. Lots of people said I did a good job. If you hire me I'd do a good job for you. You can't go wrong by hiring me because I'm the best person for the job.

Please let me know if there is anything else I can do to help get the job. If you review my attached résumé, you will see I am well-qualified.

I don't have any fresh work samples as the copy machine was broke, but I'll send some clips next week. Also, if you need to check references, just let me know and I'll send you a list.

Sincerely,

College Graduate

Far-fetched? Not really. Cover letters, however, need to be based on three considerations.

- **They need to** be thoughtful and personal. Thoughtfulness begins with learning something about the company and job, and showing that in your own words.

- **They need to** explain what you can do for the employer, not what the employer can do for you. Follow John F. Kennedy's famous statement: "Ask not what your country can do for you, but what you can do for your country." Give the employer a reason to hire you.

- **They need to** grab the interest of the hiring editor. Be creative in your writing (but not overly clever), and the best place is generally the lead. As strong as your beginning might be, you will also need a strong closing, including letting the editor know you will follow up in a few days with a phone call. Then do so!

Take a look at this creative and researched cover letter as a comparison:

> The Anytown Gazette
> 555 5th Ave.
> Anytown, USA 99999
>
> Dear Ms. Employer:
> Please consider me for the reporter's job advertised in the August 2005 edition of *E&P Magazine.* I believe we both have a lot to offer each other.
> Anytown is much like the community in which I was raised. A population of 20,000 is just about the right size—big enough to provide community and social services but small enough to run into friends at the Little League ballpark or grocery store.
> Speaking of baseball, I noticed that Anytown High School won the state title last year and the school also won the "Star City" top-school award.
> Education has always been important to me, and after reading several issues of the *Anytown Gazette* I can tell it is important to you as well. Your coverage seems very thorough . . .
>
> Sincerely,
>
> College Graduate

The job applicant, through the cover letter, has clearly shown her interest in not only the newspaper, but also the community and its educational institutions. It will make much more of an impression with a prospective employer than a cover letter that doesn't include advance research or knowledge.

Interviews

Hundreds of reporters can apply for the same position. Hiring editors, however, are not going to interview everyone who applies. Your cover letter, résumé and writing samples will go a long way toward whether or not you are invited to interview. If asked to interview, you will likely be one of three or five finalists for the position.

While it can happen, most applicants don't get a job interview just by stopping by the newspaper unannounced and asking to talk with the editor. Nor is it likely you can just call and set up an interview, if you haven't already sent a cover letter, résumé and work samples.

If you do get an interview, remember to do the following:

- **Dress appropriately:** Personal appearance and hygiene are important. A tuxedo or expensive designer gown wouldn't be appropriate, but neither are shorts and a T-shirt—or a see-through summer dress. Also, understand that while piercing and visible tattoos might be a personal lifestyle choice or decision, they might not be appropriate or accepted by some hiring editors (for some positions).

- **Conduct yourself professionally:** Make direct eye contact, but don't force or make the interviewer look you in the eye. Smile and act in a positive manner. Provide honest and concise answers to questions. Ask questions, but don't ramble.

- **Use good posture** and never interrupt, be early, be considerate, be thankful (in the interview and then afterward with a mailed thank-you note; keep in contact, but don't make a nuisance of yourself) and practice with a friend before you go to the interview.

EXERCISES

1. Using the cover letter and résumé formats provided (or other resources), put together your résumé and a cover letter for a job you would like to have or one you want to apply for.

2. Trade cover letters and résumés with another student in class, and do a critique for each other.

3. Pair up with another class member. Have one person play the role of a potential employer and the other the role of a job seeker. Practice interviewing. Switch roles.

Reporting Resources List and Internet Links

BY JOHN IRBY

Resources and information sometimes seem only a dream. Finding the truth can be hard work, but it will often open the lock to a diversity of reporting riches.

There is no substitute for knocking on doors. The best reporters are not afraid of wearing out their shoes. Reporting always has been—and always will be—about getting out of the office and interacting with people.

A sign once hung in the *Los Angeles Times* Washington bureau newsroom that read: "GOYA/KOD." It stood for "GET OFF YOUR ASS/KNOCK ON DOORS."

Hard work has made many a reporter. But it is only one of many qualities today that are necessary. The best reporters today must be knowledgeable and current with the latest computer technologies, including the Internet.

It hasn't been too many years ago that reporters didn't have to be overly adept at using computers. Many veteran reporters wrote their first stories on typewriters—without electrical assistance—and eventually used primitive word processors. All that has changed.

It's a Brave New World

Reporters and editors today have a wealth of information that is available—it's often just a matter of having the right hardware and software and understanding how to access that information.

CAR is no longer something we drive. It is *computer-assisted reporting,* and more and more newspapers are requiring at least a basic understanding of computer research.

Newspaper morgues—where clip files used to be kept—all but died at most newspapers, which today keep records via electronic archives.

Background preparation is one of the first steps in reporting and writing stories. It used to be a cumbersome process. Reporters often had to search the morgues for clippings or traipse over to the community library or hall of records to research a topic, subject or person of interest. Ask your grandparents about microfilm machines.

Far too often, the clips weren't properly filed or were simply missing because the last reporter to use them never returned them. What was the purpose? It was best to leave them in one of the many stacks of paper on your desk in case you might need them again.

And if the clipped article included a mistake, the next-day correction probably never got stapled to the original, so it was likely that a second, third or fourth mistake would be made.

Story research has been augmented and made easier today through the Internet and full-text searchable databases.

Filipino Food for Thought

A reporter in Bakersfield, California, might be assigned to write a piece about the food being sold at a Filipino celebration in nearby Delano, which is home to a large Filipino community.

Clearly, the reporter might want to do some research before attending the event and tasting chicken and pork adobo, a rich, well-marinated stew flavored with vinegar and soy, accepted as a national dish of the Philippines.

A Google search for *Filipino food* resulted in about 917,000 links and took 0.16 seconds. Much the same can be accomplished on nearly any topic.

The Internet, however, is far from perfect. It was a difficult lesson learned by the Washington State University student newspaper, the *Daily Evergreen,* when a student reporter took as gospel some information she gleaned online.

A new reporter was assigned to write an advance story on a Filipino celebration. The freshman student looked online to find information about Filipino history. In a story headlined "Filipino-American History Recognized," the author wrote that the *Nuestra Senora de Buena Esperanza* was the galleon on which the first Filipinos landed at Morro Bay, California. She then informed readers that *Nuestra Senora de Buena Esperanza* translates to "the Big Ass Spanish Boat."

A big-ass mistake, for sure. It actually translates to "Our Lady of Good Hope."

The Devil Made Me Do It

For a journalist involved in computer-assisted reporting, the Internet serves a significant purpose. It is a series of interconnected networks throughout the world, making it an international news medium. It is a source of data, including federal, state and local government information, as well as a source of information published by diverse companies, organizations or educational institutions. It has been referred to as the world's largest library.

This library is even at a reporter's fingertips, and it is a great resource for basic or background information or context. And it can be easily obtained from his or her desk.

The Internet, however, can also be compared in religious terms to "the Evil One"—or the Devil.

It is a highway that needs to be traveled with a word of caution. Everything found along the way can't be taken as gospel.

There is significant opinion and/or propaganda or persuasive writing on the Internet. Reporters must take steps to determine accuracy. Generally, if the information is obtained from what would be considered a reliable online source—such as a major newspaper, library or educational facility—it can be trusted. But if information is published by an organization that has a cause to promote, more care needs to be taken before accepting the research as fair and accurate.

Computers and the Internet might sometimes seem magical, but they are not magic. They won't make bad reporters good reporters. Technology and resources must be paired with good reporting skills.

Ed Miller, a former editor and publisher of the *Morning Call* in Allentown, Pennsylvania, said: "Tools and technology are important only in reference to their application. A baboon with a computer is a baboon."

The remainder of this appendix is a collection of Web addresses with information and tools specifically for journalists. The supplied descriptions, most often, have come from the groups or organizations. They are not listed in any particular order, but are grouped by areas of interest.

There is one site, however, that deserved special mention. Whatever a journalist is looking for, he or she should visit PoynterOnline (the Poynter Institute). The site billed as "Everything You Need to Be a Better Journalist" (and it delivers)—is at www.poynter.org.

Diversity Resources

- **Unity:** Journalists of Color, Inc. is a strategic alliance of journalists of color acting as a force for positive change to advance their presence, growth and leadership in the fast-changing global news industry. www.unityjournalists.org
- **Asian American Journalist Association (AAJA):** Goals include encouraging Asian American and Pacific Islanders to enter the ranks of journalism, working for fair and accurate coverage of Asian American and Pacific Islanders, and increasing the number of Asian American and Pacific Islander journalists and news managers in the industry. www.aaja.org/index.html
- **Native American Journalists Association (NAJA):** Serves and empowers Native journalists through programs and actions designed to enrich journalism and promote Native cultures. www.naja.com
- **National Association of Black Journalists (NABJ):** An organization of journalists, students and media-related professionals that provides quality programs and services to and advocates on behalf of black journalists worldwide. www.nabj.org/index.html
- **National Association of Hispanic Journalists (NAHJ):** Dedicated to the recognition and professional advancement of Hispanics in the news industry. www.nahj.org
- **Robert C. Maynard Institute for Journalism Education:** This Oakland, California–based nonprofit has prepared thousands of journalists to lead the industry in increasingly diverse environments. www.maynardije.org
- **The National Lesbian & Gay Journalists Association:** NLGJA is an organization of journalists, online media professionals and students that works from within the journalism industry to foster fair and accurate coverage of lesbian, gay, bisexual and transgender issues. It opposes workplace bias against all minorities and provides professional development for its members. www.nlgja.org
- **National Association of Minority Media Executives:** An organization of managers and executives of color working in both news and business operations across all media-related fields, uniting diverse leaders across departments and across cultures. www.namme.org

- **Media Reference Guide:** Over the past two decades, Americans have experienced a significant evolution in their understanding and cultural acceptance of gay and lesbian lives (source: Gay & Lesbian Alliance against Defamation [GLAAD]). www.glaad.org
- **Stand Up and Be Counted:** The largest gay and lesbian consumer census (source: Syracuse University, OpusComm Group, Society). www.glcensus.com
- **NLGJA Stylebook Supplement on Gay, Lesbian, Bisexual and Transgender Terminology:** NLGJA's 2002 *Stylebook* supplement reflects the association's mission of inclusive coverage of lesbian, gay, bisexual and transgender people; includes entries on words and phrases that have become common; and features greater detail for earlier entries. It also includes an expanded contact list of lesbian, gay, bisexual and transgender organizations, with Web sites, e-mail and mailing addresses, phone numbers and, when possible, media contacts. www.nlgja.org/pubs/style.html
- **Human Rights Campaign:** Working for lesbian, gay, bisexual and transgender equal rights. www.hrc.org
- ***N.Y. Times* to Announce Gay Unions:** Online reading (source: BBC News). http://news.bbc.co.uk/1/hi/world/americas/2201681.stm
- **International Women's Media Foundation:** IWMF's mission is to strengthen the role of women in the news media around the world, based on the belief that no press is truly free unless women share an equal voice. www.iwmf.org
- **Study: Fewer Women Hold Top Editor Jobs: A Look at Newspaper Industry's Glass Ceiling.** (source: *Editor and Publisher Magazine*). www.editorandpublisher.com/eandp/news/article_display.jsp?vnu_content_id=1695560
- **The Great Divide: Female Leadership in U.S. Newsrooms:** A study conducted for American Press Institute and Pew Center for Civic Journalism by Selzer & Company, Des Moines, Iowa, September 2002. www.pewcenter.org/doingcj/research/r_apipewstudy.pdf
- **Middle East Media Guide:** www.middleeastmediaguide.com
- **Guidelines for Countering Racial, Ethnic and Religious Profiling.** (source: Society of Professional Journalists). www.spj.org/diversity_profiling.asp

- **What You Need to Know about Race Relations:** Subjects include "white privilege," "stereotypes," "racism," "hate groups and crimes," "diversity training," "interracial issues," and "race and the media" (and others). http://racerelations.about.com/mbody.htm
- **Rainbow Sourcebook Search:** Search for sources from affirmative action to violent hate crimes. (source: Society of Professional Journalists). www.spj.org/diversity_search.asp
- **Cultural Competence Resources:** This is a list of resources that provide more information about cultural competence. Included are organizations, general information, training workshops and conferences, policy resources and implementation resources. http://cecp.air.org/cultural/resources.htm
- **2001 Minority Employment Results Tables.** (source: American Society of Newspaper Editors). www.asne.org/kiosk/diversity/2001Survey/mintabl.htm
- **Forum on Race and the Media:** The Manship School of Communication (Louisiana State University) site is dedicated to building diversity in mass communication and America's newsrooms. www.lsu.edu/raceandmedia/index.htm
- **National Center on Disability & Journalism:** NCDJ is an independent, impartial journalism organization with a mission to educate journalists and educators ab out disability reporting issues in order to produce more accurate, fair and diverse news reporting. The mission is realized through research, development and distribution of educational resources. www.ncdj.org
- **PoynterOnline Diversity:** Multiple readings (source: Poynter Institute staff). www.poynter.org/subject.asp?id=5
- **PoynterOnline Diversity:** Special reading, "Diversity across a Semester. Q&A with John Irby." Written by Keith Woods (source: Poynter Institute). www.poynter.org/content/content_view.asp?id=9527&sid=5
- **Newsroom Diversity:** The Freedom Forum works to identify, recruit and train people of color for journalism careers (source: the Freedom Forum). www.freedomforum.org/diversity/default.asp
- **Pew Center for Civic Journalism:** A word search (for *diversity*) turns up 83 documents from the Pew Center. www.pewcenter.org
- **The Rap Dictionary:** The *Rap Dictionary* is the oldest and ultimate resource for looking up hip-hop slang. www.rapdict.org

- **Journalism.org:** A series of articles on diversity (source: Project for Excellence in Journalism & Committee of Concerned Journalists). www.journalism.org
- **American Society of Newspaper Editors:** A series of articles on diversity (source: ASNE). www.asne.org/search/index.cfm
- **American Press Institute: The Journalists' Toolbox, Online Resources for Reporters and Editors:** More than 100 links to Web sites that focus on issues of diversity. www.journaliststoolbox.com/newswriting/diversity.html
- **PROUD Magazine:** People Relying on Unconditional Diversity (PROUD) is a national magazine celebrating the careers and lifestyles of professionals of color. www.proudmagazine.com
- **Fairness and Accuracy in Reporting:** FAIR, a national media watch group, has been offering well-documented criticism of media bias and censorship since 1986. It works to invigorate the First Amendment by advocating for greater diversity in the press and by scrutinizing media practices that marginalize public interest and minority and dissenting viewpoints. www.fair.org
- **Dying Tongues:** An interactive look at American Indian issues in the Dakotas. www.in-forum.com/specials/DyingTongues/
- **South Asian Journalists Association Stylebook:** www.saja.org/stylebook.html
- **Native Americans and Alcohol Abuse:** 2000 Pulitzer Prize–winning series of articles. Author: Eric Newhouse, *Great Falls Tribune.* www.pulitzer.org/year/2000/explanatory-reporting/

Other Journalism Organizations

- **American Press Institute:** The oldest and largest center devoted solely to training and professional development for the news industry and journalism educators. www.americanpressinstitute.org
- **Student Press Law Center:** This nonprofit center provides free legal assistance to student journalists. www.splc.org
- **Reporters Committee for Freedom of the Press:** This national organization keeps tabs on media law issues throughout the country. www.rcfp.org

- **National Freedom of Information Coalition:** NFOIC provides a list of links to nonprofit organizations throughout the country that provide resources, tips and information about access to public records and meetings. www.nfoic.org
- **Citizen Access Project:** This organization, out of the Brechner Institute at the University of Florida, provides information about access to public records in every state. www.citizenaccess.org
- **Associated Press Managing Editors:** Dedicated to the improvement, advancement and promotion of journalism by its own newspapers and through its relationship with the Associated Press. www.apme.com
- **The Pew Center for Civic Journalism:** An incubator for civic journalism experiments that enable news organizations to create and refine better ways of reporting the news to re-engage people in public life. www.pewcenter.org/index.php
- **Civic Journalism Interest Group:** Part of the Association for Education in Journalism and Mass Communication. www.has.vcu.edu/civic-journalism/
- **J-Lab, the Institute for Interactive Journalism:** Helps news organizations use new information ideas and innovative computer technologies to develop new ways for people to engage in critical public policy issues. www.j-lab.org
- **Committee to Protect Journalists:** www.cpj.org
- **International Federation of Journalists:** Promotes international action to defend press freedom and social justice through strong, free and independent trade unions of journalists. www.ifj.org
- **Investigative Reporters and Editors:** Provides educational service to reporters, editors and others interested in investigative journalism. www.ire.org
- **Newspaper Association of America:** A nonprofit organization representing the $55 billion newspaper industry. www.naa.org
- **National Institute for Computer-Assisted Reporting:** A program of Investigative Reporters and Editors, Inc. and the Missouri School of Journalism. NICAR has trained thousands of journalists in the practical skills of finding, prying loose and analyzing electronic information. www.nicar.org
- **Society for News Design:** A professional organization composed of editors, designers, graphic artists, publishers, illustrators, art directors, photographers, advertising artists, Web site designers, students and faculty. Membership is open to anyone with an interest in journalism and design. www.snd.org
- **Society of Professional Journalists:** Membership group of professionals dedicated to improving and protecting journalism. www.spj.org

General Journalism Resources

- **The Freedom Forum:** A nonpartisan foundation dedicated to free press, free speech and free spirit for all people. The foundation focuses on three priorities: the Newseum, First Amendment freedoms and newsroom diversity. www.freedomforum.org
- **Bob Baker's Newsthinking:** Dedicated to the proposition that there are two kinds of journalists: bad ones, and those who are improving. www.newsthinking.com/
- **Books on Media Issues:** http://members.tripod.com/~journalismcenter/bookspages.html#pages
- **CyberJournalist.net:** Focuses on how the Internet, media convergence and new technologies are changing journalism. www.cyberjournalist.net/news/000162.php
- **The Media Center:** Facilitates strategic conversations, planning and idea sharing on issues shaping the future of news, information and media. www.americanpressinstitute.org/mediacenter
- **Tapping Officials' Secrets:** Every state's open meeting law is available online by the Reporters Committee for Freedom of the Press. www.rcfp.org
- **Access experts:** Most states have a group dedicated to access to public meetings and records. You can find their Web sites at the National Freedom of Information Coalition. www.nfoic.org
- **Richard Prince's Journal-isms™:** Published Monday, Wednesday and Friday. www.maynardije.org/columns/dickprince
- **Wired Journalist:** Newsroom guide to the Internet. www.rtndf.org/resources/wiredweb/index.html
- **Facts about Newspapers:** From the Newspaper Association of America. www.naa.org/info/facts02/index.html
- **Muckraker:** Center for Investigative Reporting. www.muckraker.org
- **SlangSite.com:** A dictionary of slang, Web-speak, made-up words and colloquialisms. www.slangsite.com

- **Statistical Resources for Journalists:** From Columbia University. www.columbia.edu/cu/lweb/indiv/jour/subject/stats.html
- **The Pulitzer Prizes:** www.pulitzer.org
- **The Working Reporter:** A resource for journalists. www.workingreporter.com
- **Urban Legends, Hoaxes and Scams:** From American Press Institute. www.americanpressinstitute.org/content/3701.cfm
- **The State of the News Media 2004:** From journalism.org. www.stateofthenewsmedia.org/2005/index.asp
- **The Project for Excellence in Journalism and Committee of Concerned Journalists:** Research and resources to improve journalism. www.journalism.org
- **The Journalistic Resources Page:** Resources designed to serve scholars, journalists and other professionals to access information on the Internet. www.markovits.com/journalism/
- **Web Sites for Journalists:** Academic and professional Web sites. www.toad.net/~andrews/acad.html#Schools
- **Journalism.net:** The investigative guide to internet research. www.journalismnet.com/
- **FACSNET:** Better journalism through education. www.facsnet.org
- **The First Amendment Center:** The First Amendment Center works to preserve and protect First Amendment freedoms through information and education. www.firstamendmentcenter.org

Ethics Resources

- **Ethics on the World Wide Web:** From Fullerton State University. http://commfaculty.fullerton.edu/lester/ethics/media.html
- **Josephson Institute of Ethics:** A public-benefit, nonpartisan, nonprofit membership organization to improve the ethical quality of society by advocating principled reasoning and ethical decision making. www.josephsoninstitute.org
- **Web Resources for Studying Journalism Ethics:** From the University of Hawaii. www2.hawaii.edu/~tbrislin/jethics.html
- **Media Ethics Links:** www.people.vcu.edu/~jcsouth/hotlists/ethics.htm

- **The Journalist's Toolbox on Ethics:** American Press Institute. www.americanpressinstitute.org/content/3857.cfm

Newspaper Magazine Resources

- *American Journalism Review:* A national magazine that covers all aspects of print, television, radio and online media. www.ajr.org
- *Columbia Journalism Review:* One of America's media monitors. www.cjr.org
- *Editor and Publisher Magazine:* America's oldest journal covering the newspaper industry. www.editorandpublisher.com/eandp/index.jsp
- *Presstime Magazine:* Newspaper industry stories and information from the National Newspaper Association. www.naa.org/presstime/index.html
- *The American Editor:* Newspaper industry stories from the American Society of Newspaper Editors. www.asne.org/kiosk/editor/tae.htm

Video Resources

- *When Billy Broke His Head . . . and Other Tales of Wonder:* An irreverent road movie in the form of an hour-long documentary about disability, civil rights and the search for intelligent life after brain damage. www.itvs.org/external/WBBHH/WBBHH-Sundance.html
- *The Color of Fear:* An insightful film about the state of race relations in America as seen through the eyes of eight North American men of Asian, European, Latino and African descent. In a series of intelligent, emotional and dramatic confrontations, the men reveal the pain and scars that racism has caused them. What emerges is a deeper sense of understanding and trust. This is the dialogue most of us fear, but hope will happen sometime in our lifetime. www.tcnj.edu/~kpearson/color/program.html
- *Mickey Mouse Monopoly:* The Disney Company's success in the twentieth century is based on creating an image of innocence, magic and fun. Its animated films in particular are almost universally lauded as wholesome family entertainment, enjoying massive popularity among children and endorsement from parents and teachers. *Mickey Mouse Monopoly* takes a close and critical look at the world these films

create and the stories they tell about race, gender and class, and reaches disturbing conclusions about the values propagated under the guise of innocence and fun (source: Media Education Foundation). http://mediaed.org/videos/CommercialismPoliticsAndMedia/MickeyMouseMonopoly

- **Media Education Foundation: Challenging Media:** 26 videos on media and gender, race and diversity. www.mediaed.org/videos/index_html#MediaGenderAndDiversity
- ***Smoke Signals:*** A feature-length movie by and about Native Americans. www.fallsapart.com/smoke.html

Links to Newspapers

- **College Front Page:** By student journalists, for student journalists. www.collegefrontpage.com
- **Newspapers.com:** Find newspapers in the United States with search engine options. www.newspapers.com
- **Gebbie Press:** The all-in-one media directory. www.gebbieinc.com
- **NewsVoyager:** A gateway to local newspapers. www.newspaperlinks.com/home.cfm
- **Refdesk.com:** U.S. and worldwide newspapers. www.refdesk.com/paper.html

Online Resources for Political Reporters

- **The Campaign Finance Information Center** at Investigative Reporters and Editors (IRE) has data from many states, links to state-run online campaign finance search engines and, for IRE members, an archive of stories done using campaign finance records, including a "campaign finance story of the week." www.campaignfinance.org
- **The Hoover Institution** sponsors this site with links to history, current structure, a glossary of campaign finance terms, U.S. Supreme Court cases and recent articles about campaign finance. www.campaignfinancesite.org
- **The Federal Elections Commission (FEC)** tracks campaign contributions and spending by presidential and congressional candidates. The site also includes complaints against candidates for violating FEC rules and their resolution. www.fec.gov/
- **The Institute on Money in State Politics,** based in Helena, Montana, is a nonpartisan group that provides documentation on campaign finance at the state level. www.followthemoney.org
- **The Center for Responsive Politics** is a nonpartisan research group based in Washington, D.C., that tracks money in politics, and its effect on elections and public policy. (A "Get Local" feature allows a search by state or zip code for top donors.) www.opensecrets.org
- **A compilation of nationwide surveys** taken by news organizations and public-opinion research firms; this is useful for comparing question wording and how the timing of a poll can affect results. Some parts of the site are available only to subscribers. www.pollingreport.com
- **Stateline.org** is a nonpartisan, nonprofit online news publication that reports each weekday on state government. A "statistics" feature allows comparisons between two or more states and U.S. averages in such fields as education, environment, health care, politics, taxes and budget, welfare and social policy. www.stateline.org
- **Project Vote Smart,** based in Phillipsburg, Montana, maintains a database about thousands of candidates and elected officials at the state and federal levels. Less detailed information is available at the county and local levels for each state. A useful feature is a national calendar of primary elections and party caucuses in election years. www.vote-smart.org

Resources for Local Government Reporters

- **The U.S. Census Bureau's** user-friendly source of population, housing, economic and geographic data. Enter a zip code to generate a fact sheet about any U.S. community. http://factfinder.census.gov
- **International City/County Management Association,** the national association for appointed administrators, publishes *Public Management* magazine. Some parts of the Web site are restricted to members. www.icma.org
- **International Downtown Association,** a group that serves U.S. downtown and urban-planning

agencies. The site includes links to reports of interest to planners, such as parking, recycling, events and promotions. www.ida-downtown.org

■ **National Association of Counties** publishes *County News.* The site includes links to state associations of counties. www.naco.org

■ **New Urbanism** is an international movement of architects and designers who seek to change the way in which communities are built. New Urbanism involves fixing and infilling cities, as well as creating compact new towns and villages. www.newurbanism.org

■ **National League of Cities** publishes *Nation's Cities Weekly,* a great source of story ideas. The site includes links to member city's Web sites, organized by state. www.nlc.org/home

■ **The Smart Growth Network** was formed in response to concerns about finding new ways to grow that protect the environment and enhance community vitality. It favors finding alternatives to sprawl that make better use of existing urban infrastructure. www.smartgrowth.org

■ Funded by the Pew Charitable Trusts, **Stateline .org** provides information about political activity in the 50 state capitals, including implications of state laws for cities and counties. www.stateline.org

■ **U.S. Conference of Mayors** is a nonpartisan organization representing U.S. cities with a population of 30,000 or more. www.usmayors.org

EXERCISE

1. Compile your own list of journalism-related Internet sites that do not duplicate those previously listed.

INDEX